A Study in
Structural Semantics

The Siriono Kinship System

A Study in
Structural Semantics

The Siriono Kinship System

HAROLD W. SCHEFFLER and FLOYD G. LOUNSBURY

Department of Anthropology, Yale University

Prentice-Hall, Inc., Englewood Cliffs, New Jersey

© Copyright 1971 by Prentice-Hall, Inc.,
Englewood Cliffs, New Jersey

All rights reserved. No part of this book may be
reproduced in any form or by any means without
permission in writing from the publisher.

Library of Congress Catalog Card Number: 71-92378

PRINTED IN THE UNITED STATES OF AMERICA

13-859058-3

Current Printing (last digit):
10 9 8 7 6 5 4 3 2 1

Acknowledgements: Extracts from A. R. Radcliffe-
Brown, *Structure and function in primitive society*
(New York: The Free Press), copyright 1952, reprinted by permission of The Macmillan Company
and of Routledge & Kegan Paul, Ltd. Extracts from
M. Fortes, Kinship and marriage among the Ashanti,
in Radcliffe-Brown and Fortes, eds., *African systems
of kinship and marriage* (London: Oxford University
Press, 1950), reprinted by permission of the International African Institute.

PRENTICE-HALL INTERNATIONAL, INC., *London*
PRENTICE-HALL OF AUSTRALIA, PTY. LTD., *Sydney*
PRENTICE-HALL OF CANADA, LTD., *Toronto*
PRENTICE-HALL OF INDIA PRIVATE LTD., *New Delhi*
PRENTICE-HALL OF JAPAN, INC., *Tokyo*

Contents

v

Figures and Tables

A Study in
Structural Semantics

The Siriono Kinship System

1 Introduction

For many good reasons, Holmberg's monograph on the Siriono Indians of northeastern Bolivia has long fascinated anthropologists. For us, one of the more intriguing aspects of that study consists in the data it provides on the Siriono system of kin classification. We find this classificatory system especially interesting for two reasons. In one respect, as we shall show, it is a very unusual kind of kinship terminology, at least insofar as it features a structural principle that appears to be confined to only a few South American societies—the Apinaye, Ramkokamekra (Canella), Kayapo, and Nambikwara of Brazil, and the Inca of Peru at the time of the Conquest, in addition to the Siriono. Though these societies vary considerably in other structural features, and though their systems of kin classification differ in other details, all employ a structural principle we describe as "parallel transmission of kin-class status." In another respect, however, the Siriono system of kin classification is not an unusual one at all, for it also features a structural principle that has a fairly broad distribution in Asia, though apparently not in North or South America. This we describe as the "mother's brother's daughter and father's sister's son (MBD-FZS)–spouse equation rule in kin classification."

We show in the first part of Chapter 2 that Holmberg's data on Siriono kin classification and social structure are of exceptional theoretical interest because they present a critical "test case" for the theory of so-called prescriptive marriage systems developed by Lévi-Strauss (1949 [1969]) and by Needham (e.g., 1962b). In the latter half of Chapter 2 we demonstrate that it is reasonable to suppose that the classificatory system reported to be a "kinship" system (Holmberg 1950: 52–56) is literally that. Because this point has been called into question (see Needham 1961; 1964a), it is essential to establish that this *is* a kinship terminology before we begin to analyze it as such.

In Chapter 3 we outline our method of analyzing the semantic content

1

and structure of the system of kin classification. The method has been employed in previous shorter studies (e.g., Lounsbury 1964a; 1965) where, due to limitations of space, it was necessary to present a less-than-full account of it and of the structures of the systems in question. Here we take the opportunity to elaborate more fully on what we think are the assumptions, methods, and aims appropriate to the structural semantic analysis of systems of kin classification. We attempt also to answer some of the criticisms that have been advanced against the sort of analysis we present (see also Chapter 7).

In Chapters 4, 5, and 6 we formulate and then discuss a set of definitions and rules of genealogical structural equivalence that together constitute a formal theory, and yield a model, of the Siriono system of kin classification. We should emphasize the phrase *system of kin classification*. The words that Siriono employ to designate categories of kin have yet other semantic functions, i.e., other kinds of meanings, some of which have little or nothing to do with relations of kinship or genealogical connection, while others are closely related to the kin-category-designating senses. Some Siriono kinship terms are derived from words whose primary and most literal senses are similar to English "male" and "female"; and some, in addition to designating categories of kin, serve also to connote certain social relationships which are normatively ascribed between ego (the speaker or propositus) and kinsmen of the categories so designated. We must therefore distinguish between an account of *usage* in general and the much more simple matter of an account of *the structure of the system of kin classification*, i.e., of the kin-designating senses of the words in question. The analysis presented in Chapters 4 and 5 is concerned solely with the system of classification as such. It does not pretend to be a complete analysis of *the* meanings of Siriono kinship terms or of those Siriono expressions often used as kinship terms. Because the words *are* used to designate categories of kin we call them kinship terms, but this should not be taken to imply that they are terms solely of kinship in an absolute or exclusive sense (cf. Schneider 1968a: 101).

The adequacy of our theory of the Siriono system of kin classification rests on its ability to account for the known distribution of terms over kintypes (types of genealogical connection). On the basis of the available ethnographic data, we cannot show that Siriono themselves employ the definitions and rules that we formulate or, rather, some Siriono-language paraphrase of them. However, a structural analysis that accounts in a relatively simple fashion for Holmberg's large and internally consistent body of data probably does replicate something intrinsic to Siriono culture. We show in Chapter 7 that the posited rules of genealogical equivalence have formal analogs in decision-making criteria that could easily be employed by Siriono in the process of classifying kinsmen. The analysis may be regarded as posing a hypothesis for further testing in the field, should that still be possible.

The last two chapters take up questions of a sociological and not so formal nature. In Chapter 8 we analyze Holmberg's data on Siriono social structure, especially marriage rules and practices. We are there concerned with the probable social connotations of Siriono kinship terms and with the possible social-structural correlates of the most distinctive rules or principles of Siriono kin classification. We do not attempt to show *why* Siriono classify kin as they do, but we show that the system of kin classification is at least logically and functionally consistent with certain other aspects of the Siriono social order.

In Chapter 9 we take brief note of a few other South American Indian societies whose systems of kin classification share the feature of parallel transmission. And, finally, we return to the relevance of the Siriono case to theories about so-called preferential and prescriptive marriage systems. This involves consideration of a few other systems of kin classification, which we show to employ the MBD-FZS–spouse equation rule in kin classification, and the social systems in which they occur.

Some Notes on Concepts and Terminology

The semantic relations of linguistic signs, we shall say, are those which users of a language establish between signs and the objects to which they apply the signs (Morris 1938; 1946; 1964). "Object" is perhaps an overly concrete term for what is intended, viz., entities, qualities, conditions, relationships, etc., which are attributed existence (i.e., are posited) by the speakers of a particular language. We are concerned with the nature of certain concepts and systems of concepts: whether the conceptualized entities, their attributes, and relationships "actually exist" by some standards external to the culture of the speakers of the language concerned is a problem that we need not consider.[1]

Semantic analysis is facilitated by recognition of different *modes of reference* in the relationship between a linguistic sign and its object. It is essential to distinguish the relationship between a sign and an *object as a thing* from the relationship between a sign and an *object as an exemplar of a kind or as a member of a class of things*. The former relation has been

---

[1] We do not here attempt a statement of the more or less comprehensive general semantic theory that provides the broader context for this discussion of kinship semantics. For extended statements of the general point of view taken here, see Waldron (1967) and Leech (1969).

called *denotation,* the latter *designation.*[2] When a linguistic sign is used to "point" to a particular object, we say it *denotes* that object. At the same time it may be said to *designate* the class of such objects. An object that may be denoted by a sign is a *denotatum* of that sign; the class of all possible denotata of a sign constitutes its *designatum.* The expression "uncle" in English designates a class of one's kinsmen; a relative who is one's mother's brother (MB) is one proper denotatum of the term; a relative who is one's father's brother (FB) is another. All kinsmen properly denotable by the term constitute its designatum for a given ego.

The members of any naturally conceived class of things, arrived at pragmatically by stimulus generalization,[3] have some distinctive quality or combination or qualities in common, that furnishes the basis for their common designation.[4] These distinctive qualities are the *significant features* of the objects and the *defining features* of the class. A sign is said to *signify* these features of its objects, and its relationship to these features is described as *signification.* The defining features, the necessary and sufficient conditions for membership in a class, are the *significatum* of its sign. The primary significatum of "uncle" in one dialect of American English is "male kinsman of the first ascending generation and of the first degree of collaterality." At this limited (primary) range of the term, its significatum comprises the features or components "kinsman," "first ascending generation," "first degree collateral," and "male." Any person related to ego in this way is his or her "uncle" by definition. A more colloquial phrasing is "the brother of either of one's parents."

A statement of the significatum of a linguistic sign in terms of the features of which it is composed may be described as a *componential definition* of that sign. The semantic analysis of folk systems of classification has come to be known as *componential analysis.* The concepts and methods of componential analysis have been discussed at length elsewhere (see Goodenough 1956; 1965b; 1967; 1968; Lounsbury 1956; 1964b; Bendix 1966; Leech 1969). The reader who is unfamiliar with these discus-

---

[2] The philosopher's distinction between the extension and intension of a term merges these two semantic relations (denotation and designation) in the relation of extension.

[3] See Bruner, Goodnow, and Austin (1956), Bourne (1966), and Kintsch (1970) for reviews of the relevant literature.

[4] A natural class of this type contrasts with unnatural classes or pseudoclasses, which have no distinctive inherent qualities in common except their name, e.g., the class of objects named Peter as opposed to the class of objects named Roger, either of which may be applied to persons or to animals such as dogs and cats; or the class of things named by "masculine" nouns in German as opposed to the class of things named by "feminine" nouns in German. Such classes are not based on stimulus generalization but on random individual name bestowal from a limited stock (as in the first example) or on a traditional but arbitrary classification whose presumed former natural basis (if any) is a matter of prehistory (as in the latter example).

sions is advised to read Goodenough (1967 or 1968) before proceeding any further.

It is a commonplace observation that a linguistic sign may suggest or tend to imply additional attributes of the class, or of some part of the class of its objects, which are not proper defining features of the class (see Bloomfield 1933: 151ff.). We say that an expression *connotes* such additional but nondefining features which people associate with that expression's designatum, or with a part of it, and from which they orient themselves affectively and behaviorally toward it. The relationship of a sign to nondistinctive features of its designatum is here described as *connotation*. As noted earlier, kinship terms not only refer to the categories they designate or to particular kinsmen who are members of those categories; they may also imply or suggest certain social relationships ascribed between ego and the kinsmen so designated. We describe such meanings of kinship terms as their *status-relationship connotations*, following Goodenough (1965a; cf. Schneider and Roberts 1956: 18). To continue with our English example "uncle," men related to us as uncles are expected to behave toward us in certain ways by virtue of the fact that they are our uncles, but they *are* our uncles even if they do not conduct themselves toward us in the expected way. Thus certain modes of conduct are nondefining (nondistinctive, accidental) features of the class of kin designated by the term "uncle."[5]

To avoid confusion, we should note that philosophers, especially logicians, use some of these terms in other ways. Philosophers have distinguished between the *extension* of a term, i.e., the class of all objects to which it is correctly applied, and its *intension*, i.e., its reference to the properties possessed by all those objects and by virtue of which the term is properly applied to them. This distinction has also been expressed as that between *denotation* and *connotation* (using both these terms in ways different from those specified above) or as that between *reference* and

---

[5] Schneider (1968a: 101) speaks of the use of American kinship terms to signify *either* "biogenetic relationship" *or* "a code for the conduct of kinship (that is diffuse enduring solidarity)" *or both*, and describes both as "distinctive features of kinship terms in American culture." In our view, it is a mistake to regard the modes of conduct which American English kinship terms may *connote* as being of the same structural order as their genealogical *significata*. The modes of conduct are ascribed in the first instance between categories of kin (as Schneider notes), and the system of categories (and their definitions) must therefore be regarded as structurally prior to the system of statuses ascribed by reference to these categories. The modes of conduct that kinship terms connote may determine their use in certain social situations but are not parts of the significata of those terms, and this is conventionally recognized in American English dictionaries which seldom contain any reference to the status connotations of kinship terms. The difficulty with Schneider's argument is that it rests on a loose and imprecise use of the term "define," as in "the code for the conduct of kinship is defined in terms of the symbol of biogenetic unity which is defined as enduring" (1968a: 101).

meaning (see Copi 1953: 100–101; Alston 1964: 14–17; Ullmann 1962: 74). The philosopher's denotation is equivalent to our (and Morris's) designation, and their connotation is equivalent to our signification. As Alston (1964: 17) notes, the logician's usage is different from "the literary use, in which denotation is something like the standard meaning of a word, whereas connotation comprises the associations, which may well vary somewhat from person to person, to which this [the standard] meaning gives rise." Our usage, then, is closer to the "literary" than to the "logical."

As the quotation from Alston suggests, people may agree on the definitive attributes of a term—on what it minimally signifies—while disagreeing considerably on what is connoted or implied by it. For example, several informants, especially if taken from different English-speaking subcultures, are likely to vary in their descriptions of the conduct appropriate to uncles vis-à-vis their nephews or nieces, even more so if some of them have no uncles of their own and thus no practical experience with relatives of that kind to draw upon. This difference is a useful though hardly infallible guide to distinguishing between the essential attributes for the assignment of an object to a labeled class and its accidental attributes. In some societies the conduct appropriate to particular classes of relatives vis-à-vis the reciprocal classes is clearly and normatively ascribed, and we might therefore expect greater agreement on the connotations of the kinship terms in question. The connotative meanings of words may be relatively "standardized," i.e., consistent from one user of the term to another and from one context of usage to another.

Many words in a language have more than one significatum and serve to designate more than one class of objects. In some cases the different classes designated by the same term are quite unrelated to one another, that is, the two or more significata of the term share no features in common. In other cases the different classes designated by the same term share some of their distinctive features. The relationship between the several different significata of the same word (which is sometimes spelled differently, as in the cases of English "bear" and "bare" or "sale" and "sail") is conventionally described as "homonymy" (e.g., Bloomfield 1933: 145), but it is essential to distinguish between two kinds of "homonymy." Where the two or more significata of the same word are semantically unrelated, we speak of the relationship between them as *homonymy* and we describe the word in question as *homonymic* (see Bréal 1900: 122ff.; Ullmann 1962: 176ff.). Where the two or more significata of the word are related, sharing some of their distinctive features and suggesting derivation one from the other, we speak of *polysemy* and we describe the word in question as *polysemic*. Words that have one and only one significatum (i.e., that always signify one and the same meaning) are described as *monosemic*. Many words are both homonymic and polysemic, for example, the significata of "a sale" and "a sail" are wholly unrelated and therefore homonymous, but the verbal significatum of "sail" (as in "to sail") is semantically related to its nominative significatum, and so the word is also polysemic. (For further discussion of the concepts homonymy and polysemy, see Bréal 1900; Urban 1939; Ullman 1962; 1967; Waldron 1967; also Malinowski's distinction between "accidental" and "cognate" homonyms, 1935, II: 28).

The English kinship term "uncle" is polysemic; it may be used to designate the class of kinsmen noted above or to designate one of two different but related classes of kinsmen, namely (1) the husbands of "aunts," in which case we may speak more precisely of "uncles by marriage," and (2) the brothers of grandparents, rather than of parents, in which case we may speak more precisely of "great-uncles." These two categories of "uncle" are semantically related to the category brothers of parents, i.e., "male consanguineal relative of the first ascending generation and first degree of collaterality." The category "great-uncle" shares all the features of the category "uncle" except "*first* ascending generation," and the prefix "great" marks this specific difference between the two categories: a "great-uncle" is "like an uncle" in some ways but "unlike an uncle" in that he is a kinsman who is two generations rather than one generation removed from ego. An "uncle by marriage" is less "like an uncle" than a "great-uncle" because he is only a "relative by marriage," not a "real relative" (i.e., a consanguineal). But as a male "relative" (by marriage) associated with the first ascending generation and the first degree of collaterality (an "aunt") he is "like an uncle," too.

The several senses of a polysemic word may be related to each other in various ways, depending on their manner of derivation one from another. Of these, we may distinguish *widening* of reference, *narrowing* of reference, and *metaphor*.[6]

In the case of "uncle," the reference of the term is widened from its primary designatum (brothers of ego's parents) so as to include some more distant and differently related relatives (grandparents' brothers in the one case, parents' sisters' husbands in the other). This process is often referred to as an *extension* of the reference of the word (an unfortunate choice of term, perhaps, since it involves a different sense from that which it has in philosophical discourse about semantics [see above], but one that need not be a source of confusion since we do not here employ the term in that sense). Widening of the designatum involves an attenuation or weakening of the significatum of that term, i.e., a relaxing or diminu-

---

[6] These processes are discussed at length and with numerous examples by Bréal (1900), Stern (1931), Ullmann (1962), Empson (1967), and Waldron (1967).

tion of the conditions on the use of the term, or for inclusion in the class designated by it. Thus, "ascending generation" is a weaker condition than "first ascending generation," and "relative" is a weaker condition than "consanguineal relative" in the componential definitions of the senses of the term "uncle." More relaxed conditions allow for wider use of a term.

Additional senses of a word may result also from the opposite process, i.e., from the narrowing of the word's designatum in particular contexts of use. The French word *femme* provides an example. The wider sense of the word as "woman" is prior in this case to the special sense of "wife," and the latter can be said to be derived from the former by narrowing or specialization of the reference of the word in particular contexts. Narrowing of the designatum of a term involves the augmenting or strengthening of its significatum, i.e., the imposition of additional conditions on use of the word or of more stringent requirements for membership in the class designated by it. In the example here the additional requirement is that one be married to the woman, i.e., that one legally "possess" her. And the special contexts in which *femme* means "wife" are linguistically marked by the possessive construction (*ma femme, la femme de M. . . .*, etc.).

It was just stated that the wider sense of the term in this particular example (*femme*) is "prior" to its narrower sense, and so we may speak of this as an example of narrowing; whereas if the reverse were true in regard to the priorities, it would have to be regarded as a case of widening. We must ask, however, what we can mean by "prior," and how priority is to be judged. In the present case obviously, if we wish, we can mean "historically prior"; we can make this judgment because there is a long historical record of the language. But we may question first whether this is a kind of priority that should be of any concern to us in a synchronic structural study, and second, if we do have reasons (immediately relevant or not) for being interested in this question, whether, in languages for which historical evidence is lacking, we can still make judgments of priority among the senses of a word and so distinguish between primary senses, widened senses, and narrowed senses.

Historical priority may be established in various ways: by documentation from earlier periods of a language, by comparative linguistic study of related languages in a family, or, in some cases, by one or another kind of internal evidence solely from within the language under study. But aside from this matter of historical priority, there is sometimes another kind of priority to be ascertained: a psychological or cognitive priority or saliency. People sometimes have a clear feeling and a fair consensus (without doing any research into history) as to what sense of a polysemic word is primary, or prior to some other sense. Such intuitive "knowledge," when it exists, is not particularly mysterious; it is arrived at also from internal evidence within the language and from the conditions under which words are used with particular meanings. It is this cognitive priority that is the more relevant to synchronic studies, and especially to kinship studies. Early anthropological studies of kinship (see Radcliffe-Brown 1913: 150) perhaps naively took such priorities for granted (as we suppose their informants did also). Recent studies, however, have questioned the assumption of such priorities among the senses of kinship terms and have tended to dismiss the notion without exhausting the kinds of inquiry that would be necessary to put the assumption to a proper test.

In the study of kinship semantics, there is yet another kind of priority, one that can be ascertained by semantic analysis and which we may call *logical priority*. The nature of this kind of priority will become apparent later in this study. We should expect cognitive priority, where it can be determined, to coincide pretty largely with logical priority, since the former rests in part on the same kinds of data as the latter, though arrived at by different methods (the unconscious methods employed by a native learner of his language in the former case, the deliberate methods of structural analysis in the latter case). But more careful studies are necessary also to put this assumption to the test.

Our word "uncle" can provide us also with an example of the kind of polysemy introduced by metaphor. "Uncle," like some other English kinship terms (e.g., "father," and its more familiar forms such as "dad" and "pop"), may be employed to denote a person whom the speaker does not suppose is a kinsman or even a relative by marriage: "uncle" and "aunt" are sometimes used to denote a close friend or neighbor of the speaker's parents. As we understand this, it is an instance of metaphoric use of the word, based on connotative meaning. The use of "uncle" or "aunt" to refer to the friend of a parent has no reference to any genealogical or marital connection between the person so designated and one of the speaker's parents, for no such connection is presumed; it is only to imply solidarity of a sort, and a mode of conduct between the parties concerned, which is similar in some limited respect to that appropriate to kin (or relatives by marriage) who are designated by these terms. It implies that ego behaves toward them, or that they behave toward him, to some extent *as if* they were uncles and aunts, e.g., familiar rather than formal courtesies on ego's part ("Uncle Bill" rather than "Mr. Smith"), gift giving by the metaphoric "uncle" and "aunt" at Christmas or on similar occasions, etc.

In considering metaphoric uses of this sort when they involve kinship terms, it is important to note certain other facts about them. For example, it is a matter of some importance that whereas "uncle" and "aunt" are commonly used to denote persons not presumed to be related to the speaker, the reciprocals "nephew" and "niece" are not so used; we have heard many people speak of (or to) close friends of their parents as "uncles" or "aunts," but we have yet to hear anyone speak of (or to) the children of their close friends as "nephews" or "nieces." It is also a matter of significance that when "uncle" and "aunt" are used to denote persons not related to the speaker, they are used (whether in address or in reference) only as titles with first names, and then never with the possessive pronouns. One can speak of a relative (in an appropriate context) as "my Uncle Bill," but of a nonrelative only as "Uncle Bill." The use of the possessive pronoun in the former expression normally implies the affirmation that "Bill (or Mr.) X is my uncle," whereas in the latter case no such implication is intended. All of this suggests that the widening involved when the terms "uncle" and "aunt" are extended from their primary designata—one's parents' siblings—to include the spouses of these, as well as grandparents' siblings and their spouses, is a rather different matter from the kind of widening involved when the same terms are extended to include friends of one's parents. The former is a matter of simple widening of the range of reference within the domain of relationships of genealogical and marital connection. The latter is extension outside this domain, resting solely on considerations of affect and conduct; it is euphemism and metaphor.

One may ask how in the general case, or even in the kinship case, we are to distinguish between metaphor and simple widening. To judge from the way in which the term metaphor is used in studies of language and literature, and to register also our own preference, the difference rests on the basis for expansion of a word's meaning. In the case of simple widening, no new defining features (in a componential definition) are added to those which define the primary sense of the word in question; it is simply that one or more of those features is dropped from the definition of the wider sense. In the case of simple narrowing, on the other hand, no defining features of the primary sense are dropped, but one or more other features are taken also to be criterial and must be added to the definition. The case of metaphoric extension contrasts with both of these. At least one of the defining features (criterial attributes) of the primary sense of the word is suspended in its metaphoric use, and in its place some feature of *connotative meaning* which is associated with the primary or some simple widened sense of the word is made criterial for the metaphoric expression. Thus, a Latin dictionary gives "grandson," "nephew," and "spendthrift" or "prodigal" as meanings of the word *nepos*. Grandson is the primary sense; nephew a simple widened sense; and spendthrift or prodigal is a metaphoric sense—perhaps derived from some aspect of the jural-status relationship between mother's brother and sister's son. Similarly, the use of the Iroquois word for grandmother to refer to the moon, and of the word for mother to refer to the earth, are metaphoric. (The metaphor and its basis in the latter case—mother earth—are so common that one suspects they may be almost universal. In the other, one part of the metaphor is also, or probably used to be, almost universal: the role of the moon in governing agricultural activities. The other part, the role of lineage grandmothers in organizing these activities, was a matter of Iroquois culture.)

In the matter of kinship terms, this view of the nature of metaphor raises the question of what attributes are to be regarded as criterial in this domain, as opposed to those which are to be regarded as "accidental" and connotational. This is a matter about which anthropologists have had serious disagreements, and this is the reason for Chapter 2 in this study.

The root concept signified by a polysemic term is here described as its *structurally primary significatum* or as its *primary sense*. As we note again later, the structural primacy of a particular significatum of a polysemic term is relative to a particular "semantic domain" (Frake 1962; Conklin 1962: 124; Lounsbury 1956: 61–62; Lyons 1968: 429–34; Ullmann 1962: 243–50). The structurally primary significatum of a kinship term is not necessarily its structurally primary significatum in an absolute sense, i.e., in relation to yet wider semantic domains within the language (e.g., note the case of *femme* above).

The derivative or extended applications of polysemic words are often distinguishable from their primary or logically most prior applications by means of *lexical markers*. A term used in an extended sense may be accompanied (often optionally) by additional terms or phrases which serve to indicate that it is being used in an extended sense. The qualifying terms "by marriage," "step," "in-law," and "great" used in conjunction with English kinship terms are such markers. In the opposition "uncle" versus "great-uncle," the former term may be described as the *unmarked term* and the latter as the *marked* term. Similarly, the use of a kinship term in its primary sense may be lexically marked, as in the opposition "natural father" versus "adoptive father" or "step-father." The extended applications of polysemic terms often occur without their lexical markers: in direct address or in the use of kinship terms as titles with proper names, we seldom refer to our "great-uncles" as such but instead as "uncles." In cases like this the opposition that distinguishes the primary and derivative significata of the term is neutralized (or suspended) and the unmarked term is used to designate either the structurally primary category or the higher-order category created by this neutralization. That is to say, if we suspend or ignore the distinction between one and two ascending generations removed from ego, the result in the case of "uncle" versus "great-uncle" is the derivative category "male kinsmen of ascending generations and of the first degree of collaterality." This category is also labeled "uncle." It consists of the structurally primary category "uncle" proper and the derivative category "great-uncle." As Greenberg (1966: 72) has observed, the unmarked member of an "oppositional category" (e.g., "uncle" versus "great-uncle") typically represents either the entire category or *par excellence* the opposite member to the marked category. (For extensive discussion of the concept "unmarked" versus "marked" see Greenberg 1966; also Jakobson 1957.)

Finally, componential analysis, which has so far dealt only with signification[7]—"with definitive attributes and the ways in which they combine and are mutually ordered" (Goodenough 1967: 1204)—should be distinguished from other approaches to semantic analysis which are principally concerned with connotation, e.g., the "semantic differential" technique of Osgood (1957). There are, of course, many psychological, sociological, and anthropological concerns, including the study of kinship terminologies, for which connotation is a highly important consideration; but for many such concerns "signification is even more fundamental, for we can understand what a word signifies without reference to what it connotes, but we cannot understand what it connotes without reference to its signification" (Goodenough 1967: 1204).

---

[7] This is not quite true. Goodenough (1951: 111–19; 1965a) has presented limited formal analyses of some status connotations of Trukese kinship terms. See also Pospisil (1964: 401–4).

2 Is It a Kinship Terminology?

According to Holmberg (1950: 52) the classificatory system to be analyzed here is a *kinship system* and the class labels are *kinship terms*. Holmberg did not elaborate on this description nor did he review the ethnographic evidence that led him to describe the system in these terms. We may assume, however, that he was using "kinship" in the conventional sense to express his understanding that each of these words is the "name" of a genealogically established category, a category of kin. As such, each word may be employed in direct address or in reference to denote particular kinsmen or to designate the category itself. Insofar as any social significance is assigned to the fact of being one terminologically distinguished kind of kinsman as opposed to another, the terms may also carry status connotations.

Classificatory systems of this kind, premised on genealogical reference, are widely reported in the ethnographic literature, and many anthropologists have argued, on the basis of what they have taken to be substantial ethnographic facts, that they are a common if not universal feature of human cultures. Yet others deny this assumed universality of genealogically based systems and argue that many reputed systems of kin classification are instead some other kind of "relationship" system which the ethnographers have mistakenly identified as systems of kin classification. The mistakes, they argue, have been due largely to the fact that one's kin and other relatives (e.g., relatives by marriage) do get classified under the terms of these systems, but only accidentally, because they are related (socially) to ego in some other way too. This other way, then, forms the basis of the classifications. Since it just so happens that kin are incidentally classified under the terms of these systems, the naive ethnographer may easily have mistaken such a system for a system of kin classification— or so the argument goes—especially if he assumes, again naively, that every culture "recognizes" relations of kinship or genealogical connection

13

and has a system of kin classification (because it is "natural" to do so). Acting on this assumption, he might employ the "genealogical method" (Rivers 1914*b* [1968]) to gather data on the denotata of the terms; he would find considerable agreement on how particular types of kin are classified, and he might regard this agreement as support for his initial assumption that he is dealing with a set of kinship terms. Since he assumes that he is dealing with kinship terms, he translates them by reference to their nearest English equivalents. But, the argument goes on, such translations may be very misleading: there may be only an accidental correlation between certain kinds of genealogical connection and the kinds of relationships which are the actual bases of classification in the system under consideration, and so to translate its terms into English kinship terms may be to treat accidental or incidental features as though they were distinctive features. Since it is one of the tasks of the ethnographer to discover and to report as accurately as possible the distinctions and categories by which a people order their social lives, the mistake may well lead to radical misunderstanding of the social system in question.[1]

The Theory of Systems of Social Classification

According to Needham (1961; 1964*a*), Holmberg's report on the Siriono "kinship system" is a case in point: what we have to deal with here (and in many other cases) is not a system of kin classification but an *asymmetric prescriptive alliance system of social classification*, which is radically different from a system of kin classification (see Needham 1962*a*; 1962*b*; 1964*b*). Therefore, before we take up the Siriono system itself, we should consider the theory of *systems of social classification* in some detail. In this chapter we outline that theory and show how it has been applied, with some difficulty, to the Siriono case. We do not consider in detail many of the arguments that have been advanced in support of the theory in general or that have so far been, or might further be, advanced against it. These are considered in Chapter 3.

Needham's theory of asymmetric prescriptive alliance systems of social classification is a development from and a clarification of Lévi-Strauss's (1949 [1969]) theory of *systems of generalized exchange*. The latter is related to yet another theory now widely known as the *unity of the lineage theory* of so-called Crow- and Omaha-type systems of kin classification.

---

[1] These arguments have an interesting "ancient history," but for some more recent statements of them, which manage to avoid most of the pseudohistoricism associated with the earlier formulations, see Beattie (1964); Leach (1961); Needham (1958*a*; 1962*a*; 1966*a*); Schneider (1968*b*); Firth (1968).

In many systems of alleged kin classification, any person denotes his mother's brother's daughter (MBD) by the same term as he denotes his mother's sister (MZ) and, usually, his mother (M), and he denotes his mother's brother's son (MBS) by the same term he uses to denote his mother's brother (MB); conversely, in these same systems a female speaker denotes her father's sister's child ($\female$ FZC) by the same term as she denotes her own children ($\female$ C) and her sister's children ($\female$ ZC), and a male speaker denotes his father's sister's child ($\male$ FZC) by the same term as he uses to denote his sister's children ($\male$ ZC). These systems have become known as *Omaha-type systems*, and the "terminological equations" above are regarded as their definitive or typologically distinctive features (see Murdock 1949: 166–67). In some other systems, commonly described as *Crow-type systems* (Murdock 1949: 166), we find the "mirror image"[2] of this arrangement: father's sister's son (FZS) is classified with father's brother (FB) or father (F), and father's sister's daughter (FZD) with father's sister (FZ); conversely, a man classifies his MBD with his own C and a woman classifies her MBC with her BC.

It is important, however, to distinguish further among those systems which are of the Crow or Omaha types. In many, or perhaps most, of these systems, the most distinctive terminological equations are considerably more extensive than noted above. For example, in most so-called Omaha-type systems, the term denoting M and MBD may be further extended to MBSD, and that denoting MB and MBS may be extended to MBSS, and so on through all of the agnatic descendants of the MB. Similarly, in a Crow-type system the term denoting FZ and FZD may be extended not only to FZS but also FZDS, and so on through all of the uterine male descendants of the FZ. Furthermore, in some, but not all, of these systems, these equations appear to begin with the grandparental kintypes MF or FM, so that in some Omaha-type systems we find MF = MB = MBS = MBSS, etc., and in some Crow-type systems we find FM = FZ = FZD = FZDD, etc. It is important to distinguish between so-called Crow- and Omaha-type systems which do and do not make these more extensive terminological equations, because Radcliffe-Brown (1952: 70) intended his unity of the lineage theory of Crow- and Omaha-type systems to apply only to those terminological systems whose apparent "lineal equations" extend over at least three generations.

One way to interpret these systems is to suppose that in, say, an

---

[2] By "mirror image" we mean that if the sexual component of each of the symbols in the kintype notation is reversed, those terminological equations commonly regarded as distinctive of an Omaha-type system are "transformed" into the terminological equations commonly regarded as distinctive of a Crow-type system. For example, the mirror image (in this sense) of M is F, of B is Z, and of D is S; thus the mirror image of the equation MBD = MZ = M is FZS = FB = F.

Omaha-type system the term by which any ego denotes his or her M, MZ, and MBD, etc., is one whose primary designatum is the same category as is designated by English "mother," i.e., one's presumed genetrix, and that the term is extended to more distant kin such as MZ, MBD, etc., who are thus "classificatory mothers." Conversely, the term by which any ego designates his or her offspring as such is extended by a woman to her ZC and FZC, etc., who are thus her "classificatory children." However, it so happens that Omaha-type systems of kin classification are quite commonly found in association with patrilineal descent groups such as lineages or clans, and this association has led some anthropologists (e.g., Radcliffe-Brown 1950; 1952: 70ff.) to argue that the conceptual basis of the extensions of their terms is common descent-group affiliation:[3] in a society with patrilineal descent groups, MZ, MBD, MBSD, etc. belong to the same descent group as the mother herself. Similarly, Crow-type systems of kin classification are rather commonly, but not exclusively, found in association with matrilineal descent groups: in such a society FZD belongs to the same descent group as her mother, FZ, and thus—or so goes the argument—FZD is classified together with FZ.

Radcliffe-Brown assumed that terminological extensions are always socially motivated; the extension of a term from one type of kinsman to another is usually indicative of *and based on* the fact that ego extends to the more distant types some form of conduct, or some attitude or sentiment, which applies most properly to the closest kinsmen that term denotes. Thus, he argued, in an Omaha-type system MZ, MBD, etc. are treated terminologically as "mothers" because they are treated socially in much the same way as the mother herself, though their social equivalence to one's own mother may be limited. Moreover, socially they are treated "like" the mother herself because they belong to the same patrilineal descent group (Radcliffe-Brown 1952: 67, 70).

Although he was probably aware that Omaha-type systems of kin classification also occur in societies without patrilineal descent groups (and Crow-type systems also occur in societies without matrilineal descent groups), Radcliffe-Brown nevertheless described what he took to be their most distinctive structural principle as the principle of the unity of the lineage group. By this he meant that

> for a person who does not belong to the lineage but is connected with it through some important bond of kinship or marriage, its

[3] Murdock (1949: 167) found a fairly strong correlation between his Omaha-type systems and "exclusive patrilineal descent with exogamy." It should be noted, however, that the definitions of Omaha- and Crow-type systems employed by Murdock and Radcliffe-Brown are somewhat different; Murdock's definition would doubtless encompass all the systems encompassed by Radcliffe-Brown's but not vice versa.

members constitute a single category, with a distinction within the category between males and females, and possibly other distinctions also (1952: 70).

The presumed principle of the unity of the lineage group is thus supposed to provide both a formal account (see Chapter 3) and a sociological explanation of Crow- and Omaha-type systems of kin classification.

According to some anthropologists, this interpretation of Crow- and Omaha-type systems is seriously mistaken. As they see it, the fundamental fallacy in the argument is the unnecessary and unwarranted assumption that the terms in question have primary and extended senses; this assumption, they argue, has no basis in linguistic or sociological fact; it rests on little more than a naive, ethnocentric prejudice on the part of the ethnographer (or the theoretician). These anthropologists argue that each of the terms of a Crow- or Omaha-type system serves to designate a single *social category*, these categories being defined not genealogically but by reference to membership of descent groups. According to this "stronger" version of the unity of the lineage theory, the term that is used to denote, for example, one's MB—and which some anthropologists say is extended from that primary designatum to other kinsmen such as MBS and MBSS because the latter are members of the same descent group as the MB (in a patrilineal society)—is in fact a term whose sole designatum is the class "man of my mother's lineage (or clan) of her generation or below." Similarly, the term used to denote one's father or presumed genitor is supposed rather to designate the category "man of my father's lineage and of his generation (or age level)" (see Beattie 1958; Leach 1958; 1961: Chapters 2, 3).

According to proponents of this stronger version of the unity of the lineage theory, it provides an adequate account of the usage of the terms in question, and it does so without any assumptions about primary versus extended senses; therefore, they argue, the assumption is wholly unnecessary. Some proponents of this theory of Crow- and Omaha-type systems have noted that in some cases the words in question may at times be used quite specifically to refer to particular types of kinsmen as such (see Hocart 1937; Leach 1958; Beattie 1958). Such usages are of course inconsistent with the argument that the terms are not kinship terms, for to say that a social-category word may be used specifically to denote a particular type of kinsman as such is also to say that it has a kin-category-designating sense (though the designatum may comprise but a single kintype such as F, M, or MB).[4]

---

[4] A single-member category is no less a category than a multiple-member category (cf. Leach 1958: 124).

To save the theory of social categories from these facts, some theorists have acknowledged that the terms do have multiple category-designating senses, but, they argue, the relations between the different senses of a term are not relations of extension from a focal or primary kintype referent. These latter referents, it is argued, are to be regarded as "special cases," narrowed senses, as it were, of the more general and primary categorical senses of the terms. The primary referent is the broad social category itself, and the kin category sometimes designated by the same term is the derivative category. Thus, for example, it is argued that, in an Omaha-type system, the term designating the category "man of my lineage and of my father's generation" may sometimes be used specifically to refer to one's father (or presumed genitor) as such; it is so used to designate a special case of a man of the social category in question (see Beattie 1958; and for a parallel example in a Crow-type system, see Leach 1958; Powell 1969*b*: 603).

To the best of our knowledge, no proponent of the theory of social categories has so far elaborated on this argument or related it to what is known about the semantics of polysemic words in general. Yet the argument is not wholly implausible. As we noted in Chapter 1, French *femme*, when used in the sense of "wife," signifies a special case of "woman," but "woman" is the more general and certainly the structurally primary sense of the term. Thus, derivative senses and ranges of polysemic terms may be more restricted than their primary senses and ranges, and there is no a priori reason to argue, just because a word may designate a more specific and narrowly defined category of kin as well as a much more broadly defined social category, that the former sense is ipso facto (because of its relative narrowness) the primary sense (see Leach 1958: 123–24).

ALLIANCE SYSTEMS OF SOCIAL CLASSIFICATION.   A variant of the "stronger" version of the unity of the lineage theory of Crow- and Omaha-type systems is concerned with those systems of kin classification found in societies featuring rules of marriage between men and their mother's brother's daughters. That is to say, some Omaha-type systems are found in societies in which there is (allegedly) a rule of marriage between a man and his MBD, or, failing the availability of a MBD, any woman who is designated by the same term. It has become widely supposed in recent years that these systems of classification are not in fact systems of kin classification but that they are instead yet another kind of system of social classification, and that, although they are superficially similar in some respects to Crow- and Omaha-type systems, they are not strictly comparable to those systems based simply on lineage or clan affiliation. For it is reasoned that the terminological equations of kintypes (accidentally) effected by these systems are products of an additional structural principle which is, in a sense, more fundamental to these systems than the principle of the unity of the lineage group. The social structural and terminological principle in question has been described as *prescribed marital alliance* between unilineal descent groups. Thus, these classificatory systems have become known as *prescriptive alliance systems*, or more specifically as *asymmetric prescriptive alliance systems of social classification* (Needham 1962*b*; 1966*a*).

According to Lévi-Strauss (1949 [1969]), in a number of societies (e.g., Kachin, Batak, Gilyak, Garo, Khasi, etc.) marriage is regulated by a system of prescribed affinal (marital) alliance between exogamous and localized unilineal descent groups (which are sometimes patrilineal, sometimes matrilineal). From the perspective of any particular descent group, the other groups of the society are divided into three mutually exclusive categories: (1) those from which the men of that group may take women to be their wives ("wife-givers"); (2) those to which the men of that group must give their sisters or daughters as wives ("wife-takers"); and (3) those which are structurally equivalent to that group itself and from which its men may not take wives and to which they may not give women as wives. Such a society Lévi-Strauss describes as being ordered as a *system of generalized (indirect) exchange*. The immediate contrast is with *systems of restricted (direct) exchange*, e.g., societies in which there are only two groups, or in which the several descent groups are divided into two mutually exclusive categories, with the requirement that the men of either category must take their wives from the other category. (This is a fairly simple case of a system of restricted exchange; Lévi-Strauss also discusses a number of more complex cases such as the so-called marriage-class systems of the Australian Aborigines, which may involve sets of four or eight, rather than just two, categories.)

Lévi-Strauss observes that the systems of reputed kin classification of societies ordered as systems of generalized exchange are typically relatively simple, at least insofar as they feature a "paucity of terms of reference" (1969: 263). This "paucity," he argues, is due to the fact that

> the rule of marriage assimilates affines to a certain type of kin [e.g., wife's father (WF) to MB and wife's brother (WB) to MBS, etc.], which results in an initial terminological economy, and because family relationships are thought of in terms of groups [e.g., "wife-takers" versus "wife-givers"], so that individuals need be denoted only summarily, and with respect to their position in the structure (1969: 263).

The "structure" in question is a system of prescribed affinal alliance between unilineal descent groups. Thus, although Lévi-Strauss does *not* specifically argue that the classificatory systems at issue are not systems of kin classification in the strict sense, his interpretation of them is a permutation of the "stronger" version of the unity of the lineage theory of Crow- and Omaha-type systems.

The specific difference between the alliance system theory interpretation and the unity of the lineage theory interpretation of certain systems of kin classification is the emphasis given by the former to relations of prescribed affinal (marital) alliance between lineages or clans *as such*. The stronger version of the unity of the lineage theory argues that the mother's lineage, for example, is treated terminologically as a more or less undifferentiated whole because all of ego's kin in that lineage are somehow "socially equivalent" to one another vis-à-vis ego. Alliance theory, on the other hand, (glossing over the ego-oriented or egocentric nature of the systems) locates the reputed "social equivalence" in the alleged wife- giving versus wife-taking relationship between the lineages as such. The argument is that the lineages are treated terminologically as wholes because they are allied as wholes, not simply because, from ego's perspective, the women of his mother's lineage are *his* potential wives. As Lévi-Strauss puts it, "The *connubium* [or marital relationship] is between the lineages considered as entities. In such a system there is an immediate confusion of generations" (1969: 369). Both the alliance system theory and the stronger version of the unity of the lineage theory argue that lineages are treated terminologically as wholes. Thus both posit the same structural principle, but they attribute its presence to different social causes.

What then of the fact that many ethnographers, reporting on societies and systems of "kin" classification which Lévi-Strauss interprets as systems of generalized exchange, have reported that in these societies there is either a prescription of, or a preference for, marriage between a man and his MBD? What, also, of the ethnographic reports that the classificatory systems in question are systems of "kin" classification premised on this kintype–specific marriage rule? Obviously, Lévi-Strauss's theory of the nature of these classificatory systems would seem on the surface to treat the latter reports as invalid, although Lévi-Strauss does not attempt to show how such misunderstandings might have arisen. However, Lévi- Strauss treats the former reports as valid. He argues that, in many systems of generalized exchange, kinswomen such as MBD are singled out from the category "women of wife-giving groups" as "the most satisfactory representatives" of women of this category (1969: 272), and a rule of marriage to the MBD in particular, be it prescriptive or preferential, provides the "simplest illustration" (1969: xxxii) of the more general rule of indirect exchange between unilineal descent groups. It is, moreover, the most direct and effective means of instituting or maintaining such a system of intergroup exchange (1969: Chapter 27). In other words, in these societies the marriage rule is one implicating unilineal descent groups; the further prescription of or preference for MBD-FZS marriage is a product or function of that rule. Thus, Lévi-Strauss argues, "from marriage with the matrilateral cross-cousin, to the exclusion of marriage with the patrilateral cousin, we can immediately infer a system of generalized exchange, one which thus involves more than two exchange *groups*" (1969: 363, italics ours).

In short, Lévi-Strauss's theory explains rules of matrilateral cross-cousin marriage and their associated systems of kin classification by reference to systems of prescribed affinal alliance between unilineal descent groups. The systems of classification, he argues, are not products or functions of the kintype–specific marriage rules (see Rivers 1914*b*); both are products or functions of the system of intergroup alliance, and all of these phenomena are expressions of the fundamental structural principle of generalized or indirect exchange between groups.

It should be noted that Lévi-Strauss does not insist that all cases of prescribed or preferred cross-cousin marriage rest on systems of exchange between unilineal descent groups. He notes that in some cases rules of bilateral cross-cousin marriage constitute modes of direct exchange in and of themselves, for the societies in which they occur lack unilineal "rules of descent," i.e., of "transmission of the family name." He argues (1969: 159, 315, 410) that there are "two methods for determining the spouse, viz., the method of classes and the method of relations" and both constitute modes or rules of exchange. The *method of classes* is exemplified by rules of marriage to women of particular categories, and these may be kin categories, or unilineally defined groups, or major social categories (such as the Australian so-called marriage classes or sections). The *method of relations* consists in rules of marriage to women of particular kintypes. As already suggested, he argues that both kinds of marriage rule may coexist in the same society and that rules of bilateral cross-cousin marriage (a form of direct exchange) may occur in the absence of unilineal descent groups and rules of direct exchange between them. *But he does not concede as much for rules of matrilateral cross-cousin (MBD-FZS) marriage.* These are consistently interpreted as noted above, and he states: "generalized exchange can originate only in a harmonic regime" (1969: 266); i.e., a system of indirect exchange (including a rule of MBD-FZS marriage) is possible only in a society composed of localized, exogamous unilineal descent groups, and the "rule of residence" must be congruent with the "rule of descent."

Certain scholars, given more strongly than Lévi-Strauss appears to be to the theory of social categories, have found certain aspects of his theory unsatisfactory. Most pertinent here is Needham's contention that it is essential to distinguish between "prescriptive" and "merely preferential" marriage rules implicating men and their MBD (see Needham 1958*a*;

1962*b*). Needham argues that, for a number of reasons (e.g., simple demographic contingencies), it is fairly unlikely that any society does in fact literally prescribe marriage between MBD and FZS, though it is clear that in some societies marriage is quite literally prescribed between a man and a woman, any woman, of the "kin" category of which his MBD is a member. In other societies, Needham argues, there is no doubt an expressed preference for marriage between MBD-FZS, but such marriages are not prescribed, and neither is marriage prescribed with a woman of the "kin" category which includes a man's MBD. In the former societies, Needham argues, a man is required to take his wife from among the women of one specific category and marriages to women belonging to other categories are flatly forbidden (though they sometimes occur). In contrast, where MBD-FZS marriage is merely preferred, men may marry women belonging to categories other than the one containing their MBD, and no stigma attaches to such marriages. The distinction is important, Needham argues (1958*a*), because prescriptive marriage rules have "structural entailments" that merely preferential rules do not have. One of these is the system of "kin" classification: prescriptive rules affect the system of "kin" classification, preferential rules do not (see also Dumont 1968). Thus, in an *asymmetric prescriptive system* we find (incidental) terminological equations of kintypes such as

WF = MB, WB = MBS, WM = MBW, WZ = MBD,
HF = FZH, HB = FZS, HM = FZ, HZ = FZD, etc.,

and (incidental) terminological distinctions of kintypes such as

WF ≠ HF, WM ≠ HM,
WB ≠ FZS (MBS ≠ FZS),
WZ ≠ FZD (MBD ≠ FZD), etc.

Although such terminological equations and distinctions are only incidentally affected by the terms of an asymmetric prescriptive alliance system of social classification, they are nevertheless confined to such systems, and therefore they may be taken as indicative of the existence of such a system (or such a marriage rule) where more direct evidence is lacking (see Needham 1966*a*: 32).

According to Needham's view, as we understand it, Lévi-Strauss's theory is really concerned—or ought to have been concerned—solely with societies featuring prescriptive marriage rules. For Lévi-Strauss defines "the elementary structures of kinship," the focus of his study, as those societies whose systems of "kin" classification *are* affected by a rule of marriage with a specific type or category of "relative" (Lévi-Strauss 1969: xxiii); and Lévi-Strauss frequently appeals to certain terminological equations of kintypes (such as those noted above) to demonstrate that the society in question is ordered by a rule of generalized exchange between unilineal descent groups even where the ethnography is silent on the possible existence of such a system of exchange, or sometimes does not report even a preference for MBD-FZS marriage (Lévi-Strauss 1969: 274–75). In other words, according to Lévi-Strauss's theory, the structure of the system of "kin" classification is a distinctive feature of an "elementary structure of kinship," and it is, according to Needham, only where there is a prescriptive marriage rule that the system of "kin" classification meets the requirements of the theory.

Moreover, Needham argues, truly prescriptive marriage rules occur only in societies ordered by what Lévi-Strauss terms systems of generalized or restricted exchange between unilineal descent groups. In these societies the requirement of marriage to a woman of a specific category of relationship is the *one and only* marriage rule. In a system of generalized exchange, the rule is that a man must marry a woman of a group related to his group as a wife-giver, and, conversely, he may not marry a woman of a group related to his group as a wife-taker (e.g., a FZD), nor may he marry a woman of a group that is terminologically equivalent to his own group. The prescribed category is "woman of a wife-giving group." Thus, to say that a man must marry a woman of a specific category of relationship, *one* specific "social category," is merely to assert in another way that he must marry a woman of a wife-giving group.

In Needham's view, the systems of kin classification of societies with prescriptive marriage rules have essentially nothing to do with relations of genealogical connection (or kinship) and so they are not, strictly speaking, systems of kin classification (1966a: 31). They are better termed *asymmetric prescriptive alliance systems of social classification*. It just so happens that, because in a patrilineal society a man is obliged to take his wife from the same group (or from the same type of group) as his father took his wife, his MBD is one of his proper potential spouses; MBDs are inevitably members of wife-giving groups, and they are classified as they are *because* they are members of wife-giving groups, not because there is any rule of or preference for marriage to a MBD as such. Further still, since the term that designates the category which inevitably (albeit incidentally) contains WF and MB is one designating the category "man of a wife-giving group," such kinsmen as MBS and such affinal relatives as WB are typically denoted by the same term, or so it is concluded from this line of argument.

As for the common report that in these societies there is a rule of marriage between MBD and FZS, this can be disposed of by the argument that such reports are typically based, again, on little more than our naive ethnocentric supposition that all societies, to one degree or another, order social relations by reference to relations of presumed genealogical connection and utilize systems of kin classification to facilitate this ordering. Because certain types of kin are consistently, though only incidentally, included in the social categories of these societies, and because in some of these societies there is in fact a secondary, though "structurally" insignificant, preference for MBD-FZS marriage (Needham 1962a: 247), ethnographers have been misled into thinking they were dealing with MBD-FZS marriage rules and systems of kin classification based on the assumption of MBD-FZS marriage. To some extent, however, they have misled themselves with their ill-founded assumptions about the universality of systems of kin classification and terminological extensions—or so the argument goes. According to Needham, a "protracted series of comparative investigations," has shown that

> in a prescriptive alliance system the relationship terms are applied completely generally within the recognized bounds of the society; i.e., that the terms are not "kinship" terms, distinguishing a limited range of relatives from all other members of the society who are not kin, but they are general terms of *social classification*. Non-prescriptive terminologies, however, do by contrast denote recognized relatives of varying degrees of closeness, as against unrelated members of the society who are distinguished by other means (1964b: 310–11).

Lévi-Strauss and Needham agree, then, that in dealing with systems of reputed matrilateral cross-cousin marriage and their associated systems of kin classification, we have in fact to deal first and foremost, or according to Needham, only, with systems of prescribed asymmetric affinal alliance between unilineal descent groups (but see Lévi-Strauss 1965: 17; 1969: xxx–xxxv).

There is, however, a further difference between the theories of Lévi-Strauss and Needham. Lévi-Strauss maintains that in some societies there are rules of FZD-MBS (i.e., patrilateral cross-cousin) marriage (1969: 438ff.). But, he argues, these are never aspects of systems of generalized exchange between unilineal descent groups, the reason being that consistent FZD-MBS marriage must operate as follows: Group A gives women to group B in one generation, but in the next generation B may (or must) give women back to A. A rule of FZD-MBS marriage cannot, that is, lead to or be a part of a system in which some groups are defined exclusively as wife-givers and others as wife-takers, and so it cannot be part of a "total structure of reciprocity" implicating all of the groups of the society in a system of *unidirectional* exchange of women in marriage. Thus, despite the fact that FZD-MBS and MBD-FZS marriage rules are both "unilateral," they amount to radically different kinds of things. The latter belong to a special kind of marriage-class system—one involving a

number of groups (an odd number of types of groups) in systematic indirect exchange—but the former can never be aspects of such a system for
they violate its most fundamental principle.

Needham agrees, but he adds that, if we take the notion of prescription seriously, it is evident that a society alleged to prescribe FZD-MBS
marriage must in fact be ordered as a system of symmetric alliance (or
direct exchange), in which there is merely a preference for FZD-MBS
rather than MBD-FZS marriage, though both are permitted. Thus, Needham argues, there is only one kind of system of generalized or indirect
exchange, i.e., the kind of system in which marriage is prescribed with a
woman, any woman, of a "social category" which happens to include the
kintype MBD, but which excludes the kintype FZD; systems of prescribed
patrilateral cross-cousin marriage are a figment of the anthropological
imagination.

Needham argues that Lévi-Strauss was correct, however, in maintaining that the laterality of the prescribed marriage (matrilateral or
patrilateral) is not related to the "mode of reckoning descent": it is not the
case that matrilateral cross-cousin marriage is a function of the presence
of patrilineal descent groups and that patrilateral cross-cousin marriage
is a function of the presence of matrilineal descent groups (see Homans
and Schneider 1955; Eyde and Postal 1961). For, in the first place, prescriptive rules of patrilateral cross-cousin marriage or, better, patrilateral
asymmetric alliance systems, do not exist, but this has nothing to do with
the nature of the descent groups of which a society may be composed.
In the second place, asymmetric alliance (or so-called matrilateral cross-
cousin marriage) is possible in matrilineal as well as patrilineal societies.
Unfortunately, Needham argues, the two matrilineal cases—Garo and
Khasi—adduced by Lévi-Strauss in support of the argument, do not in
fact possess prescriptive rules of marriage of the sort required by the
theory: the systems of kin classification of these societies are symmetric,
not asymmetric (Needham 1961: 241; 1962b: 56, 65; but see also 1966c:
143–48). Thus, although there would seem to be no formal or structural
reasons for the nonexistence of *matrilineal* asymmetric alliance systems,
"it has not been empirically demonstrated" that such systems do exist
(Needham 1961: 241).

NEEDHAM ON THE SIRIONO.   This brings us, at last, to the Siriono.
According to Needham (1961: 241), Siriono is one of at least three societies
ordered as *matrilineal asymmetric alliance systems*, the other two being
Mnong Gar of central Vietnam (Condominas 1960) and Belu of central
Timor, Indonesia (Vroklage 1953). That Siriono society is so ordered, and
that the Siriono system of kin classification is in fact a matrilineal asym-

metric prescriptive alliance system of social classification, is demonstrated, Needham argues, by the following ethnographic facts. Holmberg (1950: 80–83) reports that for the Siriono the "preferred" form of marriage is that between a man and his MBD; marriage between FZD and MBS is forbidden; marriage between parallel cousins is likewise forbidden. However, if a MBD is not available, a man may marry a "second cross-cousin," a "classificatory cross-cousin" or a "nonrelative," and it is clear that by "second cross-cousin" and "classificatory cross-cousin" Holmberg means women whom a man designates as *yande*, the term by which he designates his MBD, and which Holmberg glosses as "potential spouse" (1950: 54). Holmberg notes also that he found a few cases of marriage between a man and his "first cross-cousin once removed," but these, he says, are "exceptional" and "secondary," i.e., they occur only in cases of polygyny and not as initial marriages (1950: 81). Needham concludes that "from the combination of 'preferred' matrilateral cross-cousin marriage and prohibition of patrilateral crosscousin marriage we may immediately conclude upon the probable existence of asymmetric alliance" (1961: 243), and he then proceeds to analyze the "relationship terminology, which may be expected definitely to reveal whether or not Siriono society is so organized" (1961: 243).

Needham's analysis consists of the following observations. The system features certain "minimal equations and distinctions" which are "typical" of "lineal descent systems" (1961: 243–44): for male ego,

$$F = FB \qquad FB \neq MB$$
$$M = MZ \qquad FZ \neq MZ$$
$$B = MZS/FBS \qquad B \neq MBS, FZS$$
$$S = BS \qquad S \neq ZS$$

This is, if certain kinsmen are terminologically equated because they are unilineally related to one another, or because they belong to the same unilineally defined group, then FB, for example, will belong to the same "relationship category" as F, but MB will belong to a different category, and so on. Moreover, the system lacks any special affinal terms; all relatives by marriage are terminologically equated with certain kinds of kinsmen, the following terminological equations and distinctions, again, being typical of an asymmetric prescriptive alliance system of social classification (Needham 1961: 244): for a male ego,

$$FB = MZH \qquad MBS \neq FZS$$
$$MZ = FBW \qquad MBD \neq FZD$$
$$MB = WF \qquad ZH \neq WB$$
$$MBW = WM$$

Furthermore, the system may be represented, according to Needham, in the form of a genealogical diagram in which every man is married to his MBD and every woman to her FZS (1961: 244). The implication is that the diagram provided by Needham constitutes an adequate representation of the structure of the system and, of course, of the distribution of its terms.

From these observations Needham concludes that it is "perfectly clear" that marriage is in fact *prohibited* with any woman of any category other than *yande*, the category which contains a man's MBD but not his FZD; marriage is thus *prescribed* with a woman of the category *yande*; "therefore, Siriono society constitutes a clear instance of asymmetric alliance" (1961: 246). The occasional marriages between men and kinswomen who are not their *yande* are attributed to necessary adjustments to demographic contingencies (e.g., the unavailability of MBDs or other women classified as *yande*), or, possibly, they indicate "an incipient breakdown of the alliance system" (1961: 246).

From preceding and subsequent discussion of asymmetric alliance systems (see Needham 1958a; 1958b; 1962b), it would seem that to describe a society as so ordered, in Needham's sense of the phrase, is to say that it is a society composed of a set of unilineal descent groups engaged in the prescribed unidirectional exchange of woman in marriage. However, the Siriono, according to Holmberg, are not ordered into any such groups. They are ordered instead into a number of relatively small and effectively endogamous *bands*, and each band is further organized into a small number of *matrilocal extended families*. The extended families have no corporate properties and, to all appearances, they are not even named; they appear to be little more than relatively transient residential clusters within the band (Holmberg 1950: 49–52; see Chapter 8 for further discussion of Siriono social structure). Therefore, it is unclear how, or in what sense, Siriono society may be said to be organized as a *matrilineal* asymmetric alliance system.

Needham (1961: 246ff.) acknowledges that the ethnography offers little or no evidence to support the contention that Siriono society is so ordered, in the sense that it is composed of a set of matrilineal descent groups implicated in a system of prescribed unidirectional exchange of women in marriage. These are no signs, other than the alleged structure of the system of kin classification, that the Siriono distinguish in any way, terminologically or behaviorally, between wife-givers and wife-takers. The indications are that "the Siriono extended family is not in effect a corporate group" (1961: 249), and there is nothing in the ethnography to suggest that, corporate or otherwise, these are the units of an asymmetric alliance system. Indeed, the endogamous nature of the nomadic groups, together with the very small scale of social life, means that we cannot expect to find in Siriono society the confrontation of corporate descent groups, clans or lineages, localized or dispersed, which in other societies of the type gives the alliance system such vital importance (1961: 249).

So it is not surprising that here "the alliance system has no political or other corporate significance" (1961: 248–49). (In these passages the phrase "alliance system" obviously refers only to the system of classification.)

Thus, Needham argues, the conclusion that Siriono society is ordered as an asymmetric alliance system "appears to hold in little more than a formal sense" (1961: 246). That is to say, we have here a society with an asymmetric alliance system of social classification, and, moreover, a *matrilineal* asymmetric alliance system of social classification—because, as in Crow-type systems, it equates FZ with FM and FZD with FZ, and this is a "matrilineal equation" (Needham 1961: 249; 1964a: 233) —but, curiously enough, there is no evidence for any "lineal" ordering of social relationships and, thus, no evidence for any concrete alliance system.

It is difficult, if not impossible, to reconcile this claim with many of Needham's previous and subsequent observations on what he calls asymmetric alliance systems and their associated systems of social classification. For he has consistently treated the system of intergroup alliance and the system of social classification as inherently associated phenomena. For example, the "lineal equations" of kintypes in these systems of classification are said to "denote corporately the lineal descent groups which are distinguished and related by the alliance system" (1961: 250), and here "alliance system" can refer only to a system of intergroup relations. And in numerous places Needham has argued that certain terminological equations and distinctions of kintypes such as those noted above are "totally incomprehensible" except as the incidental products of a system of classification which is an *integral* part of a system of asymmetric alliance between unilineal descent groups (see 1960; 1964a: 233). In other words, Needham has consistently treated both a system of maritally allied descent groups and a system of social classification consistent with such an arrangement between groups as being *equally* diagnostic of an asymmetric alliance system. The categories are said to "order social relations" within such a system (1964a: 237). Thus, for Needham as for Lévi-Strauss, the system of social relationships between groups and the system of classification are parts of an "indissoluble whole" (Lévi-Strauss 1969: 365; Needham 1960: 99–106). This is not, from Needham's perspective, to claim that the system of intergroup alliance is in any sense the "cause" of the system of classification, but it is, nevertheless, to claim a regular and consistent association between the two such that from the (incidental) pattern of kin classification a system of intergroup alliance may reliably be inferred (see again Needham 1960: 99–106).

So, it requires a substantial reformulation of the theory of alliance systems in order to argue that Siriono society is ordered as an asymmetric alliance system even though it features no corporate groups formally engaged in the indirect exchange of women in marriage, but simply because it features a system of kin classification that appears similar to those of societies which *do* feature systems of intergroup alliance. This reformulation is evident in Needham (1964*a*; 1964*c*; 1966*c*; 1967).

In 1964 (1964*a*: 233ff.), Needham returned to the question of Siriono "matriliny," and specifically to the crucial question of whether or not Siriono have matrilineal descent groups. Although in 1961 (1961: 249) Needham argued, as indeed appears to be the case, that Siriono "matrilocal extended families" are not to be regarded as corporate groups, in 1964 (1964*a*: 234) he described them as corporate, but without adducing any reasons for doing so, and he then proceeded to argue that, by some definitions of the terms, they might be regarded as corporate unilineal "descent groups." However, he noted, even if we should regard the matrilocal extended families as matrilineal descent groups, "we still have no evidential warrant to argue that [they] are corporate in the sense that they are alliance groups" (1964*a*: 234–35). Thus, he asked, "are lineal descent groups essential to prescriptive alliance?" (1964*a*: 236).

His answer, then, was that they are not: what is essential is a system of unilineally defined *categories* and relations of prescribed asymmetric alliance between them (1964*a*: 236–38). In the Siriono case, he argued, there is no doubt that the categories Holmberg describes as "categories of kin" are lineally defined and that asymmetric alliance or unidirectional exchange is prescribed: "These terms, when analyzed, cohere into a consistent terminology of asymmetric alliance . . . and *it is by this feature itself* that we determine that we are in the presence of such a system" (1964*a*: 236, emphasis ours). In other words, *the* distinctive feature of an alliance system is the structure of the system of classification, and this system may or may not be associated with a system of asymmetric alliance between corporate unilineal descent groups. But if the terms of an asymmetric alliance system of social classification need not designate "corporately" (i.e., as wholes) any unilineal descent groups, what else may they designate and still be regarded as the terms of an alliance system of social classification, rather than as, say, kinship terms?

According to Needham (1964*a*: 237), it is not possible to determine from Holmberg's data what the terms "denote" (i.e., designate): "they could apply to persons or to extended families or to shallow matrilineages. . . ." The important thing is that they designate categories which are somehow unilineally defined, and it is unimportant (for typological purposes anyway) whether the constituent units of the categories (the units which are regarded as unilineally related to one another and thus co-classified), are "persons," "extended families," or "lineages." However, if we may say with assurance of a particular terminological system that it is an asymmetric alliance system of social classification, and of the society which possesses it that it is ordered as an asymmetric alliance system, simply because the terminology in question features certain "minimal" terminological equations and distinctions of kintypes, what is left, then, of the presumed sociological distinctiveness of the category "asymmetric alliance systems"? (It should be recalled here that Needham *inferred* the existence of a prescriptive marriage rule in Siriono society from the pattern of kintype equations and distinctions, and from the report that MBDs are "preferred" whereas FZDs are prohibited as spouses, but in the final analysis the decision rested on the terminological data, not the jural.)

Consistent with this revised and sociologically weakened definition of the essential features of an asymmetric alliance system, Needham notes that, when he describes the Garo system of kin classification as a "terminology of symmetric prescriptive alliance,"

> It will be realized that this is a purely conventional description of the case, couched in terms which have become usual in discussions of prescriptive alliance and are convenient for comparison; it neither states nor implies anything about matters of fact in Garo society or about the concerns of Garo individuals (1966c: 144, note 5; but see also 1966a: 31–32).

The same considerations must apply *pari passu* to the designation "asymmetric alliance system of social classification." Thus it is no longer puzzling that the Siriono should have an asymmetric alliance system of social classification but no system of asymmetric alliance between unilineal descent groups (see Needham 1961: 246ff.), because there is, by definition of the two phenomena, no longer any necessary relationship between them.

But the Siriono case and Needham's analysis of it present two further difficulties for the theory of alliance systems, and Needham has yet to deal with or even to take note of them. First, if we are to describe a particular system of alleged kin classification as an asymmetric alliance system of social classification simply because it features certain "minimal" terminological equations and distinctions of kintypes, we must at least be clear about what those "minimal" equations and distinctions are (as per Murdock 1949 on Crow, Omaha, and other types of kinship terminologies). However, it is not yet clear from Needham's discussions of alliance systems of social classification just exactly which terminological equations and distinctions of kintypes are supposed to indicate quite definitely that we have to deal with a special kind of system of monosemic "social-category" labels and not, for example, a system of polysemic kinship terms. In his original Siriono analysis, Needham stated: "there is a structural necessity in asymmetric alliance systems to distinguish wife-givers from wife-takers, and they are usually categorically distinguished in the terminology of social classification" (1961: 251). But shortly thereafter the "necessity" of this terminological distinction was put somewhat more strongly: "The first and most obvious" of the "essential and general features of asymmetric classification" is the "distinction . . . of at least three lines of different term composition, corresponding to the minimally triadic and cyclic character of the system" (Needham 1962a: 242), the latter system being, of course, a system of inter-descent-group alliance. However, "in the Siriono terminology we find that in certain respects they [wife-givers and wife-takers] are on the contrary identified, e.g., in the equations FZ = MBW and FZH = MB" (1961: 251).

Now it would seem that, insofar as the terminology fails to distinguish systematically between kintypes that would belong to wife-giving and wife-taking groups or categories in an asymmetric alliance system, it is not accurate to say that "in some respects" it "identifies" wife-givers and wife-takers. It must be said that it simply fails to make what is, by definition, the most "essential" and "general" distinction characteristic of an asymmetric alliance system of social classification. Indeed, the only terminological equations and distinctions of kintypes that approach being typical of all those classificatory systems Needham describes as asymmetric alliance systems are WF = MB, WM = MBW, HF = FZH, HM = FZ, WB = MBS ≠ FZS, WZ = MBD ≠ FZD, HB = FZS ≠ MBS, and HZ = FZD ≠ MBD, and their reciprocals. It is obvious that these could be pure and simple products of a rule of MBD-FZS marriage. It need not follow from such a rule that FZH ≠ MB and MBW ≠ FZ, for the co-classification of these types of relatives could be the product of yet another rule of kin classification, that is, yet another rule of terminological extension (see Chapter 4).

This brings us to the second difficulty. Although Needham argues that "what the terms denote is indeterminate and cannot be inferred from the classification [of kintypes?]. . . they could apply to persons or to extended families or to shallow matrilineages" (1964a: 237), he does in fact conclude that "The units associated in the alliance system appear . . . to be simply the elementary families" (1961: 249). Insofar as the terms of an asymmetric alliance system of social classification are supposed to refer to relative positions within and between the allied units, it would seem to follow that, in this case, the terms signify relative positions within and between maritally allied "elementary families." Moreover, Needham asks, if the Siriono do not distinguish systematically between wife-givers and wife-takers (as seems indicated by the equations FZ = MBW and MB = FZH, and of course their reciprocals), how do they "preclude the possibilities of bilateral confusion" (1961: 251); how do they know that a particular woman is to be classified as *yande* rather than as, say, *ari* (which category includes the prohibited kinswoman FZD)? How, in other words, is the marriageable category of woman defined? There are no named, corporate wife-giving versus wife-taking descent groups, so she cannot be a "woman of a wife-giving group"; she cannot be defined as the daughter of an *ami*, for *ami* denotes FZH as well as MB, and FZD is prohibited as a spouse; nor can she be defined as the daughter of an *ari*, for *ari* denotes FZ as well as MBW, and so on (Needham 1961: 251). Thus, by process of elimination, Needham comes to the conclusion:

> A possible method is to say that she is the daughter of a man who is *anongge* [B] to one's *ezi* [M]. . . . Given the scale of this society, this leads to the inference that the definition of *yande* is determined mainly, it seems, by genealogical means, tracing connection from the mother through particular individuals. This genealogical emphasis is consistent with the preference for the daughter of the maternal uncle, with the place of the elementary family in social life, and with the general lack of lineal features in the society; but it is an unusual procedure in an asymmetric alliance system . . . (1961: 252).

The last remark is of course something of an understatement. In the first place, no evidence other than the terminology itself has been adduced to show that there is any concrete alliance system present in this case. In the second place, if "the definition of *yande* is determined mainly . . . by genealogical means," it is ipso facto a kinship term, a word that serves to designate a category of kin. If the terms in question comprise a natural set, and Needham's analysis presumes that they do, then it follows that they are *all* kinship terms. What we have here, then, is a system of kin classification, although in 1961 (see also Needham 1962b: 83; 1966a: 31) alliance systems of social classification and systems of kin classification were regarded as radically different kinds of things.

Now it should be relatively obvious that the only reason that can be offered for treating the Siriono system of kin classification as an asymmetric alliance system of social classification (rather than the kind of system the ethnographer reported it to be) is that it makes certain terminological equations and distinctions of kintypes, which, it would have to be presumed, can result only from a system of asymmetric alliance between unilineal descent groups. Needham's more recent contention that the alliance may be between unilineally defined "categories," not necessarily corporate unilineal descent groups, is vitiated in the Siriono case by the fact that the sole evidence for the existence of such categories is the set of terminological equations and distinctions of kintypes which, he once argued, can result only from some sort of concrete intergroup alliance system. The sole ethnographic evidence bearing on the possible designata and significata of the terms of this system, and cited by Needham, consists of the data on kintype classification provided by Holmberg (but see also Schermair 1948; 1952; 1962). Thus, it is merely tautological to assert, as Needham does, that this is the terminology of an asymmetric prescriptive alliance system of social classification because it features certain "minimal" terminological equations and distinctions of kintypes. *To describe the system in this way, and on these grounds, tells us nothing about its inherent structure.*

The Relevance of Semantic Theory

Needham's original presumption about the factual basis of these terminological equations and distinctions of kintypes was itself presumed to rest on substantial ethnographic evidence (which has not been reviewed here, but see Needham 1962b), but the data that constitute that evidence do not "speak for themselves" and have to be interpreted in the light of sociological and, in this case, semantic theories. The fundamental semantic tenet underlying the alliance-theory interpretation of many systems of reputed kin classification is that the terms of those systems are monosemic: each designates a single unitary category. If, to the contrary, it were presumed that the terms may be polysemic, a good many of the empirical claims put forth by proponents of alliance-theory interpretations would have to be reckoned as ill-founded. Most importantly, if each of the terms of an alleged asymmetric system of social classification serves to designate more than one category, it could be that some of these *are* kin categories while others are, perhaps, "lineages as wholes" or "positions" within concrete alliance systems. And without the presumption that the terms designate *only* "lineages as wholes" or "positions" within concrete alliance systems, there would be no necessity to argue, as per Lévi-Strauss (1969), Needham (1962b) and Dumont (1968), that what we have to deal with in such cases are "total social systems" whose most distinctive structural principle is "prescriptive alliance."

Proponents of alliance-systems theory, to the best of our knowledge, do not argue that polysemy and extensions of meaning do not exist in the realm of systems of kin classification (see Needham 1964*b*: 310–11). What they do argue is that there is no evidence that the terms of what they describe as alliance systems of social classification have these semantic properties. Yet there are certain aspects of these systems for which alliance theorists have yet to account; indeed, they have for the most part simply ignored the existence of the linguistic and semantic data we have in mind. It is a matter of ethnographic fact that, in even the most commonly accepted indubitable cases of asymmetric prescriptive alliance social classification, distinctions *are* drawn between the closer and more distant kintype members of the categories.

Consider, for example, the case of the Kachin. According to Leach (1945 [1961: 29ff.]), the terms of the Kachin system of kin classification have primary and extended senses, though he provides no data on how the Kachin distinguish between the several different categories that may be designated by the same term. Leach has subsequently disavowed this claim and attributed his error to the fact that, in 1945, he "was still dominated by the views of Malinowski and . . . accepted uncritically the biographical approach to kinship advocated by Malinowski" (1961: 28). Yet there are good reasons to suppose that Leach's original claims were based not merely on theoretical presuppositions inherited uncritically from Malinowski but on what he then took to be substantial ethnographic facts.

Hanson's dictionary (1906) and grammar (1896) of the Kachin language report that Kachin distinguish between, for example, M and MZ as *nu* versus *nu dim* or *nu doi* in the case of mother's younger sister, or *nu tung* in the case of mother's elder sister. FBW is included among the "qualified" *nu*. Similar distinctions are reported for other Kachin kinship terms. It would appear that the kinship category designated by Kachin *nu* comprises in its primary range only women of the kintype M, whereas the derivative categories designated by the same term comprise certain more distant kintype denotata. Moreover, it would seem that inclusion in one or the other of the derivative categories depends on the relative age of the designated kinsman in relation to one's own mother (or, in the case of FBW, it depends on the relative ages of F and FB). In short, this linguistic evidence suggests quite strongly that the kintype M is the focal or primary denotatum of *nu*, that is, that the primary sense of *nu* is "mother," and the term is extended to certain other kinswomen and relatives by marriage who are thus treated as classificatory mothers and who can be properly categorized (as *nu dim, nu doi,* or *nu tung*) only by reference to one's own mother, in the literal sense of this term. (See also Leach 1954: 306–8.)

Linguistic distinctions of this sort are not atypical of those terminological systems that have been variously described as systems of generalized (or restricted) exchange or as systems of asymmetric (or symmetric) alliance. The data in the Siriono case are unusually full (see Schermair 1958; 1962). We argue in the following chapters that, contrary to the arguments of proponents of alliance theory, these linguistic distinctions are not readily interpretable in any other way than that in which we have interpreted the Kachin distinction between the various classes of *nu*, "mother."

In brief, the argument of the following chapters is that what we have here is a fairly simple system of kin classification. It is an unusual kind of system of kin classification insofar as it features one structural principle that is, so far as we know, restricted to only a few South American societies. But it is not an unusual kind of system insofar as it features what we term a "MBD-FZS–spouse equation rule in kin classification," because it shares this structural principle with a great many other systems of kin classification, viz., many of those that have been variously described as systems based on generalized exchange or asymmetric alliance systems of social classification.

The MBD-FZS–Spouse Equation Rule

We should note at this point, in order to avoid any possible confusion, precisely what we mean by the phrase "MBD-FZS–spouse equation rule in kin classification." Note in particular that in this expression the "rule" in question is one of kin classification, not of actual marriage transactions or of obligations to marry. The rule is that, for purposes of classifying kin, any man's MBD as a linking kinswoman is to be regarded as equivalent to his wife. As far as the ethnographic data permit us to determine, this rule does not rest on a prescription of MBD-FZS marriage, if by prescription we refer to an obligation or duty encumbant on each man to marry one or more of his MBDs, if such a kinswoman is available. Nor does it seem to rest on a general preference for MBD-FZS marriage, at least insofar as "a general preference" suggests that MBD-FZS marriage is generally regarded as, for some resaon, the best possible or most desirable kind of marriage that can be contracted. To all appearances, the rule of kin classification rests here on nothing more or less than the *right* of each man to claim one or more of his MBDs as a wife or wives (see Holmberg 1950: 81; and Chapter 8 of this study). We suggest in Chapter 9 that the same jural principle, or one very much like it, is probably the factual basis of many reports of prescribed or preferred MBD-FZS marriage, even in the cases of those societies that some anthropologists insist can be understood only as cases of asymmetric prescriptive alliance. Insofar as, in these societies, marriage between MBD-FZS rests on a rightful claim ascribed to men in respect of their MBDs, and this in itself constitutes a prescription in the most general sense of the term, these societies may be said to prescribe MBD-FZS marriage, even though they do not enjoin it.

II

At this point we might assume heuristically that what we have to deal with here is a system of kin classification and then go on to attempt to ascertain its structural characteristics—by subjecting the kintype data provided by Holmberg to formal or structural analysis. Should it prove possible to show that the distribution of terms over kintypes in the Siriono language can be understood as the product of a few relatively simple principles of kin classification, which presumably any Siriono could employ, we might then argue that it is highly probable that this is a system of kin classification and that it has the structure revealed by the formal analysis. But to do so would certainly prove unsatisfying to some anthropologists, especially those critics of componential analysis who maintain that, insofar as the data to be analyzed were gathered by "the genealogical method" (see Holmberg 1950: 51), there is little that the system can appear to be other than a kinship system, and that when analyzed the data will of course yield a genealogically structured system. Therefore, they argue, no such analysis can reasonably be said to show that the system is a system of kin classification, nor can it reasonably claim to tell us what are *the* meanings of the terms comprising that system (see Schneider 1968*b*; Tyler 1969).

The argument of the critics is correct, as far as it goes, but at least two points should be added. First, it is not at all certain that Holmberg's description of this as a system of kin classification rests solely on the genealogical data presented on pages 53–56 of his monograph and gathered by "the genealogical method." The ethnography provides other evidence to support the claim (see below). Second, it is true that if we analyze only genealogical data, we can obtain only genealogical results (and we cannot legitimately claim any others without going beyond the data). However, if this is not a system of kin classification and if "the genealogical method" was indeed misapplied in gathering data concerning the denotata of its terms, it seems rather unlikely that formal analysis of those data would be at all possible or that it would yield *sensible* results. Analysis of those data might result in something describable as a system of definitional and extension rules, but it is likely that, if the data really are not the data we ought to be working with, we should be forced to posit a set of rules so numerous and so complex that it would be obvious that they could not be the rules (or a paraphrase of the rules) that the Siriono themselves employ in classifying their kin. (For further discussion of the problem of the "cultural" and "psychological" validity of formal semantic analyses see Chapter 7.)

Be this as it may, it has to be acknowledged that the formal semantic analysis of systems of kin classification presents certain difficulties which have yet to be resolved and which make it difficult for the analyst to claim that his model of the system in question is *the* proper model, that is, the model which best represents the intrinsic semantic structure of the system in question. Some of these difficulties are dealt with in the following chapter (and others in Chapter 7), where we show that the problem of "alternative solutions" (see Goodenough 1956) is not as insurmountable as it has sometimes been made to appear. In any event, it is best not to let our claim that this *is* a kinship terminology rest on a "formal proof" that certain data provided by Holmberg can be made to appear systematic if we assume heuristically that it is one. The proper use of formal or structural analysis is not to show what the object of analysis is or may be but what its *structure* is or may be. "What is it?" is a question whose answer ought to be known before any attempt is made to determine how it is organized or structured. So before proceeding any further let us determine what evidence the ethnography offers to support Holmberg's description of this terminology as a kinship system.

Genealogical Connection

We must ask first whether or not there is any evidence that Siriono themselves posit some sort of interpersonal relatedness or connectedness that might reasonably be described as "genealogical connection." Is it because he presumes that such a relationship exists between himself and some other person that a Siriono addresses or refers to that other person by one of these words, the particular one being determined by the culturally posited distinctive features of the specific genealogical chain in question? In other words, does a Siriono refer to his presumed genetrix as his *ezi* precisely because he presumes she is his genetrix? Does he refer to his presumed genitor as his *eru* precisely because he presumes he is his genitor?

The critical term is "genealogical." The problem of defining it, and thereby "kinship," in a way that is cross-culturally useful has given anthropologists considerable difficulty (see Malinowski 1913: Chapter 6). Without entering into the history of the problem (as we hope to do at a later date), let us simply state that by "genealogical connection" we designate those *culturally posited* forms of interpersonal connectedness that are held to be direct consequences of processes of engendering and bearing children and that have the property of indissolubility.[5] To phrase this another way, genealogical connection is employed here as a general cover term for a wide variety of culturally postulated forms of *congenital* relatedness between persons.

So defined, genealogical connection may entail an enduring and indissoluble relationship of "sharing" of one or another component of a person's being with those two parties presumed to have been responsible for bringing that person into being. "Body," "bone," "blood," "flesh," "soul," and even "appearance,"[6] are some of the more common culturally posited shared components of being. In some cases, however, the enduring and indissoluble relationship is only vaguely defined; it is simply a matter of two persons' being jointly responsible for another's being, with no particular aspect (or aspects) of the other's being singled out as somehow critical. The terms of this stipulative theoretical definition of genealogical connection only require that, in local theories, sexual intercourse is considered necessary to the processes of engendering and bearing children. They do *not* require that local theories regard sexual intercourse as *the* sufficient condition for the initiation of these processes.[7] Beyond this, the processes may be (and are) conceived in a variety of ways.

Relations of genealogical connection, or kinship proper, are fundamentally different from and are logically and temporally prior to any social relations of kinship. Relations of genealogical connection may be

---

[5] We do not assume that concepts of genealogical connection, as they are defined here, are a cultural universal, but we suspect that they are far more common than much of the ethnographic and theoretical literature might lead one to believe. Few if any of the numerous alleged cases of "ignorance of physiological paternity" (or even "maternity") or of "the [sic] role of sexual intercourse in reproduction" can withstand detailed scrutiny (see Read 1918).

[6] Malinowski's account (1929b: 179–210) of Trobriand beliefs makes it clear that each person is presumed to resemble his or her presumed genitor in facial appearance, and Powell's (1956: 277–78; 1968) account reveals that the Trobrianders are no more "ignorant" of "the role of sexual intercourse in reproduction" or of "physiological paternity" than are most other folk who know nothing about the sciences of physiology or biology. The Trobriand theory is like many others in that the component of being that a child is thought to share with this presumed genitor is different from but complementary to that which he shares with his presumed genetrix. Compare the theory propounded by Aristotle, and mentioned in Singer (1959: 505), that the function of the sperm is to *form* all parts of body by action on the "egg."

[7] Most well-documented folk theories of human reproduction hold that sexual intercourse is a necessary part of the process, not merely that virgins cannot conceive. It is not always held to be sufficient for conception or pregnancy because, for example, it is widely appreciated that not all acts of sexual intercourse result in pregnancy. To account for this fact many folk theories hold that other-than-human or "supernatural" agencies may also play a part. According to some theories (see Meggitt 1962: 272–73; Powell 1956: 277–78; Grottanelli 1961: 3–4), certain spiritual entities *activate* the foetus which itself results from events or processes associated with sexual intercourse. Theories about the role of such spiritual entities (theories of *vivification*) have sometimes been confused with theories about *conception* per se.

described as components of "ethnoscientific" (sometimes "ethnobiological") theories. In contrast, the social relations of kinship consist of any rights or duties, or privileges and obligations, that a culture ascribes between kin in general or between the particular reciprocal kinds of kinsmen that it distinguishes. Anthropologists recognize and distinguish such rights and duties—those of kinship—not by their "content," which may be economic, political, religious, or whatever, but by means of the criteria for their distribution or allocation (see Beattie 1964). Where the distributional criteria are genealogical and egocentric, we speak of relations of kinship. The *social* relations normatively entailed by kinship are not conceived as congenital or indissoluble, no matter how binding they may be in law or morality: it is a matter of some concern to many of the world's peoples that one *cannot* choose his kinsmen whereas he *may or may not* choose to fulfill the duties and obligations of being a kinsman or a particular kind of kinsman (see Schneider 1968*a*: 24; Fortes 1949: 16–18).

Concerning the Siriono, Holmberg notes, "With respect to conception, there is no lack of knowledge that it is caused by sexual intercourse. All informants agreed that a woman could have a child by no other means" (1950: 65). Also:

> When first conceived, the child is believed to be a miniature replica of the infant at the time it is born, and intercourse is thought to stimulate the growth of the infant in the mother's womb. Thus, intercourse is desirable throughout pregnancy (1950: 66).

The Siriono notion that intercourse during pregnancy stimulates the growth of the infant in the womb is similar to that of many other peoples who hold that the foetus grows by accretions of sexual fluids (see Evans-Pritchard 1932 [1964]), so that each individual is thought to share the physical substance of his being with those two individuals who brought him into being. We do not know that this is what Siriono believe, but it is clear that they posit what we may describe as "genitors" and "genetrices" (Barnes 1961). It may well be that they also posit some sort of enduring physical or metaphysical connection between presumed parents and their common offspring. Holmberg does not specifically report that they do. He remarks that "no crystallized theories of how the process of conception takes place have been formulated" (1950: 65), though sexual intercourse is regarded as a necessary element in the process. This does not rule out the possibility of a theory of shared components of being, and in one context (1950: 57) Holmberg speaks of "kinship" among Siriono as though it were a matter of being "related by blood." He does not state explicitly that Siriono regard themselves as "related by blood," and it is possible that he employed the phrase without intending to imply that they do. On the other hand, the implication may have been intended.

In any event, it is hardly necessary to let the question of whether or not Siriono posit relations of genealogical connection rest on Holmberg's intensions when he used the phrase "related by blood." We have already seen that they posit the existence and necessity of genitors and genetrices. Moreover, like many other South American peoples, they impose a number of food taboos on pregnant women and some on their husbands, the presumed genitors of their unborn children. They also practice a form of couvade and apparently rationalize it on the ground that there is some sort of continuing "intimate connection" between both parents and the child, such that an event affecting them will affect it, too, and the child is particularly in danger just after birth when it is still "delicate" and vulnerable.[8] Moreover, in order "to protect the life of the infant and to insure its good health," both parents are ritually scarified (on the legs) on the day after the birth. The Siriono rationale for this rite is that the scratching "gets rid of old blood, which might cause the child to be sick" (Holmberg 1950: 69). Such beliefs and customs are virtually incomprehensible unless Siriono presume some sort of substantial and enduring connection, physical or spiritual, between the child and its presumed genitor and genetrix. Because of their nature, these connections cannot be undone, and for each person there can be one and only one set of such relationships. They come into being with him and cannot be created at any other time (e.g. through adoption). Of course, such relationships might be denied where their existence was once affirmed, e.g., a man might deny that he is the genitor of a child he once accepted as his own, in which case he necessarily imputes that identity to some other (perhaps unspecified) man.

PATERNITY AND SOCIAL FATHERHOOD.   Some of Holmberg's observations might be taken, however, to reflect negatively on the argument so far. He noted, for example: "Of course, considering the sexual freedom allowed by Siriono, the true paternity of a child would be difficult to determine, but, as far as the group is concerned, it is only the social role of the father that is important" (1950: 73). This might be taken to suggest that Siriono are in fact little concerned with the question of "true paternity," but rather with "social fatherhood," and that the latter might be "determined by marriage," as Radcliffe-Brown once argued was true of human societies in general (1950: 4). But to all appearances this is no more true of the Siriono than it is of human societies in general. It was Holmberg's *inference* that Siriono could not accurately assign the identity of the genitor; he does not report that they themselves experience

---

[8] See Crawley (1927: 177ff.) for an important discussion of the relevant comparative data.

difficulty in assigning the identity *to their own satisfaction* and, of course, according to whatever criteria they find acceptable. It is ethnographically irrelevant whether or not these criteria lead them to assign the identity to the man who is the *genetic* father, as we would wish to do if we were conducting a biological study of the Siriono.

Furthermore, to speak of the "social role of the father" is to suggest that the fact of being the presumed genitor of a particular child is a matter of some social significance. Holmberg's account of a case of "disputed paternity" shows clearly that Siriono *are* concerned about specifying a particular man as the genitor of each child (1950: 73–74). In this case a man refused to acknowledge his presumptive paternity of the child of a woman whom, he claimed, he had recently "divorced." The Siriono, like many other peoples, appear to assume that, in the absence of specific knowledge to the contrary, being the husband of the mother at the time of conception is sufficient presumptive evidence of paternity, since a husband and wife living together are assumed to be in regular sexual association. Here the presumptive genitor appears to have argued that he was not the father because he was not married to the mother at the time the child was *born*. Other Siriono, particularly the mother's female relatives, refused to accept this unreasonable argument and eventually coerced him to acknowledge his presumptive paternity, at least to the extent that he finally agreed to perform the ritual cutting of the umbilical cord. The man said he did this only to save the child's life, not because he recognized the child as his own, thus clearly expressing the normal significance of the rite. (See below for further discussion of the significance of this rite.)

Holmberg also notes that on the second day after the birth, a father and mother are decorated with feathers and "these decorations are sometimes applied to other members of the family, especially to a co-wife, or, in the case of a multiple birth, to either the co-wife or sister of the mother who is designated to take immediate care of one of the babies" (1950: 69). Moreover, in two cases observed by Holmberg, young boys who were the mother's *yande* ("potential spouses" with privileges of sexual access to her) were also decorated in this fashion. Holmberg observes this was "doubtless because they, too, had been having intercourse with the mother before and during pregnancy." This, again, might be taken to suggest that Siriono may have some doubts about "true paternity" and attach little importance to it. It may even suggest that they, like some other South American peoples, have a concept of possible "multiple paternity" (see Nimuendaju 1946: 78, 107). But it would be dangerous to draw any such conclusions. Holmberg does not state that he was specifically told either that these boys had been having intercourse with the mother or that this was *why* they were so decorated. Only some of her *yande* were decorated, and there is no evidence that she had not been having sexual relations with other *yande* who were not decorated. It would seem that Holmberg was only drawing an inference for which little support could be offered. Further still, it is at least plausible that the *yande* who were so treated were ritually decorated for the same reason as the "other members of the family," but it must be acknowledged that we do not know what that reason might be—because the ethnography is silent on this matter.

There is, then, nothing in the ethnography to indicate that Siriono do not concern themselves with the question of "true paternity" (and "true maternity"!). There is much to indicate that they do and that they assign considerable social significance to the fact of being the (presumed) genitor of a child.

Kinship Terms

There are good reasons to suppose also that the Siriono terms *ezi* and *eru*, glossed as "mother" and "father" by Holmberg, denote first and foremost those two persons who are presumed to have brought ego (an individual) into being through sexual intercourse. For example, Holmberg translates the Siriono utterance *dezi erangkwi*, a statement made by several women as another woman was giving birth to a male child, as " 'penis for the mother,' i.e., the boy for the mother" (1950: 71). Here we have the use of *ezi* in the context of a birth with apparent reference to the "mother" as the genetrix. It is difficult to imagine what else *ezi* could signify in that context. We therefore gloss *ezi* as "mother," because mother in its logically prior (or literal) English sense denotes the genetrix. To gloss *ezi* in this way is not, of course, to imply that it has precisely the same denotative range as "mother" or that it has the same connotations; it is only to take account of the fact that these Siriono and English words have the same primary or logically prior designatum, regardless of any other designata they may or may not share.

POLYSEMY.   However, the Siriono term *ezi* is a form comprised of the root *zi* and the third person pronoun, *e*. The first person singular form is *sezi*. (Schermair [1958] renders *zi* as *si* or *ŝi*, but Holmberg's orthography is retained here except where we quote from Schermair.) The morpheme *zi* may serve to signify not only "genetrix" but also "woman" (Schermair 1958: 373), and it may serve as a "feminine" class marker (Schermair 1958: 90). Therefore, *zi* in and of itself is not a kinship term but a word with a variety of closely related meanings, only some of which belong strictly to the domain of kin classification. It seems relatively unlikely that Siriono employ a word whose most literal sense is "mother" to designate women and feminine objects in general; it is more likely that they employ a term whose most literal sense is "woman" to indicate feminine objects, or as a kinship term. That is, the case of zi is probably structurally comparable to the case of French *femme*, though with a different connotative emphasis ("birth giver"?): zi, when marked by the possessive pronoun with a human antecedent, signifies a "special case" of zi in general, namely, "*the* woman who gave birth to ego." Thus "mother" is not the absolute primary sense of zi; it is the primary sense of the possessed form, $-zi$, occurring with a prefixed pronominal element. Thus, although the Siriono form zi is not a kinship term in any absolute sense, it does serve to designate a category of kin, and so there is no reason for not speaking of it as a kinship term. After all, when we describe a word as being of one kind or another on the basis of its semantic functions, we have to recognize that, because of polysemy and homonymy, the categories we establish are unlikely to be mutually exclusive.

We have said that the primary sense of $-zi$ (possessed) is "mother," which is to imply that the term has yet another kin-category–designating sense, as it does. Schermair (1958: 373) gives the following forms and translations:

e-si te	:	"madre verdadera," i.e., "one's true mother, own mother, proper mother,"
e-si tyono	:	"madrasta," i.e., "one's stepmother,"
e-si avarea	:	"madre no propria," i.e., "not one's proper mother."

He gives the form *te* as an augmentative or accentuative particle (1958: 411), which must here serve to signify that the reference is to the $-zi$ par excellence. Schermair indicates elsewhere, in connection with other kinship terms, that the form *tuti*, "truly," may be used to signify the same thing (1958: 329, 442). He does not indicate whether the form *aeae*, "own, proper," may be used with $-zi$, though it may occur with *edidi*, "offspring." *Tyono* and *avarea* are not semantically opposed froms. *Avarea* signifies "false, simulated, apparent, unreal, nonexistent" (1958: 46), and *tyono* signifies "falsely, without truth or sincerity" (1958: 478–79). Schermair indicates that *edidi* (his *e-riiri*) *avarea* signifies "one's not-true child, one's stepchild, or one's adopted child" (1958: 329). We may conclude that *tyono* and *avarea*, though they have slightly different significata, do not mark different classes but are synonymous in the context of kin classification: either may serve to indicate that a kinship term is being used in an extended sense. In contrast, the forms *te*, *tuti*, and *aeae* all serve to indicate that a kinship term is being used in its primary sense.

Although neither Holmberg nor Schermair reports that the collateral kinswomen MZ, MMZD, etc., whom Holmberg reports as denotata of *ezi*, are classified as *ezi tyono* or *ezi avarea*, it is obvious from the fact that these forms signify extensions of *ezi* that these collateral kinswomen must be so classified. They are women who may be called or referred to as *ezi* but who are not in fact one's genetrix (*ezi te, ezi tuti, ezi aeae*, "proper mother"). The conceptual distinction signified by *te, tuti* or *aeae* versus *tyono* or *avarea*, when added to a kinship term, is commonly described by anthropologists as one between "own" or "true" kin and "classificatory" kin. A "classificatory" kinsman of one kind or another is a kinsman to whom a particular term is applicable but who is not a kinsman of the type or types denoted by the term when it is employed in its primary sense.

We have just seen that *zi*, when employed as a kinship term (*-zi*), is potentially ambiguous. If necessary, any ambiguity of reference may re-resolved by the addition of certain suffixes which serve to distinguish the two different categories designatable by the term. Both the primary and the derivative applications are potentially markable, and it is not simply the fact of lexical marking that enables us to single out *ezi tyono* or *ezi avarea* as derivative applications or as extensions of *ezi* from its primary sense; it is rather the very nature of the semantic distinctions indicated by the lexical markers themselves. These semantic relations may be diagrammed as in Figure 1.

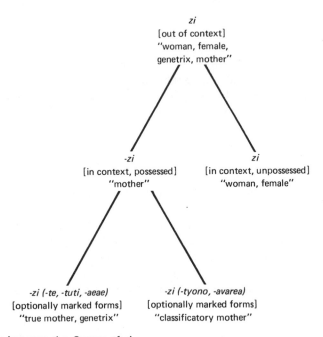

Figure 1.   Relations between the Senses of *zi*

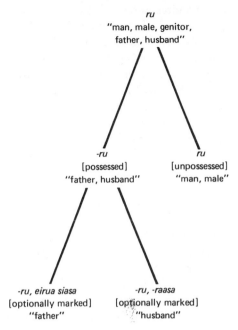

Figure 2.   Relations between the Senses of *ru*

Zi has places in two semantic domains, one having to do with the distinction between men and women (or males and females) in general, and the other with distinctions between kinds of kin. Structurally, and perhaps etymologically, we may say that *zi* has been "taken from" one semantic domain and put to use in another.

The case of *eru* is comparable. The distinction between primary and extended applications in the domain of kin classification is made in the same way as in the case of *ezi* (Schermair 1958: 349; 1962: 322). *Eru*, however, has an additional meaning, viz., "husband" ("marido") (Schermair 1958: 349). This arrangement is directly comparable to that of French *femme*. The relations between the several senses of *ru* may be diagrammed as in Figure 2.

One's husband may also be designated by the term *e-raasa* (Schermair 1958: 302), and "husband" is the primary sense of this term. Schermair indicates that "in case it is necessary to distinguish rigorously between *eru*, 'father,' and *eru*, 'husband,' " Siriono distinguish between *eiruã siasa* and *eraasa*, respectively (1958: 349). *Eiruã siasa* is translated by Schermair as "he who cut the umbilical cord," (*iruã* = umbilical cord, and *siasa* is a form of the verb "to cut"), and this is the "right and privilege of the father exclusively." Holmberg reports that, "After a child has been born, a man addresses his wife as *akesi* (mother-of-child) and he is addressed by her as *akendu* (father-of-child)" (1950: 54).

We have the testimony of both Holmberg and Schermair that *ezi* signifies a person's genetrix and *eru* his genitor, but unfortunately neither author provides an account of how he knows this. Neither states, for example, that any Siriono told him in so many words that he calls a particular woman *sezi* ("my mother") precisely because she is his genetrix, or a particular man *seru* precisely because he is his presumed genitor. Perhaps, then, Holmberg and Schermair only inferred the meanings (or these particular meanings) of these terms from utterances such ad *dezi erangkwi* (see p. 42). Though, as we noted earlier, it is difficult to imagine what *ezi* might signify in this context if not "the genetrix," evidence of this kind has not always been found convincing. Despite reports by other ethnographers that certain words in certain other languages also signify "mother" (i.e., "genetrix") or "father" (i.e., "genitor")—reports that are often based on evidence similar to that reviewed above—many anthropologists have argued that, in some cases, the words at issue *really* designate categories defined by reference to social rather than genealogical relationships.[9] These social relationships are said not to be ascribed on genealogical (or presumed genealogical) grounds, even though the parties to them may be and often are persons who are assumed to be mother and child (see Powell 1969*a*: 192 on the Trobriand distinction between "own" and other *ina*). These arguments have been used to support the contention that, in some cases, so-called kinship terms "are not the names of genealogical connections, even though they may be associated with such connections; they are the names of categories, sometimes groups, of people, socially defined" (Beattie 1964: 101).

Since this contention is widely accepted by anthropologists, some might suspect that what the Siriono term *eru* "really" designates is the category "mother's husband," i.e., "the man who was married to one's mother when one was born." And they might suspect that it is the mother's husband, not necessarily the presumed genitor, who has the reported right (perhaps the obligation) to cut the umbilical cord. Some might also suspect that *-zi te* "really" designates a social category too, e.g., the category "the woman who is rearing (or who has reared) ego."

As far as we know, however, there is no evidence to support these possible, though to us highly improbable, interpretations of the Siriono

[9] In some cases, however, the argument has involved a confusion between accurate genealogical relationships as defined by, say, a professional biologist, and presumed genealogical relationships as understood by the people within the culture in question. (See Radcliffe-Brown 1950: 4–5, 25).

terms -*zi* and -*ru*, but there are additional reasons to suppose that these terms really do signify "genetrix" and "genitor," as Holmberg and Schermair report. Note that the reciprocal of both *ezi* and *eru* is *edidi* (Schermair's *e-riiri*), which Holmberg glosses as "child" in the kinship sense of this English word, meaning "son" or "daughter." In English the kinship sense of this word is related to its nonkinship sense, "immature human being," in much the same way that Siriono -*zi* ("mother") is related to *zi* ("woman"), but this is not the case in Siriono. The Siriono term for "child" in the nonkinship sense is *ake* (Holmberg 1950: 54, Schermair 1958: 32), a term that also has a kinship sense, viz., "grandchild." Since we have no need here to refer to this nonkinship sense of *ake*, we employ "child" as a gloss for *edidi* in its kinship sense. Schermair derives the noun *e-riiri* from the verb *ri*, "to be," and -*rii*, "joined to (him or her)," and he translates the noun thus formed as "one who is joined to, one who is tied to (mother being intended)." But, recognizing that this is a translation of the construction, not of the significatum of the noun thus formed, he adds "child." This term figures in utterances such as *se eriiri atea*, "to conceive (or engender) a child"; *giiri mingo*, "to engender a child"; *giiri teakuka*, "to give birth"; *eriiri ubua he* or *eiiringi*, "fetus"; *tiiri*, "one who was joined with her (in the stomach), viz., child"; and *tiiri-mbae*, "one who has or can have no children, viz., sterile."

There can be no doubt about the genealogical significatum of *edidi*. Moreover, it is the common reciprocal of *ezi* and *eru*, and if a man and a woman both call ego *edidi*, it must be because there is something either similar or identical about their relations to or connections with ego. Siriono beliefs clearly require the sexual cooperation of a man and a woman to account for reproduction; therefore, *ezi* and *eru*, like *edidi*, must signify a genealogical relationship.

It follows that there is an implicit "parent" class: both men and women call their offspring *edidi*, a "parent" is a contributor to one's being, and *ezi* and *eru* are "kinds of parents." It does *not* follow that there is a single, special term for this class. In many languages the concept "parent" is expressed by juxtaposing the "father" and "mother" terms, thus naming the category by their union (see Scheffler 1970a). In others (Spanish, for instance), the "father" term is used in the plural (or dual), i.e., in a specially marked form. The Siriono expression is not reported.

If each person is immediately genealogically connected to two other persons, then he is less immediately so related to many others—those who are so connected to his parents or to his children, if he has any. In many other societies, all persons presumed to be genealogically connected to a given ego, though sometimes only within a limited range, are conceptually aggregated into a single category. The verbal label for this category, where such a label exists, is appropriately glossed as "kin" or "kindred."[10] The Siriono expression is *e-nonge* or *enonge renda* (Schermair 1958: 272, 312). *Enongge* (Holmberg's form) also designates the category "sibling." Thus, the category "kin" (in general) is expressed by an extension of the sibling term—or it may be. According to Schermair, the concept may be expressed in other ways, e.g., *e-tiesenda,* "those who pertain to one another; those who are joined; those who are related," or simply "relatives" or "relations." Schermair indicates that the same expression is used to signify "family," but he does not explain what he intends by "family" in this context (1958: 423). A related expression is *e-renda* or *e-resenda,* but this seems to refer primarily to the so-called bands, for the root term signifies "place, site, camp." etc. (Schermair 1958: 312). The expression is used to signify kinship perhaps on the basis of a presumption that the members of one band generally are kin of one another.

We may now assume that the several "kinship terms" reported by Holmberg are in fact kinship terms (though, as already noted, in some cases their root forms have yet other semantic functions). It remains to be shown how the "core terms" (*ezi, eru, edidi*) of this set are related to the other terms, and how the primary and extended senses of the terms are related to one another. These matters are dealt with in Chapters 4 and 5.

[10] Of course, relations of genealogical connection are often employed in other ways, e.g., nonegocentrically in order to define the boundaries of those groups of major social categories which anthropologists describe as lineages, clans, descent groups, etc. There is a tendency among some social anthropologists to describe the totality of a society's modes of ordering social relationships by reference to ties of genealogical connection as its "kinship system." Our usage is somewhat more restricted and, we hope, somewhat less conducive to confusion.

3 Concepts, Methods, and Aims

I

Chapters 4 and 5 present a formal or structural semantic analysis of the Siriono system of kin classification. In this chapter we consider some of the concepts, methods, and aims appropriate to such an analysis.

We may say that a formal account of a collection of empirical data has been given when there have been specified (1) a set of primitive elements, and (2) a set of rules for operating on these, such that by application of the latter to the former, the elements of a model are generated; which model in turn comes satisfactorily close to being a facsimile or exact replica of the empirical data whose interrelatedness and systematic nature we are trying to understand. A formal account is thus an apparatus for "predicting back" the data *at hand*,[1] thereby making them understandable, i.e., showing them to be the lawful and expectable consequences of an

---

[1] This limitation is noted but misunderstood by Powell (1969a: 182). Powell notes Lounsbury's (1965: 174) observation that his (Lounsbury's) analysis of Malinowski's Trobriand data might be relied on to predict correctly the terms that would be applied to any of the other types of relatives not included in Malinowski's schedule but whose genealogical connections might be known to a Trobriander. This, of course, is the test of whether the "rules" posited in the analysis of Malinowski's data are the rules of the system as such or whether they are just those that are necessary to account for Malinowski's data on the system. Since Powell reports that FBC are classified as "siblings"— as he notes, this is unclear from Malinowski's account—we must now suppose that the analysis presented in Lounsbury (1965) must be revised by positing the structural equivalence of paternal half-siblings, as well as maternal half-siblings, with full siblings. So far as we can tell from Powell's data, this is the only revision that is required. Powell (1969a: 182) mistakenly imagines that Lounsbury's account describes the paternal parallel cousins as half-siblings. To do so would be absurd. The half-sibling merging rule was restricted as it was in Lounsbury (1965) because the more general and more conventional form of that rule would result in the terminological identification of FBC with one or another full sibling via the same-sex sibling merging rule which would first equate FB with F.

underlying principle or set of principles that may be presumed to be at work at their source.[2]

Formal Accounts of Systems
of Kin Classification

In the case of systems of kin classification, a formal analysis aims to discover the structure of the system, i.e., the criteria or "rules" of kin classification that distinguish among and at the same time relate to one another the several categories belonging to any particular system. The "data at hand" in this case consist in Holmberg's and Schermair's accounts of how Siriono classify a large number of types of kin, and the goal of the analysis is to discover the genealogical discriminations underlying the distribution of terms over kintypes as reported by Holmberg and Schermair. As noted in Chapter 1, this is not to be confused with an account of *the* meanings (all the meanings) of those words which Siriono employ as kinship terms. Our goal, in Chapters 4 and 5, is only to formulate a model of the semantics of certain Siriono words as they are employed to designate categories of kin. Since Holmberg's and Schermair's reports clearly indicate (and demonstrate) that Siriono regard certain denotata of these terms as their "proper" or primary denotata and other kintypes as derivative denotata, one of the goals of the analysis must be to discover the primary denotata (or *focal types*) for each term and then the rules whereby the terms are extended from the focal types to the derivative denotata, i.e., the rules of terminological extension.

The procedure is as follows. We assume (on the basis of the argument of the preceding chapter) that the primitive or fundamental element of this system is the parent–child relationship. The terms *ezi, eru,* and *edidi* refer to parties to this relationship with respect to one another. We represent these parties by the symbols F, M, S, and D. (Our reasons for employing this rather than some other form of kintype notation are given below.) The other terms of the system, we assume, designate categories (or subcategories) of kintypes that are relative products of parent–child relationships. One or more members of each terminological kin class—the genealogically closest members of that class—are regarded as the focal member or members of that class. We then formulate simple, conjunctive componential definitions (*definitional rules*) for each of the class labels (kinship terms) at this, its primary range. The primary senses of the terms, as expressed in these definitions, are then expanded to define those ranges of denotation which encompass the more distant kintypes

----

[2] This statement of the nature of a "formal account," and those concerning the conditions of sufficiency and parsimony on p. 52 are drawn from Lounsbury (1964*a*).

known to be denotable by the same terms. The expanded sense (or senses) of each term is then related analytically to its primary sense by means of certain *extension* or *equivalence* rules. These rules do no more than relate the primary and extended senses of the terms, senses which are, of course, equally capable of being defined componentially.[3]

These rules may be expressed analytically in either of two ways: (1) in the form of simple verbal statements specifying the neutralization or suspension in certain genealogical contexts of certain distinctions made by specified components in the definitions of the primary senses (or previously derived expanded senses) of the terms (see our treatment of the extensions of "uncle," Chapter 1, pp. 7–8, and see also Lounsbury 1965: 151 on certain extensions of Trobriand *tabu*); or (2) in formula written in kintype notation and specifying a limited genealogical structural equivalence between two or more specified kintypes as linking or as designated kinsmen (see Lounsbury 1964*a*; 1965: 152–70). These latter may be written either as reduction or, conversely, as expansion rules, depending on the problem at hand. Expansion rules derive genealogically more distant members of a class from the basic member or members; reduction rules reduce the distant to the basic member or members.

We have found it convenient to express most of the extension rules of the Siriono system in kintype formula, but it should be emphasized that rules expressed in this fashion are no less neutralization rules than are rules written or expressed in the other way; a rule expressed in one way might just as well be expressed in the other. The convenience of which we speak is partly a matter of economy of expression and partly a matter of facilitating comparison of the structure of this—the Siriono—and other systems of kin classification (see Chapter 9).

We take it as demonstrated beyond a reasonable doubt that many kinship terminologies are structured in such a way that statements of equivalence rules of one kind or another will form an essential component of a structural semantic description of them. Note carefully that we say many, not all. Whether or not any particular system is so structured is a matter to be determined empirically. We are equally confident that many

---

[3] It should be added—since this point has been the source of much theoretical confusion (see Wallace and Atkins 1960: 74; Riddington 1969; Berlin and Kay 1969: 13; Burling 1970)—that, where kinship terms are polysemic, componential definitions and extension rules are not properly regarded as competing kinds of analysis but as *necessarily* complementary means of dealing with *different aspects* of the semantic structure of the system being analyzed. It is seriously misleading to suggest that the necessity to posit extension rules in order to account for the polysemy of kinship terms (or of any other kinds of words) indicates that "current formal theories of lexical definition are not able to deal naturally with such phenomena" and that "simple Boolean function theories of lexical definition" may have to be revised "in favor of more powerful formalisms" (Berlin and Kay 1969: 13). The defect is not in "current formal theories of lexical definition," but in the failure of many anthropologists to make adequate use of those theories.

systems of kin classification do not employ extension rules; instead of expanding the denotative ranges of their terms they designate the more remote kintypes "descriptively" by means of relative products (combinations) of their few basic terms (see Morgan [1871] on Esthonian and some of the Scandanivian and Semitic systems).

A formal account should be distinguished by its sufficiency and by its parsimony. Its sufficiency consists in its ability to account in toto for what is at hand in the empirical data, with no elements of this collection wrongly predicted or left unpredicted in the model, and with none of the predictions of the model remaining empirically unverifiable (assuming adequate documentation or documentability of the source). A structural model or formal account should not underpredict, overpredict, or wrongly predict. To the extent that it achieves this goal, a formal account satisfies the requirement of sufficiency. Of course, these criteria are applicable to nonformal theories, also. Theories, formal or otherwise, purporting to account for the application of terms of relationship (or for the application of any linguistic signs) can and should be judged against this criterion of sufficiency.

The parsimony of a formal account consists in its specifying only the absolute minimum of assumptions that are necessary to account for the data of the empirical collection, or to generate an exact replica thereof. Nonformal theories may be judged against this criterion too. One that purports to be formal is expected to be so judged.

It is a fact, deriving from their parsimony, that formal accounts are likely to be peculiarly unsatisfying to many anthropologists. A simple rule or set of rules that tells one the exact minimum he needs to know in order to account for the proper applications, or a natural sub-set of the proper applications, of the terms of a particular classificatory system, *and nothing else,* is quite likely to be rejected because it fails to tell him other (and doubtless, from his point of view, more important) things that he wants to know about the society, its culture, its legal structure, its patterns of social interaction, and so on. In fact, it may well reinforce in him the common prejudice that kinship terminologies are of no importance to the study of social structure and that the concern with them is but a relic of antiquarian diddling and the presociological days of anthropology. This, we hope to convince the reader, would be a premature and unfortunate conclusion.

Previous analyses similar to the one presented in Chapters 4 and 5 have been the subjects of a variety of critical comments, many of which, we think, are founded on misconceptions about the assumptions, methods, and aims that are appropriate to them. These should be clarified before we proceed with the analysis itself.

II

Perhaps the most fundamental objection that has been or can be raised against analysis of a body of data giving the distribution of terms over kintypes in any language was noted in Chapter 2, viz., that these data are only peripherally related to the "real" meanings of the terms, which designate kinds of socially, not genealogically, defined categories; and that their apparent use to designate categories of kin is just that— only apparent—the appearance being due to the method of data collection (i.e., "the genealogical method"). That is to say, the terms in question are not kinship terms to begin with and to analyze their distributions as though they were cannot lead to any genuine understanding of their meanings. We saw, in our review of the unity of the lineage and the alliance-system theories, that proponents of these theories have sometimes argued that such data, since it is all that is available in many cases, may be employed to determine whether a particular system is or is not, say, one or another kind of prescriptive alliance system of social classification. But, it is acknowledged, this is merely a methodological convenience, necessitated by the nature of the available data, and it does not require or prove the assumption that the systems under consideration are "kinship" systems. Indeed, the analytic procedure is based on the assumption that they are not kinship systems (see, again, Needham 1966a: 32). Certain terminological equations and distinctions of kintypes are treated as incidental or accidental by-products of nongenealogical principles of classification, and it is argued that these nongenealogical principles may reliably be inferred from these equations and distinctions.

As noted earlier, this argument is based on certain *interpretations* of matters of reported fact. The kinds of facts and the interpretations are, briefly:

1. A term reported as designating first and foremost "the father" is reported also as denoting, for example, FB. A term reported as designating first and foremost "the mother" is reported also as denoting MZ. The same holds true for the other terms of these systems. The interpretations have questioned the reported priorities, arguing that there is no warranty to assume that the terms do not *equally* denote all of the kintypes to which they may be applied, arguing, that is, that there is no warranty for assuming polysemy.
2. The same terms may be used to denote persons whom the speaker does not presume are his kinsmen, i.e., persons whom he does not suppose are genealogically connected to him. Therefore, it would seem that the terms do not essentially designate categories of kin.
3. The same terms usually imply kinds of social relationships which

may appropriately be ascribed on grounds of relative age, sex, descent group affiliation, etc. The interpretation then is that we can assume that these are their central or only referents, and that this assumption permits us to account for their usage.

Deficiencies of the Argument
Against Extensions

We have shown, however, that in the Siriono case, as in many others, there is abundant evidence for polysemy. F and FB are not equal denotata of *eru*, and M and MZ are not equal denotata of *ezi*; the classes containing FB but not F and MZ but not M are lexically and semantically marked as "not true or proper" *eru* or *ezi*, i.e., as extensions of those terms. It is only because it is not obligatory to distinguish at all times between the proper *eru* and other kinsmen who are merely *eru* by extension of the concept that it may appear that no distinction is or can be made. Indeed, in many societies it is considered ill-mannered to make these distinctions, especially in direct address to the designated kinsman, because they connote invidious social distinctions based on closeness of kinship (Beattie 1958: 321–22; Scheffler 1970*a*). It may be too much to assert, as Malinowski once did (1930: 29), that "It is only through the extraordinary incompetence of the linguistic treatment in kinship terminologies that the compound character of primitive terminologies has, so far, been completely overlooked," but it is certainly true that some sociological theories are founded on exclusive attention to the immediately apprehensible surface features of systems of kin classification and either ignore or deny the very existence of some of the more important structural features of these systems.

As for the second and third points, we have noted that kinship terms, like many other kinds of words, often have two distinct kinds of meanings, but there is an orderly relationship between these meanings. If a word may designate a genealogical kin category (thus providing the reason for describing it as a "kinship" term) and connote a kind of social relationship, there must be some systematic relationship between these two kinds of meaning. It is difficult to imagine what that relationship might be, if it is not that the kind of social status connoted by a given term is ascribed between ego and his kin of the kind designated by that term. If, however, persons who are presumed not to be kin are permitted to *assume* social relationships like those which are *ascribed* as proper between certain kinds of kin, then the appropriate kinship terms may be used (metaphorically) to denote the parties to those social relationships. That is to say, the terms may be extended to nonkin along with the kin-like statuses they connote. It cannot be denied that this is possible in the realm of kinship, for metaphorical extensions (based on connotative meaning) are common enough in other semantic domains. What may be questioned is whether or not it occurs. It has been reported, however, by more ethnographers than we could possibly list here and we can see no good reason to deny the validity of these reports, once we admit the possibility of the process just described.

Meaning and Usage

It may be that in some societies kinship terms are *used* more often to connote kin or kin-like statuses and to denote parties to them (whether kin or not) than they are to denote kinsmen or to designate kin categories. The possibility cannot be dismissed out of hand, even though so far nothing more than impressionistic evidence has been offered for it (e.g., as in Schneider and Roberts 1956). We know from ethnographic reports that in some societies kinship terms are seldom used in direct address unless there is a specific intention to invoke their status connotations, that is, unless the speaker wishes to make a particular point of the fact that the designated party is the speaker's kinsman of a certain kind and therefore should behave as such. In any event, these are observations about usage, about the frequency of occurrence in actual speech of the different kinds of meanings that kinship terms may imply; they are not observations about the structure of kin categories, or systems of kin categories, or the intrinsic relations between the category-designating and status-connoting senses of kinship terms. Thus, regardless of the relative frequencies in actual usage of the several senses of a term, if it is a kinship term and if it has multiple significata, its structurally primary sense is probably the narrowest of its kin-category–designating senses. It would be illogical to argue that where a term designates a kin category (or categories) and connotes a kin status (or statuses) that the latter sense is structurally prior or unrelated to the former. If a term may be used to refer to both things, it must be because it is presumed that in the normal state of affairs both are found together, because one implies the other, because the status connoted is one belonging properly to members of the designated category. Pragmatically, of course, category and status are separable, for nonkin may optionally model their social relationships after those presumed to be proper between certain kinds of kin; but, in the conceptual structure of the system, category and status must be associated in an orderly and hierarchical fashion.[4]

In brief, the very fact that a kinship term may be used to connote a status (and a kin status at that!), without implying that the person denoted

---

[4] Of course, in some societies there are status relationships between kin which are *not* associated with categories of kin distinguished by single lexemes. For a case in point see Tax (1955*b*: 255, 282) on the Fox Indians, and Radcliffe-Brown's (1952: 74–75) misleading comments on that system. See also Opler (1937).

by the term is presumed to be a kinsman of the category designated by the term, is dependent on a hierarchical relationship between kin class and normative kin status. It follows that there can be no adequate account of *all* usage until there is an adequate account of category designation to build on, for usage is dependent on the structure of meaning as well as its content, and in kinship terminologies the genealogical level is the structurally prior level.

Social Categories as Extensions

In addition to their extensions to broader categories of kin, kinship terms may also be extended to label "social categories." For example, in some, but by no means all, societies with Crow- and Omaha-type systems of kin classification, the terms (or some of the terms) of these systems may be extended beyond the range of known or traceable genealogical connection to designate categories such as "man of my mother's lineage (or clan) and of her generation or below." According to Beattie (1958) this is the sole, or at least the central, meaning of Banyoro *nyinarumi*; it is not an extension from a primary designatum "mother's brother." Furthermore, as we noted earlier, Beattie maintains that Banyoro kinship terms "are not the names of genealogical connexions, even though they may be associated with such connexions; they are the names of categories, sometimes groups, of people, socially defined" (1964: 101). The "social" criteria have to do with relations of clanship. Now we do not know what relations of clanship are if they are not, at base, relations of genealogical (or presumed genealogical) connection. Therefore, it would seem that Beattie's glosses of Banyoro "kinship terms" *do* involve reference to kinds of genealogical connections. But, according to Beattie, Banyoro do not conceive of clanship as a matter of agnatic genealogical connection, although clan affiliation is ascribed "patrilineally by birth" (1958: 320), for Banyoro do not suppose that all members of one clan are in fact agnatic kinsmen of one another. Thus, he argues, their "kinship terms" do not necessarily refer to relations of genealogical (or presumed genealogical) connection.

Yet Beattie notes that the word *ruganda*, which signifies "clan," also "implies, in behavioral terms, kinds of social relationships which are thought about in the *idiom* of agnation," and although Banyoro are quite capable of distinguishing between agnatic kinship and clanship when they want to, "they see them as merging into one another" (1958: 320, italics added). Now to assert that certain kinds of social relationships are "thought about the idiom of agnation" is surely to say that they are ascribed between persons who are presumed to be—at least distantly and at least probably—agnatically related; clanmates are by definition agnatically related and thus, of course, the two notions must "merge." Apparently,

Banyoro realize that because of the scope of their clans, some clanmates may not be agnatically related, or at least they may be unable to demonstrate to their own satisfaction that they are. But this, of course, does not reflect on the fact that Banyoro *conceive* of clans as agnatically constituted units. It is plain from Beattie's account that Banyoro model social relations of clanship after social relations that are ascribed, in the first instance, between agnatic kinsmen. Beattie shows quite clearly that when Banyoro suppose that clanmates may not be agnatic kinsmen, or when they know that a clanmate is a distant rather than a close agnatic kinsman, they are at some pains to gloss over these facts, precisely because they know full well that people do not feel as socially constrained by attenuated or fictitious agnatic connections as they do by what they know to be the real thing.

Furthermore, Beattie argues that Banyoro "kinship terms cannot and are not designed to indicate [the] genealogical nearness or remoteness of the relative designated" (1958: 319). Yet he notes that, by means of "qualifying terms," they can and often do (in reference but not in direct address) indicate "whether the relationship is lineal or collateral," that is, in the case of *ise*, "father," for example, whether the designated kinsman is in fact one's father (or presumed father) or one's father's brother, and in the case of *nyina*, "mother," whether the designated kinswoman is in fact one's mother or one's mother's sister, etc. The distinction between "lineal" and "collateral" kin in this context is a distinction between one's direct ascendant kin and the collateral descendants of their parents, and this is of course a distinction between nearer and remoter kinds of kin.

Thus Beattie offers us no good reasons to suppose that Banyoro "kinship terms" are not in fact kinship terms in the strict sense, and he offers an abundance of evidence that they are. The "idiom" by which Banyoro order their social lives is the idiom of genealogical connection. In dealing with questions of semantics we are concerned precisely with the content and structure of "idioms." Thus it would seem that the Banyoro are not different from, say, the Tallensi in this respect (see Fortes 1949); they are fully aware of the partial structural isomorphism between their system of kin classification and their system of clans, and they extend words which belong properly (primarily) to the former system into contexts which have to do with the latter. *Nyinarumi*, when used in the sense of "a man of my mother's clan and of her generation or below" is derived from the Omaha-type extension of the term's primary sense "mother's brother," which extension results in the category "my mother's agnatic kinsmen of her generation or below"; this category is readily converted or expanded to "man of my mother's clan of her generation [or age level] or below" on the assumption that clanmates are probable agnatic kinsmen, or like agnatic kinsmen, and must be treated (terminologically and socially) as such, whether or not it can be shown that they are. It follows from the facts that Banyoro kinship terms have status connotations and that clan-mates who are not presumed or who cannot be shown to be agnatic kins-men must nevertheless be treated as though they are, that kinship terms must be extended to these clanmates. Not to do so would be to deny the social implications of common clan affiliation.

Extension via Alter-Ego

Yet another interesting form of terminological extension should be noted here, for it has led some anthropologists (e.g., Guemple 1965) to question the adequacy of structural semantic analyses of systems of kin classifica-tion insofar as they purport to account for *all the uses* of all the terms of a particular system. As we have noted several times already, this is not our aim; our aim is to describe the structure of a system of kin classification, not to account immediately for all known applications or uses of the words that serve as kinship terms. It is quite clear that the category-designating senses and the status-connoting senses of kinship terms constitute two quite distinct, though nonetheless related, sets of senses which must be analyzed separately, the former before the latter. The form of termino-logical extension to be noted now demonstrates this quite clearly.

Many Eskimo groups indulge in the practice of naming children after other persons, most often a kinsman, and they posit special "name-giver-namesake" relations and, since two persons may be named after the same other person, "namesharer" relations (Guemple 1965: 326). These entail certain, but not particularly distinctive, social relations (Guemple 1965: 327ff.), and they affect the use of kinship terms, both vocatively and referentially: "In the most general case, any Ego can address and refer to the relatives of anyone whose name is the same as his (i.e., namesake, namegiver, or namesharer) by the appropriate terms used by that other in addressing and referring to them" (Guemple 1965: 330). However, if ego is otherwise related to the designated kinsman of his namegiver, name-sharer, or namesake, as he usually is, he may employ the term which is appropriate because of the presumed genealogical connection between himself and that person. Thus, the use of kinship terms based on name relations is one of at least two options open to the speaker, and it is clear that one of these options can be understood only with reference to the other. All that is involved here is that ego treats his namegiver, namesake, or namesharer as his alter-ego, as a projection or extension of himself; he puts himself in the place of the other. When ego speaks of (or is it only to?) his alter-ego's father as "my father," it is not the category "father" that is extended but the category "I," "me," or "my." Obviously, since ego applies kinship terms to the kinsmen of his alter-ego exactly as his alter-ego applies them, according to their proper kin-category–designating senses, this form of usage does not involve any modification of the *structure* of the system of kin classification. It, in fact, depends on and simply makes use of that structure.

Why people choose sometimes to take the perspective of their alter-egos, and sometimes not, we cannot say; the relevant data are not available. But the important point is that this choice, whatever its basis, does not affect the structure of the system of kin classification, and adequate understanding of which is an obvious prerequisite to understanding why anyone calls another person one thing or another once the choice has been made.

Fabian (1965) notes a similar practice among the Kung Bushmen (Marshall 1957) and he suggests that "Kung kinship relations are *constructed* on the basis of the factor of the name [i.e., name relations], they are measured in the language of the *generation* method" (1965: 684); that is, the basic relationship underlying the terminological system, and to which its terms refer, is the name relationship and not any presumed "biological" relations. According to Fabian, "kinship" here is a matter of namesharing, not of relationships established by the reproductive process. However, as Fabian notes, the Kung system of kin classification features a set of "core terms" which are in fact nothing more than simple parent, child, and sibling terms, which (except for the sibling terms) are not extended to other kinsmen, namesharers, or the kin of namesharers. The persons designated by these terms serve as the focal points for the application of kinship terms as determined by relations of namesharing. Fabian (1965: 716) attempts to accommodate these terms to his analysis by noting that ego's parents are the persons who give him his name, and so the core terms may be seen as signifying "relations of production," i.e., as designating those persons who "produce" new members for the namesharing system by conferring names. This rather tortuous argument, which turns Marshall's eminently sensible ethnographic account on its head, overlooks the fact that it is paternity per se that gives the right to confer names, and the names conferred are typically those of ego's parent's parents. In the final analysis, the system of namesharing and all it implies about social relations and the extended use of kinship terms is founded quite simply on the (presumed) "biological" (genealogical) facts.

Structural Semantics and Etymology

Another source of considerable confusion in the study of kinship semantics has been the common failure to distinguish between diachronic and synchronic issues, which have to be distinguished just as much in studies of semantics as in studies of linguistic morphology or social structure. Thus,

Hocart (1937) and many others before him were fully aware that in contemporary usage kinship terms may have multiple senses which are obviously semantically related to one another. Hocart (1937: 546, 550) noted that Fijian *tama*, for example, is used sometimes to designate a broad category of kinsmen which, he argued, is "socially defined" by the criteria of "generation" and "side," and is used at other times to designate the quite specific category "father." The former, he argued (following but not acknowledging Lubbock 1875 and Westermark 1891), is the "original" sense of the term; "father" is a narrowed sense, derived etymologically from this original sense; it is not that the original sense was "father" and that the term has been extended to designate a broader category of kin.

To illustrate his point, Hocart drew on the English example, "king." He noted that "If an Englishman says 'The King,' everyone understands, the King of England. It does not follow that originally the title meant that king only, and has been extended to other kings" (1937: 550). In the case of *tama*, he argued, the specific referent, *the* special case, is "the *tama* of [one's] family circle" (1937: 550). Of course, Hocart's argument about king is correct, and the reason every Englishman understands "The King" to refer to the King of England is because he is an Englishman and because "king" is here lexically and semantically marked by the definite article, or in writing by capital initial letter on both the article and the noun. But the analogy is a poor one; the situation in the case of *tama* is not the same.

As Hocart noted, in Fiji, as in much of Melanesia, classificatory terms such as *tama* "are constantly used like ours," i.e., like English kinship terms, in that "*tama* is often understood to mean the father and no one else" (1937: 550). Hocart even went on to note how "words designating whole classes of men are restricted by the singular, the definite article, or some other sign of definiteness, to one person; the context and custom further define who that one person is" (1937: 550). Hocart suggested that the possessive pronoun "my" marks the particularized, restricted, and derivative sense of *tama*. So far this may not seem inconsistent with his "king" analogy, but note how Hocart defined the coexistent and "original" sense of *tama*: "*tama* = all males of the previous generation on the father's side" (1937: 546). This definition treats one's father not as a special case of one's *tama* in general but as *the* kinsman with reference to whom the broader extension of the term is determined! That is, it treats one's father as *the* focal member of the category, *the* man who must be one's *tama* before any other, both logically and temporally.

The case of "The King" is, of course, not the same. This expression does not refer to any focal member of the category "kings (in general)" by reference to whom and in relation to whom other men are entitled to be described as kings. It refers to a particular king who is no more entitled to the designation "king" than is the king of any other country. The difference between the two cases is further demonstrated by another linguistic fact which Hocart noted (1937: 548) but whose significance he failed to appreciate. In many Fijian dialects a distinction is drawn between the elder and younger brothers of the father, all of whom are designated *tama*, but with the addition of suffixes which indicate their ages or seniority relative to one's own father. This indicates in another way that the kintype F is focal to *tama*, not just one among several structurally equivalent kintype denotata. No such situation exists in the case of "king," and this shows quite clearly that the two cases are in no way analogous.[5]

We do not deny the possibility of a "narrowing" or "particularization" process whereby a word designating a broad category may come to designate also (or instead) a much narrower category whose members are (or were) contained within the broad category. This is known to have happened in the case of some well-documented English words (see Stern 1931: 416ff.; Ullmann 1962). As might be expected, however, when a word acquires a more restricted and special meaning (as "king" has not), its unrestricted and general meaning tends to become archaic; it is either taken over by another word, perhaps a loan word, or lost from the language altogether, unless the new meaning is confined to special context or clearly indexed by special lexical markers (as in the case of *femme, ezi, eru*, etc.). Thus, from what we know of well-documented cases, Hocart's analysis of Fijian *tama* is at best improbable. In any event, even if the broad sense of a term were to survive along with a more recent, narrow, and special sense of the same term, in the way that Hocart claimed for Fijian *tama*, the former may become regarded as derivative in relation to the latter. In the Fijian case, the contemporary lexical and semantic relations between the various significata of *tama* are such that, if we were to accept Hocart's etymological reconstruction, we would have to suppose also that this had been its end result.

Structural and etymological relations are two quite different things; we cannot assume any simple, universal correlation between them, and serious mistakes can result from confusing structural primacy with historical priority, or, what is worse, from confusing questions of "origins" with questions of meaning per se (as in Lubbock 1875: Westermark 1891; Lang 1903).

Structural Semantics and Learning

Furthermore, as Hocart (1937: 551) noted, the order in which a child learns the several distinct meanings of a word cannot reasonably be used

---

[5] For more recent examples of the same errors, minus the etymological speculations, see Leach (1958: 123–24) and Powell (1969b: 603) on Trobriand *tama*.

as evidence for the etymological relations between those meanings. Similarly, it cannot reasonably be regarded as evidence for the structural relations between them. Such data can contribute to our understanding of how children acquire their knowledge of and ability to use a pre-existing "organized language" (Hocart 1937: 551), including its semantic distinctions. The child's conception of these distinctions may well differ from the adult's, but it is the adult's conception, which the child has to learn if he is to communicate satisfactorily with his fellows, that must be the focus of our attention when we study the content and structure of folk systems of classification (cf. Burling 1970). An adequate understanding of these is prerequisite to an investigation of how they are learned. Thus, the fact that a child first applies the term "father" (or its local equivalent) to one man before he applies it to others is not, we think, to be taken as evidence for determining what is the structurally prior or primary sense of the term. The evidence for this has to come from adult usage, from the conceptual and terminological distinctions made by adults. It follows, of course, that the fact that certain conceptual and terminological distinctions may be learned within the context of the domestic unit or from the adults who are members of that unit, has nothing whatsoever to do with why we describe the system to which those distinctions belong as a "kinship system" (see Hunt 1969: 49). This specification must rest on the nature of the distinctions, not on when, where, how, or in what circumstances they are learned.

Sentiments and the Nuclear Family

Many anthropologists, even some who have made use of methods similar to those we employ in Chapters 4 and 5, have supposed that, if they admit they are dealing with kinship terms, whose primary category-designating senses undergo extension and whose status connotations may also be subject to attenuation, they must accept certain theories about "the extension of sentiments and attitudes." Or they suppose that they must accept certain propositions about the universality of the "nuclear family" and its significance as a sort of structural building block (see Malinowski 1913; 1929a; 1930). But no such suppositions are necessary to anything we have said about systems of kin classification. Some anthropologists treat the "recognition" (i.e., cultural postulation) of parent–child relationships per se as though this in itself constitutes "recognition of the nuclear family." Others prefer to speak of "the nuclear family" only where husband and wife and their offspring form a distinct domestic unit or are otherwise distinguished as a special type of social unit or group. The nuclear or elementary family in the former sense is, of course, relevant to kin classification because the cultural postulation of genealogical connections is a necessary precondition for a kinship terminology. The nuclear or elementary family in the latter sense is not necessarily relevant, because it is possible to posit parent–child relationships per se without also instituting social groups or units composed exclusively of persons so related to one another. The question of the *universality* of the nuclear family in either sense is not necessarily relevant to the analysis of systems of kin classification; but the question of the universality of the nuclear family in the former sense is relevant to the question of the possible universality of systems of kin classification—because its distribution is, by this definition, coextensive with the distribution of the predication of genealogical connections. We do not assume (in spite of strong suspicions to the contrary) that all human societies have kinship terminologies or that all alleged kinship terminologies are just that. Whether or not systems of kin classification are a cultural universal is an interesting but essentially unanswerable question. It is also essentially irrelevant to the formal analysis and comparison of systems that are known to be or can be shown to be systems of kin classification. That is to say, even if it were true that certain peoples do not predicate relations of genealogical connection, this would have no direct bearing on the matters with which we are concerned here, for by our definition these people would not and could not have any systems of kin classification and they would not and could not have any systems of social relations between kin (cf. Malinowski 1913: Chapter 6).

Structural Semantics and Sociology

Yet another source of confusion in the study of kinship semantics is that, being in a hurry to get on with sociological investigations, anthropologists have often emphasized, and perhaps overemphasized, the fact that "the reality of a kinship system as a part of a social structure consists of the actual social relations of person to person as exhibited in their interactions and their behavior in respect of one another . . . . What we have to seek in the study of kinship systems are the norms" (Radcliffe-Brown 1950: 10). Now all of this is true enough: if we are interested in the sociology of kinship systems, we must direct our attention to the jural and moral norms which ascribe different right- and duty-statuses to different types and kinds of kinsmen. But also, and even more fundamentally, we must consider the cultural distinctions drawn between different kinds of persons, such that some are defined as kin of one another and others are not; and of those who are, some are defined as one kind of kin and others are defined as other kinds of kin.

Radcliffe-Brown's treatment of "kinship" as "genealogical connection recognized for social purposes" (1929) may have helped him to get on with the sociological analysis of kinship systems by enabling him to assume that terminological distinctions are "usually" socially motivated: "The general rule is that the inclusion of two relatives in the same terminological category implies that there is some significant similarity in the customary behavior due to both of them, or in the social relation in which one stands to each of them. . . ." (1950: 9; see also Lowie 1929). But this led him to fuse social-structural and cultural (or conceptual) "principles," as in his *principle of sibling solidarity* and *principle of the unity of the lineage group*. But these two kinds of "principles"—the social-structural and the conceptual—must be clearly distinguished, for although terminological extensions probably are sometimes socially motivated in the way Radcliffe-Brown imagined that they generally are, this is not an unexceptionable arrangement, and some of the cases assumed by Radcliffe-Brown to be so motivated are not.

The exceptional cases, whatever their relative frequency may be, show quite clearly that it is a serious mistake to assume that the overt, readily observable terminological equations and distinctions of types of kin are always socially motivated, especially in the way Radcliffe-Brown supposed. They show also that one cannot investigate these social motivations without first determining the structure of the terminological distinctions in and of themselves. Even if they are socially motivated, even if one does extend a term to some relative *because* one treats that relative more or less like one treats the primary designatum of that term, we still have to consider why and according to what principles one treats the former like the latter.

Suppose that it had been established that in a society with an Omaha-type system of kin classification, the "mother's brother" term is extended to MBS, MBSS, etc. because, for some reason, men of these kintypes are ascribed right- and duty-statuses with respect to ego which are more or less similar to those ascribed between MB and ZC. Further, suppose that the reason for this extension of jural status is that men of these kintypes belong to the same lineage or clan as the mother's brother. This seems to tell us how the extension works and why it occurs, but it is in fact only a superficial analysis of the situation. MBS, MBSS, etc. are members of the MB's clan or lineage only by virtue of the fact that they are the sons of MB or the sons of MBS, etc. The principle of the clan or lineage affiliation is that children take the affiliations of their fathers vis-à-vis the world at large, but this cannot be the principle of jural-status and kin-term extension in a case such as that noted above. A system of kin classification is ego-centric and any extension of terminological (and perhaps jural) status within it must be vis-à-vis a particular ego. A system of this kind cannot employ the simple "lineage principle" that children shall take the statuses of their fathers; it must instead employ the somewhat similar but nonetheless distinct principle that the sons of certain of ego's kinsmen shall take the classificatory statuses of their fathers vis-à-vis ego, and the daughters of these same kinsmen shall take the classificatory statuses of their fathers' sisters; conversely, some of ego's kinsmen (the reciprocals of the above) shall take the reciprocal classificatory statuses with respect to ego. This is perhaps the hard way of stating what has elsewhere been described as an Omaha-type skewing rule of kin classification (Lounsbury 1964*a*), but it makes the point that the rule of terminological extension in these systems is not the same thing as the "lineage principle." The two systems of classification, the lineage system and the kinship system, are only *similar*—i.e., partially isomorphic, but not wholly so.

Looking at the matter of the structure of Omaha- and Crow-type systems of kin classification in this way, rather than in terms of Radcliffe-Brown's principle of the unity of the lineage group, helps us to understand some of the variation among these systems (Lounsbury 1964*a*). True, it does not immediately offer a sociological explanation for any particular Omaha- or Crow-type system or for the variations among them, but it does have the advantage of not presupposing such an explanation, as did Radcliffe-Brown's unity of the lineage theory, which is not a generally satisfactory sociological theory even if it were a satisfactory structural theory. There are many societies with Crow-type systems of kin classification (as those types that were defined in Lounsbury 1964*a*) but *without* matrilineal descent groups (see Deacon 1934; Layard 1942; Meek 1931; Netting 1968); and in none of these cases, so far as the available data permit us to say, is the Crow-type extension of terms correlated with any form of matrilineal extension of jural statuses. Indeed, the most prominent structural feature of all of these societies is a system of corporate *patrilineal* descent groups.

The foregoing observations on Crow- and Omaha-type systems suggest quite strongly that, in analyzing any system of kin classification, most especially if our ultimate aim is to understand the social system of which that cultural system is a part, we must hold open the possibility that the terminological equations and distinctions effected in that classificatory system are *not* socially motivated. This must be our heuristic procedure, for we must allow for the possibility that extensive terminological equivalences between close and distant kintypes may be merely the cumulative end result of the consistent and repeated operation of a few, and perhaps more significant, equivalences of a much more limited scope (such as those that may be formulated as equivalence rules).

Primary Meanings

We should note in passing that some linguists have suggested that the "primary" meaning of a word be regarded as that which a child learns first.

Others have suggested the criterion of frequency of usage of the various senses of a word; and still others have suggested "psychological saliency" (i.e., the sense which comes to mind first if a person is presented with the word outside any linguistic or social context), or, as noted already, historical priority. It seems to us that to use "primary" in any of these senses would be rather pointless and certainly would be risking confusion with structural primacy. It remains to be demonstrated that there is any correlation, weak or strong, between structural primacy, etymological priority, priority of acquisition by the individual, frequency of usage, and psychological saliency. While there may be good reasons for suspecting some interesting relationships here (see Chapter 1 and Greenberg 1966), no good can come of confounding the questions at the outset by using "primary sense" to refer to anything other than structural position—and it must be remembered that even this has to be regarded as a relative matter, insofar as a word may have positions in more than one semantic domain and, thus, primary and derived senses within each of those domains.

Once questions of structure *per se* are clearly separated from questions of usage, etymology, cognitive saliency, the acquisition process, and the possible social causes of those structures, and once the concepts of polysemy, extension, and metaphor are given a fair hearing, it becomes apparent that most reputed systems of kin classification are just that, though the terms of which they are composed may have yet other semantic functions. To recognize this fact is not to reduce social structures to kinship systems. It is merely to recognize, as Evans-Pritchard (1951) and Fortes (1949) have demonstrated, that in many societies (but not in Siriono), and to varying degrees, cultural models of and for interpersonal relationships are the keystones of models of and for intergroup relationships.

Formal Inadequacies of Social Category Interpretations

Since proponents of the social categories interpretation of systems of kin classification have so often and so consistently failed to make use of any systematic semantic theory, overlooked or ignored many linguistic facts about the systems they have dealt with, and confounded etymological and structural issues, among others, it is not surprising that their models of these systems are structurally inadequate. Some of the inadequacies of the unity of the lineage theory have been dealt with above and elsewhere (Tax 1955a; Lounsbury 1964a) and need not be reiterated here. To these it may be added that, to the best of our knowledge, no proponent of this theory, or of the alliance system theory, has ever provided an analysis that deals with anything more than the classifications affected by the terms of a particular system when employed by a *male ego*. The fact that women also use these terms has been glossed over in many ways, none of which are at all convincing. It is commonly supposed that an analysis that considers the distribution of terms for a male ego alone can lead to a satisfactory understanding of the system. But for the majority of cases this assumption merely serves to save the analyst from rethinking his theory. In any system where there is a difference between the ways in which males and females distribute terms, such a difference must be a function of the structural principles of the system; any analysis that fails to consider this will be incomplete at best. While social category interpretations of Crow- and Omaha-type systems only come close to accounting for the distribution of terms when employed by males, they fail miserably when called upon to account for the distribution of terms when employed by females. In most such systems a woman refers to her children by the same term as a man refers to his children, and this is quite inconsistent with the unity of the lineage theory. The stronger version of that theory maintains that the terms of any such system are monosemic and designate categories or subcategories of lineages to which ego is (genealogically!) connected; in any such system male and female ego are necessarily related to the lineages of their children in different ways. The same objection applies to the alliance system interpretation of many systems of kin classification, for the arrangement in them is precisely the same.

Furthermore, in the great majority of systems of kin classification that have been dealt with by proponents of the unity of the lineage theory or the alliance system theory, there are only two or three terms embracing all kintypes in the grandparental and grandchild generations. According to the theory of alliance systems, these are not kinship terms but "general terms of social classification" based on a system of intergroup alliance, but of course this distribution of terms over kintypes is inconsistent with the theory. An asymmetric alliance system would require at least three terms at the grandparental level (see Lévi-Strauss 1969: 364, note 3). Proponents of alliance theory interpretations have yet to explain why the requisite distinctions are never present; they merely note that it is a general feature of asymmetric systems that such distinctions are not made and that distinctions between "own," "wife-giving," and "wife-taking" groups or "lines" are made only in "the three medial generations" (see e.g. Needham 1964c: 1379). It is plainly unsatisfactory to leave the matter at that.

In some alleged asymmetric alliance systems of social classification, the term that denotes MF and FF is extended, Omaha-fashion, down the entire "patriline" descended from the MF. According to proponents of alliance theory, this is not an extension of the "grandfather" term, for the term that designates the category containing the kintypes MF, MB, MBS, MBSS, etc., is really one that designates the category "man of a wife-giving group (or line, or category)." But these theorists have yet to explain why it is that the same term is also applicable to FF and, indeed, to all male relatives of the second ascending generation. And why is it that the wives of wife-givers are so often designated by the same term as that for MM and FM and, indeed, all women of the second ascending generation? These are unresolved difficulties for the alliance system theory, and for the unity of the lineage theory of Crow- and Omaha-type systems; so, even if these theories did take account of the matter of polysemy in some way, they are seriously inadequate as they now stand.

Finally, on the inadequacies of alliance theory, it should be noted that in most so-called symmetric alliance or two-section systems of "social classification," there is but a single term (or two terms distinguishing sex of alter) for a man's sister's children and a woman's brother's children. This is inconsistent with the two-section system hypothesis because, if the sections really did exist, regardless of whether they were matrilineal or patrilineal, a man's sister's children would belong to the section opposite that of a woman's brother's children. Thus, this term (or these two terms) fails to make the distinction required by the two-section system hypothesis. Again, because proponents of alliance theory have been content to "analyze" only the classifications affected by male ego, this defect in the theory has been obscured. A few, however, have noted the inconsistency, and to save the theory they have argued that the point of view or perspective of either male or female ego is imposed on the system as a whole. In the light of the many other defects of the alliance theory interpretations this tortuous argument must be seen as but one further attempt to shore up a wholly inadequate theory.

III

A great deal has been written in recent years about the "psychological" or "cultural" validity of formal semantic analyses of systems of kin classification, and many such analyses have been dismissed as unrealistic. As a consequence of such criticism, some "formalists" have retreated to the sophistic position that their methods and findings are useful for comparative purposes whether or not they have any cognitive, psychological, or cultural validity. However, if an analysis is to claim the name "semantic" it must necessarily formulate hypotheses about cognitive phenomena, and the issue of cognitive validity cannot fairly be ignored, dismissed, or minimized. Nevertheless, many of the demands that have been placed on formal semantic analyses by "formalists" and their critics have been quite unrealistic, and this issue does require some clarification.

Some aspects of this issue are dealt with in Chapter 7, but others must be dealt with here.

The Status of Kintype Notation

The most important issue, it seems to us, is the question of the ethnographic appropriateness as opposed to the analytical usefulness of employing kintype notations of one sort or another in the analysis of kinship terminologies. In our view, and as we have defined the analytic category "kinship terms," if the analyst is dealing with such a system of terms he has no choice but to make use of one or another kind of kintype notation. Kintype notations represent nothing more than genealogical chains connecting ego and persons properly denotable by the terms, and these are the veritable objects of classification! As we have defined the analytic constructs "kinship" and "kinship terms," it is evident that if the object of analysis is a kinship terminology—in that the terms of the set designate egocentric and genealogically established categories—the descriptive and analytical use of kintype notation is not merely legitimate, it is mandatory!

Some critics will doubtless conclude that our argument is tautological, but this would be a mistake. Kinship terminologies comprise a natural class of cultural phenomena, and our argument is *not* that a particular terminological system may be identified as a kinship terminology because it may be analyzed by the method employed here (or one similar to it) and shown to "make sense" as a kinship terminology, but rather that the method works—it produces systematic, coherent, and descriptively satisfactory results—and can work only where the object of analysis *is* a kinship terminology. Whether or not a terminological system is a kinship terminology is a matter to be determined prior to a full-scale structural semantic analysis of it (see Chapter 2, Part II). In the absence of data permitting such a determination, a body of kintype data that has been reported for a particular system may be subjected to structural analysis, and if the analysis yields an adequate, simple formal model we may assume with a fair degree of confidence that the system is a kinship system. Of course, such an analysis cannot "prove" that the system in question *is* a kinship system (cf. Tyler 1966) or that it has the structural properties indicated in the model (cf. Buchler and Selby 1968: 39–46); it can only add a *degree of confirmation* to these hypotheses. But as noted earlier, the probability of being able to construct a simple and adequate formal model of a system on the basis of utterly false assumptions about it is virtually infinitesimal.

It should be evident, then, that we do not agree with those who have argued that a kintype notation is a kind of "etic grid" (see Hammel 1965b: 4–7; Kay 1966: 21), insofar as the use of "etic" here implies that whatever relationships and concepts one intends to represent by kintype notation, they have no place in the culture of the people whose words are being analyzed for their semantic content and structure.[6] If that were so, there could be no justification for analyzing the terms by reference to such a "grid." As Wallace has rightly observed, one might as well analyze them by reference to the periodic table of elements or the Linnaean system of classification (1965: 230), if he assumes that kintypes may not be their proper denotata. It is wholly mistaken to describe kintypes as "objectively defined" and "universal," or as constituting a "primitive reference language" or a "target language," as though they represented something external to the language or culture being analyzed (cf. Hammel 1965b: 4–7; Pospisil 1965: 188; Tyler 1969: 71). The genealogical relations they represent are themselves *conceptual* phenomena. In this respect, the distinctive genealogical (and other) features that serve to define and distinguish classes of kin are not different from the kinds of culturally conceptualized features by reference to which different kinds of plants and animals are distinguished in folk-classificatory systems concerned with such things.

Nor do we agree with Buchler and Selby's contention (1968: 45) that "transformational (or componential) analysis neither requires nor proves the extensionist hypothesis." In the first place it is erroneous to associate the postulates of an equivalence rules analysis with the postulates of "transformational linguistics," as Buchler and Selby do but without demonstrating that there is any similarity beyond the fact that the practitioners of both kinds of analysis employ arrows in their respective notational systems (see also Fox 1969). The semantic theory that serves, along with certain ethnographic and linguistic facts, to justify such analyses of systems of kin classification is not in the least dependent on the postulates of any particular current general linguistic theory.[7]

---

[6] "Etic" elements might also be regarded as those elements of content and structure which are common to a variety of different systems but which combine differently to produce the overt differences among those systems. From this point of view, the relationships expressed in kintype notation are etic. However, so far as we have been able to determine, this is not the sense given to etic by Hammel, Kay, Tyler, and others who describe kintype notation as an "etic grid."

[7] This is not to suggest that there are no important similarities between the theory or theories that go under the name of "generative grammar" and a theory of designative semantics that takes account of polysemy and extension. There is, for example, the formalism common to both: both posit "basic" underlying forms and relations between them that may be operated on by specific rules of combination and contextual permutation to yield a wide variety of derivative forms, or applications of forms, and structures. But this formalism is equally characteristic of yet other current general linguistic theories (see Lamb 1964; 1965); it is indeed a property of most general linguistic theories, though in some it is a relatively unelaborated feature. Beyond this, it is equally characteristic of many other kinds of theories. Fox's description (1969: 469) of the structural analysis of semantic fields as "transformational analysis (from Lounsbury out of Chomsky)" is uninformed and misleading.

In the second place, the sole empirical and theoretical justification that can be offered for employing equivalence rules in the analysis of systems of kin classification is "the extensionist hypothesis," i.e., the hypothesis that the terms (or some of the terms) of the system under consideration are polysemic, that they may have more than one significatum each. Without that hypothesis, which is of course a hypothesis about the nature of the object of analysis, the use of equivalence rules would be reduced to nothing more than a methodological gimmick which we could not expect any competent scholar to take seriously. Thus, it is utterly false to assert that polysemy is "operationally" (sic., heuristically) eliminated in an analysis such as that presented in Lounsbury (1965) (cf. Buchler and Selby 1968: 45). The hypothesis that Trobriand kinship terms are polysemic is the very keystone of that analysis, as was carefully noted (Lounsbury 1965: 181–84), and the hypothesis was founded on ethnographic facts reported by Malinowski (1929a: 494 ff.).

As we see it, the sides in the anthropological dispute over "whether kinship 'is' or 'is not' genealogical," i.e., whether kin classification is reckoned genealogically or otherwise, are not merely statements of "alternative strategies" (Hammel 1965b: 7; see also Buchler and Selby 1968: 45). Nor is it simply being "interested in the neatness, the closure, the sufficiency of an analysis in a formal sense" (Hammel 1965b: 7) that should lead us to formulate a genealogically based analysis of a particular terminological system (see also Tyler 1969; Buchler and Selby 1968: 44, 45). Again, if the object of analysis is not a system of kin classification there can be no justification for analyzing it as though it were one, and no such analysis could have any reasonable claim to being "neat" or "sufficient." The dispute over what kinship "is" is real enough. It has been badly muddled by being at once a largely unacknowledged dispute over the meaning of a word used by anthropologists to describe an aspect of other people's cultures and a dispute over the meanings of words in other people's languages (and even in the English language—see Goodenough 1965b; Schneider 1965a; 1968a). It is, thus, a dispute about the very nature of many classificatory systems in many languages, about matters of ethnographic fact, and cannot be settled by mere common adherence to stipulative theoretical definitions such as those offered here for "kinship" and "kinship terms" (i.e., the ordinary, conventional, uncomplicated definitions). But such an adherence could save us from the pointless exercise of noting that in society X, Y, or Z "kinship" is not a matter of genealogical connection and its "kinship terms" do not refer to genealogically established categories—if not, then what possible reason could there be for calling them kinship terms to begin with? (See Ruel 1962; Glick 1967; Beattie 1958; and many others.)

Some Limitations of Componential Analysis

It is unfortunately true that many of the formal semantic analyses of systems of kin classification that have been published so far are quite probably unrealistic, for the formulators of these analyses have seldom taken adequate, if any, account of the phenomena of polysemy and extension. Most conventional componential analyses suffer from this defect, and it has led to a number of pseudoproblems to which a great deal of attention and discussion have been needlessly devoted.

The by now traditional form of componential analysis has concerned itself almost entirely—especially in analyses of kin categories—with the formulation of sets of single-sense, conjunctive definitions, almost as though it had to be assumed that the words under analysis were monosemic.[8] Yet, as we have seen, the linguistic phenomena of polysemy, center-oriented categories, and extension have to be reckoned with just as much in analyzing kinship terms as in dealing with meaning in other lexical domains (e.g., the taxonomies of plant and animal forms, diseases, geographical features, and so on). Thus, most of the sets of definitions formulated in numerous published componential analyses of kinship terminologies deal only with categories in their maximum extension. In these analyses much of the inherent organization of the terminological systems has been glossed over or has gone completely unnoticed (see Lounsbury 1956; Goodenough 1956; 1965b; 1968; Wallace and Atkins 1960; etc.), and in some instances disjunctive definitions have been admitted to the analysis without being acknowledged as such (see, for example, Goodenough 1956: 205 on the dimension of "generation," and 1968: 187 where the disjunctive component "kinsman by blood or marriage" is left out of the definition of "uncle," thus making the category appear to be conjunctively defined). Thus, for reasons quite different from those so far advanced by most critics of componential analysis, it is probably true that most such analyses are inadequate. The fact that they deal only with signification, not with all the different kinds of meanings that kinship terms may have, does not make them inadequate or unrealistic, but they are inadequate and unrealistic even as accounts of signification insofar as the terms they deal with have multiple significata.

In Lounsbury (1956) it was found to be apparently impossible to formulate a single, conjunctive componential definition for each Pawnee kinship term, and disjunctive definitions were admitted to the analysis. The need for such definitions suggested that the terms in question are

---

[8] For some notable exceptions, though not in the analysis of kinship systems, see Bright and Bright (1965), Berlin, Breedlove, and Raven (1968), and Friedrich (1969).

polysemic, that they have multiple and semantically interrelated significata. Thus it was reasoned (Lounsbury 1964b: 1088) that analysis should start from a set of hypothesized central meanings and then attempt to discover the rules peculiar to a system, which is may also share with other systems, that govern extensions from the central to the various peripheral denotata and to more attenuated senses of the terms. The analyses of Crow- and Omaha-type systems presented in Lounsbury (1964a; 1965) illustrate some aspects of the theory and method whereby such rules may be discovered and expressed analytically. (Similar methods were developed at more or less the same time by K. Romney, D. Metzger, E. Hammel, and perhaps others.)

Problems of Equivalence Rule Analysis

The method has been widely applied to a variety of systems of kin classification (see Hammel 1965c; Buchler and Selby 1968; Bock 1968; Elkins 1968; Hopkins 1969; Keesing 1968; etc.), but more often than not without sufficient regard for the necessary semantic postulates, or for the criteria of adequacy and parsimony, or for alternative possibilities. The necessary semantic postulates have been discussed above. Here we should take brief note of some of the erroneous assumptions and faulty procedures that have motivated numerous so-called equivalence rule analyses and criticism of them.

PARSIMONY. In some cases (see Hopkins 1969), an exceedingly large number of equivalence rules has been posited in order to account for terminological assignments in a simple Omaha-type system, though much simpler analyses of virtually identical systems have been presented (Lounsbury 1964a). But in this case, as in the others, only a few such rules are necessary. Many of the rules posited in Hopkins' (1969) study are but special cases of more general rules which, if posited, would drastically reduce the number of distinct and required rules.

FOCI. It is sometimes assumed that each and every kin class has one and only one kintype as its class focus (see Buchler and Selby 1968; Hammel 1965c; Coult 1967), though no general theoretical or empirical reasons have ever been offered to support the assumption. Yet the assumption has led Buchler and Selby (1968), for example, to posit what they call *transformation rules*, rules which do not reduce distant to closer kintypes but "cycle" equally close kintypes "through" one another. The "direction" of the cycling as required by these transformation rules—which do not in fact "transform" anything—is arbitrarily chosen. Arbitrary assumptions and procedures have no legitimate place in any kind of analysis, scientific or otherwise, and analyses based on them may be summarily rejected.

INADEQUACY.   Previously published analyses, by Lounsbury (1964a; 1965) of Crow- and Omaha-type systems have been deemed inadequate because, it has been argued (Coult 1967; Bright and Minnick 1966; Hopkins 1969), they do not account for extensions of grandparent and grandchild terms to kintypes more than two generations removed from ego. As Bright and Minnick observe (1966: 382), these extensions were not dealt with in Lounsbury's (1964a: 359–66) discussion of the Fox system, where kintypes more than two generations removed were covered in statements of the primary meanings or foci of their respective terminological classes (1964a: 362). As Coult (1967: 31) points out, in the Fox system there are (or would seem to be) kintypes in these generations which are not members of the grandparent or grandchild classes, and so the specifications in Lounsbury (1964a: 362) should have been that all "grandfathers," for example, reduce to male, *lineal* kintypes of second or higher ascending generation (rather than simply male kintypes of second or higher ascending generation). Moreover, strictly speaking, lineal kintypes more than two generations removed from ego are not primary foci of the grandparent and grandchild classes but are covered by what we describe below (p. 125) as *first-extended senses* of their terms. In order to account for these extensions, Bright and Minnick (1966: 382) argue, we must posit two additional rules and introduce an order into the total set of rules. A somewhat similar, but simpler, procedure was followed by Lounsbury (1965: 151), but (for reasons not stated by them) that discussion is not noted by Bright and Minnick or Coult (1967), though they cite other aspects of the analysis presented in the same paper. The problem of accounting for such extensions of grandparent or grandchild terms is further discussed below (pp. 124–25).

Some of those who have attempted to employ equivalence rules in analyses of systems of kin classification have assumed, again arbitrarily, that if a term is self-reciprocal one of the sets of reciprocal kintypes has to reduce, or as per Buchler and Selby "transform," to the other (Hammel 1965c; Coult 1966; Hopkins 1969; Bright and Minnick 1966). For example, in the Commanche kinship system, the four grandparent and grandchild terms are self-reciprocal; the term *kinu*, for example, designates the category "father's father," male or female ego speaking, *and* the reciprocal category "male ego's son's child." In Hammel's analysis of this system, where a term is self-reciprocal the senior kintype is chosen as the "root" or focal type of the category (Hammel 1965c; 74 and Table 1). Hammel offers no justification, empirical or theoretical, for this choice, though it leads to the rather abstract and elaborate mathematical analysis he subsequently presents. Coult (1966) objects to the mathematical aspects of the analysis and finds it unnecessarily complex, as indeed it is, but Coult offers no adequate substitute and makes some of the same arbitrary assumptions.

A general theoretical justification can be offered, however, for regarding the senior kintype foci of a self-reciprocal term as its focal denotata, to the exclusion of their junior reciprocals. In Lounsbury (1965: 150) it was noted that several Trobriand kinship terms were self-reciprocal; their senior kintype denotata were listed first and it was then noted that, "by self-reciprocity," the terms are used also to denote the junior reciprocals of these. Although the matter was there passed over without further discussion, this procedure amounted to treating the senior kintype denotata as class foci, to the exclusion of their junior reciprocals. However, in a componential definition of one of these terms, *tabu*, the senior and junior denotata (FF, FM, MF, MM, SS, DS, DS, DD) were implicitly treated as equivalent foci, when the primary sense of the term was given as "lineal consanguineal relative two generations removed from ego" (1965: 150). This is not entirely satisfactory, since a "seniority" dimension (with the values senior vs. junior) has to be employed in the componential definitions of certain other Trobriand kinship terms (unfortunately, this matter is not fully discussed in Lounsbury 1965), and it must be assumed that, in the case of the definition of *tabu* given above, this distinction has been neutralized and thus suspended. Prior to this neutralization, the term's definition must be understood as "lineal consanguineal relative two generations removed from ego, senior," or "grandparent." On this analysis, it is the neutralization of the seniority distinction that results in the self-reciprocity of the term, or in other words, in its extension from the category "grandparent" to the category "grandchild" (which has no distinctive term of its own).

As Greenberg (1966: 103–4) has observed, ascending (or senior) generation categories of kin are often treated as unmarked in relation to their junior reciprocal categories, and it is simply neutralization of this opposition that results in self-reciprocity of the terms for the senior categories. (Note that the reverse is more often the case with affinal categories.) Although, on the surface of it, the case of *kinu* (and the other Commanche "grandparent" terms) may seem much more complex, it is not. The Commanche system differs from the Trobriand in distinguishing four grandparent classes to begin with; neutralization of the seniority opposition in a case like this logically entails that terms marked for sex of alter in ascending generations become marked for sex of ego in descending generations.

ALTERNATIVE DESIGNATION.   Finally, we have heard it argued that a formal analysis of the kintype denotata of kinship terms cannot account for the "alternative classifications" of kintypes that are frequent in some kinship systems, e.g., the Zuni, Cochiti, and Navaho systems (see Schneider and Roberts 1956; Fox 1967; and Landar 1962 for some of the relevant data). It should be noted first that in these cases, as in others, the range of alternate classifications for a particular kintype (and its reciprocals) is never very broad; there are usually only two or three permissible classifications for a given kintype (and its reciprocals), and it appears that these alternatives are not "free" but are regarded by the speakers of the language concerned as appropriate to particular social contexts. As we noted above, the contexts are sometimes simply differentiated as vocative and referential usage; in speaking directly to a particular type of kinsman it is appropriate to use one term, but in referring to him in his absence it is appropriate to use another. If the uses of kinship terms in these two contexts are clearly separated from one another, as they are sometimes quite explicitly separated by informants (see Schneider and Roberts 1956: 11–12), it usually becomes apparent that the same terms are ordered into different systems appropriate to different contexts of usage. What we have to deal with, then, are *alternative systems* of classification, not simply alternative classifications for isolated types of kin. Of course, the vocative and referential systems constituted by the same terms, but differently distributed, are both *systems* of classification, and both may be analyzed formally as such.

Most published formal analyses of systems of kin classification have been concerned with referential systems, and it has been suggested that vocative usage is more difficult to account for, as indeed it is, because vocative usage is more likely to be affected by considerations of status connotation and is therefore prone to exhibit more variation from speaker to speaker and from one social context to another (see Murdock 1949: 97–98, 106–7).[9] The Zuni, for example, are quite clear about the fact that a FZD is properly classified as a kind of "father's sister," and a FZS is

---

[9] There is some tendency in Murdock's discussion to treat "terms of address" as though they had only connotative meanings and "terms of reference" as though they had only designative meanings. What we usually have to deal with, however, are systems of address and systems of reference, the same terms appearing in both and having category-designating senses in both. It is probably true that when the terms are used vocatively (in direct address), it is often with the specific intention of implying their status connotations, and their status connotations within the vocative system may differ from their status connotations in the referential system.

properly classified as "father"; conversely, MBC is properly classified as "child" by male ego and as "brother's son" or "brother's daughter" by female ego (Schneider and Roberts 1956: 3, 11–12). Zuni children are taught that these are the proper classifications and they use them to indicate respect, but "face to face" cross cousins call one another one or another kind of "sibling." However, some Zuni appear to disagree and assert that "there isn't really any rule" that governs these different classifications and they may be used indifferently in direct address and reference. Yet others clarify the situation by noting that the choice depends not only on the vocative versus referential distinction but also on the status connotations of the terms. Thus, one Zuni noted that when cross cousins are "living right in the same family" they call one another "sibling," because they are "very close" and "it's more polite and in the right way" (Schneider and Roberts 1956: 11–12). Otherwise, cross cousins follow the Crow-skewing principle. It would seem from this that the sibling terms connote closeness and nonsexual intimacy in interpersonal relations, whereas the "father," "father's sister," "child," and "brother's child" terms, at least in their attenuated senses, connote social distance and fairly formalized relations of respect. Thus the sibling terms are used perhaps both vocatively and referentially between cross cousins reared in the same domestic unit. Note, however, that these alternative classifications of cross cousins are generationally appropriate classifications. The alternatives no less than the proper nonsocially conditioned classifications are governed by genealogical considerations.

Of course, a particular individual may follow the *Crow-skewing principle* (see p. 107) in classifying some of his cross cousins and the generational principle in classifying others because his social relations with them may differ. It would not be inconsistent of him to do this, but it would be inconsistent for him to call, say, his FZD "father's sister" and for *her* to call him "brother," for this would violate the structural principle of *consistency of reciprocals*. To all appearances, Zuni do not violate this principle (cf. Schneider and Roberts 1965: 11).

If we were to analyze only those classifications that Zuni regard as proper referential classifications unaffected by status connotations, we would probably find a relatively simple Crow-type system. Of course, this analysis would not, in and of itself, provide an account of all uses of Zuni kinship terms, but it would provide the essential base for such an account, just as the linguist's grammar, constructed from speech, provides an essential base by reference to which the variation within speech may be understood and accounted for. In many instances, the terms are applied according to the principles of this "ideal model," while in others they are applied according to these principles supplemented by others. These others are no less a part of the total system of kin-term usage, but they may have to be distinguished as supplementary and contextually conditioned principles which may, as it were, override the Crow-skewing principle which is the principal distinctive rule of the basal referential system.[10]

IV

As we noted in Chapter 2, it follows from the assumption that each person is immediately genealogically connected to two other persons (his presumed genetrix and genitor) that he is less immediately so related to many other persons. For analytical purposes, the several parent–child and sibling–sibling links connecting ego (any individual) to his various kinsmen may be represented by means of a kintype notation, and such chains may be mapped onto genealogical trees. The ethnographic appropriateness of these reportorial and analytical devices was discussed above and is further considered in Chapter 7. We should note that in recent years several systems of kintype or genealogical notation have been employed by different anthropologists engaged in the formal semantic analysis of kinship terminologies (see Romney 1965; Keesing 1968). The differences among these notational systems are perhaps rather minor, and it seems to us that an analysis employing one of them will always be readily "translatable" into an analysis employing another—provided of course that the two analyses take similar account of the phenomena of polysemy, extension, etc. If the two analyses are equally satisfactory (i.e., equally parsimonious and equally sufficient), and if they make the same general semantic theoretical assumptions, we may say they are formally equivalent and differ only in trivial ways, even though they are expressed in different notational systems.

The most "traditional" notational system and the one most often employed here, differs from some others in overtly distinguishing the two sexes of parent, child, sibling, and spouse by means of the symbols:

F	= father	M	= mother
S	= son	D	= daughter
B	= brother	Z	= sister
H	= husband	W	= wife

[10] Another possibility, suggested by Kroeber's (1917) data, is that the Zuni case is similar to the Mnong Gar (Condominas 1960; Lounsbury 1964a: 368–69), that is, the Crow-skewing rule may apply only to father's *elder* sister as a linking kinswoman, thus leaving the children of father's younger sister to be classified as "siblings" (the generationally appropriate classifications). It is interesting to note that in the Zuni system the paternal cross cousins, when classified as "siblings," are classified only as "elder siblings," and the maternal cross cousins, when classified as "siblings," are classified only as "younger siblings." Unfortunately, Schneider and Roberts did not

However, the Siriono system (like many others) makes some distinctions covertly that it does not make overtly, and, vise versa, so that we occasionally find it convenient to employ the symbols P and C for "parent" and "child," respectively. For example, in the Siriono system, the two sexes of parent (but not of child) are distinguished overtly, but not covertly when considered as links to more distant lineal kin (grandparents)—the male parent of a parent (male or female) is an *ami*. Similarly, male and female siblings are *anongge*, but as links to more distant kin (e.g. their children) they are differentiated as same- and opposite-sex siblings. Thus, in listing the foci of Siriono kin categories we could emphasize the overt distinctions and employ a single symbol for "sibling" rather than the two symbols B and Z; but for other purposes, such as writing the equivalence rules of the system, we would have to employ subscripts with that symbol and with the symbols for ego and linking kinsmen to indicate sex or relative sex; alternatively, we could employ the two symbols in the kintype formula stating the extension rules but only the one symbol in the statements of the class foci. As far as we can tell, it makes no substantial difference to the analysis which of these conventions is chosen. In any event, the overt distinctions have to be expressed in the componential definitions of the primary senses of the terms and the covert distinctions in the equivalence rules (though they may express certain overt distinctions as well).

Thus, the notation FFZS is to be read "father's father's sister's son." We sometimes enclose kintype notations in quotation marks, e.g., "MB" or "MBD" vs. MB or MBD. This indicates a kinsman of a kintype more distant than the one so enclosed but terminologically equivalent to that kintype, i.e., what anthropologists have conventionally described as "classificatory" MBs or MBDs, etc. A "MB" or "classificatory MB," for example, is a kinsman who is not presumed to be one's mother's own brother but who is nevertheless classified as "brother" by one's mother.

In addition, the Mars ($\male$) and Venus ($\female$) symbols are used for male and female, respectively, to designate either ego or one of his or her kinsmen or kinswomen, and in each case specify the sex of the party designated by the symbol. In the text and in the various tables listing the kintype denotata of Siriono kinship terms, these symbols are sometimes prefixed to kintype notations. In these contexts they serve only to indicate the sex of ego who so employs the terms in question. Where a kintype notation occurs in the text or tables without such a prefix, it may be understood that the sex of ego is immaterial, unless the sex of ego is other-

---

consider the possibility that the relative ages of linking kinsmen are taken into account by the Zuni, but this consideration would account for most of the so-called irregularities and alternatives in Zuni kin-term usage.

wise indicated, e.g., "a man's MBD," "a woman's FZS." Thus, where the reader encounters these symbols in the text or in the tables, he should understand them as follows:

♂ MBS = male ego's mother's brother's son
♀ MBS = female ego's mother's brother's son
   MBS = any person's mother's brother's son (i.e., male or female ego's mother's brother's son).

In contrast, in the equivalence rule formulas the Mars and Venus symbols are used more broadly to designate either the sex of ego and/or that of his (or her) kinsmen or linking kinsmen to whom the rule applies. Thus, unless interpretation of the symbols is otherwise restricted (as noted below), the Mars sign may be read (in the equivalence rule formulas) as "male ego, or any male relative of any ego or of any relative of ego," and the Venus sign as "female ego, or any female relative of any ego or of any relative of ego." But in these formulas it is often necessary to distinguish specifically nonterminal positions in the genealogical chains (i.e., a linking kinsman) from unrestricted positions (i.e., ego or the designated kinsman). A single dot (·) and a sequence of three dots (. . .) are used for these purposes. A single dot preceding a male or female sign means this sign must be interpreted as ego and precludes any other interpretation. A sequence of three dots before a male or female sign means this sign must *not* be interpreted as ego, but must be interpreted as a linking kinsman of the appropriate sex but of unspecified genealogical position. A single dot following a kintype abbreviation means that the given abbreviation must be understood as referring to the designated relative only. Three dots following a kintype abbreviation mean that the given abbreviation cannot be interpreted as referring to the designated relative, but must be interpreted as a linking relative. Contrast the following when they occur in the equivalence rule formulas:

     MB = anyone's mother's brother.
  ♂ MB = any man's mother's brother.
. ♂ MB = male ego's mother's brother.
. ♂ MB . = male ego's mother's brother as a designated relative.
    MB . . . = anyone's mother's brother as a link to some more distant relative.
♂ MB . . . = any man's mother's brother as a link to some more distant relative.
. . . ♂ MB = a male linking relative's mother's brother.
. ♂ MB . . . = male ego's mother's brother as a link to some more distant relative.

We can offer no ethnographic justification for employing the symbols F, M, S, D, B, Z, H, and W to represent the units or relationships of the Siriono system of kin classification.[11] We employ them simply because they are familiar to most anthropologists and, perhaps most importantly, to most students of anthropology who are not yet familiar with similar analyses employing different notational systems. To choose another notational system would not simplify matters of importance. Perhaps the equivalence rules developed in Chapter 5 could be written more briefly or more compactly in another notational system, but this would not alter the number or the basic nature of those rules. In short, the notational system employed here is readily intelligible to us, and we believe that it is the one that will be most readily intelligible to the reader.

[11] The inclusion of H and W in this list does not imply that we regard the spouse relationship as on a par with the parent–child relationship and as one of the primitive (irreducible) elements of a system of kin classification (cf. Tyler 1969: 73). The spouse relationship is essential to any system of consanguinity *and affinity*, to use Morgan's (1871) phrase, but not to systems of consanguinity, i.e., systems of *kin* classification *per se*.

4 Siriono Kinship Terms: Ranges and Primary Senses

Holmberg's data on Siriono kinship terminology are reproduced here as Figures 3, 4, and 5 and Table 1. From his account (1950: 54) it appears that these terms are employed both in direct address and reference. Elsewhere, however, Holmberg gives *paba* for F and FB, *tain* for M and MZ, and *eco* for S and D (1948: 459). These terms are also reported by Priest (1964: 1151) and Schermair (1948: 427; 1958: 410; 1962: 322), whose orthography is slightly different (*pava, tai* or *tay*). The conditions governing the use of these terms are not clearly reported and it is not stated whether or not they may be further extended as in the case of *eru*, *ezi*, and *edidi*. It seems probable that these are special independent (i.e., nonprefix-taking), first person singular forms of *eru*, *ezi*, and *edidi*: Schermair glosses *tai* as "my mother, mama" and *pava* as "my father." Special forms of this sort are common to a great many kinship systems and we may assume that, in this case as in the others, the terms may be extended in the same way as their dependent forms. There is nothing in the available ethnographic literature to suggest the existence of differently structured vocative and referential systems. Therefore, we may assume that insofar as their significata are concerned *pava, tai,* and *eco* are equivalent to *seru, sezi,* and *sedidi,* the first person singular possessed forms of *eru*, *ezi*, and *edidi*.

In addition to the terms reported by Holmberg, Schermair reports the terms *erikii*, "elder brother or sister," and *eribi*, "younger brother or sister" (1948: 428; 1958: 333, 141). These terms may be glossed as "elder sibling" and "younger sibling," respectively; they designate subclasses of *anongge*, "sibling" without regard to considerations of sex or relative age.

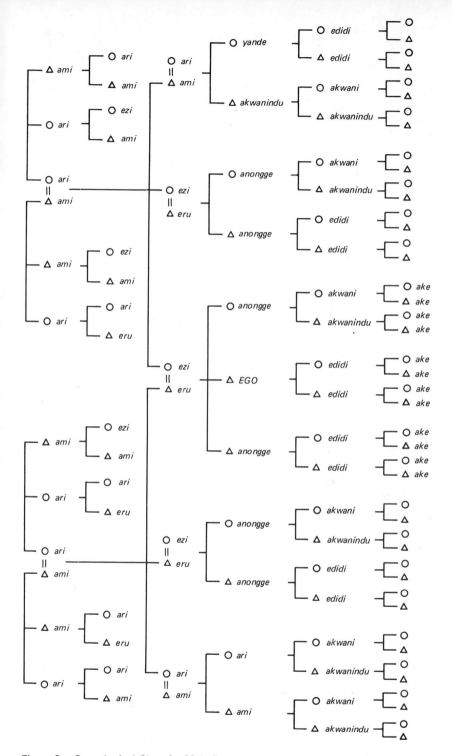

Figure 3. Genealogical Chart for Male Ego

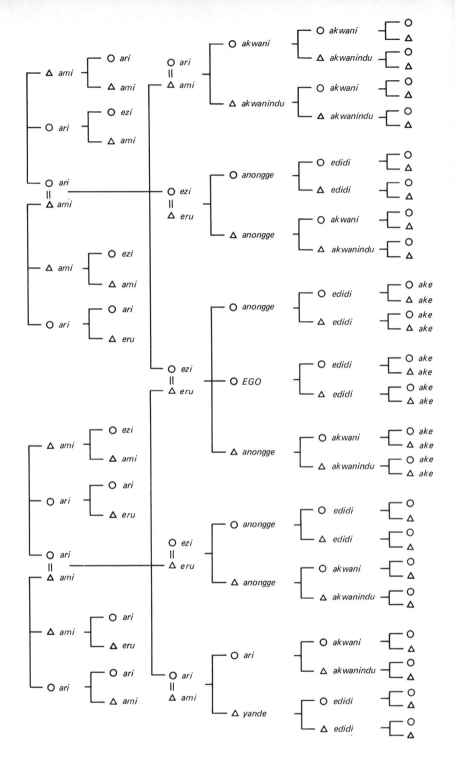

Figure 4. Genealogical Chart for Female Ego

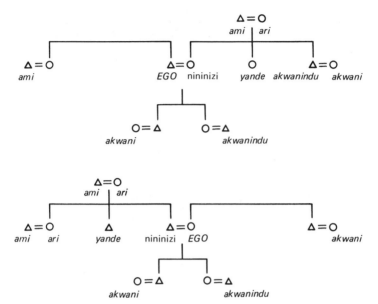

Figure 5.   Terms for Affinal Types

That is to say, one who is my *anongge* but who is older than I am is also my *erikii*, but if younger than I am he or she is also my *eribi*. It is unreported whether or not these terms are extended in the same way as *anongge*. Even if we assume they are so extended there is no need to give them any further attention here, because whatever rules govern the extension of *anongge* must also govern the extensions of *erikii* and *eribi*, if they are extended. In order to determine whether some kinsman is or is not an *erikii* or *eribi*, it must first be determined whether or not he or she is an *anongge*. After that, criteria of relative age serve to differentiate between the two different kinds of *anongge*.

Apparently, the terms *ami, ari, anongge, ake, akwani, akwanidu,* and *nininizi,* reported by Holmberg without the prefixed possessive pro-

Table 1

DENOTATA OF SIRIONO KINSHIP TERMS

Term	Denotata
1. *ami*	FF, MF, FFB, MFB, FMB, MMB, WFF, HFF, MB, FFZS, FMBS, MFBS, MMBS, MMZS, FZH, WF, HF, ♂ FZS, ♂ ZH, HZH
2. *ari*	FM, MM, FMZ, FFZ, MMZ, MFZ, WMM, HMM, FZ, FMZD, FFBD, FFZD, MMBD, MFZD, MBW, WM, HM, FZD, HZ
3. *eru*	F, FB, FFBS, FMZS, MFZS, MH, MZH
4. *ezi*	M, MZ, FMBD, MMZD, MFBD, FW, FBW
5. *anongge*	B, Z, MZS, FBS, MZD, FBD, FS, MS, FD, MD
6. *yande*	♂ MBD, ♀ FZS, WZ, HB
7. *edidi*	S, D, ♂ BS, ♂ BD, ♂ FBSS, ♂ FBSD, ♂ MZSS, ♂ MZSD, ♂ MBDD, ♂ MBDS, ♀ ZS, ♀ ZD, ♀ FBDD, ♂ FBDS, ♂ FZSS, ♀ FZSD, ♀ MZDD, ♀ MZDS, WS, WD, HS, HD
8. *akwani*	♂ ZD, ♂ MZDD, ♂ FBDD, ♂ FZSD, ♀ BD, ♀ MBDD, ♀ MZSD, ♀ FBSD, ♀ MBD, ♀ FZSS, MBSD, FZDD, SW, WBW, ♀ BW
9. *akwanindu*	♂ ZS, ♂ MZDS, ♂ FBDS, ♂ FZSS, ♀ BS, ♀ MBDS, ♀ FBSS, ♀ MZSS, MBS, MBSS, FZDS, DH, WB
10. *ake*	all second-descending generation kintypes
11. *nininizi*	W
12. *eru$_2$*	H

Data are from Holmberg (1950: 52–56). See also Needham (1961: 244–45) for some minor corrections authorized by Holmberg and included here.

noun (*se-*, ,"my"; *nde-*, "your"; *e-* "one's"), i.e., as independent noun forms, may also be treated as dependent nouns. Schermair indicates that all of them may be prefixed by *e-* or the other pronominal forms.

Holmberg (1950: 54, note 1) indicates that he was not certain that *nininizi* is in fact applied to both husband and wife. Schermair reports *enindisi*, "wife," and *eraasa*, "husband," but notes that a woman usually refers to her husband as *eru*, "her man." The term *eraasa* can be employed to distinguish a woman's husband from her father in a context where *eru* might be ambiguous. There is no evidence that *eraasa* is subject to simple extension. We may take it, then, that the normal term for "husband" is *eru* and that the Siriono clearly distinguish between the two categories labeled by this term. Henceforth *eru$_2$* will stand for "*eru* in the sense of husband." *Eru* without a subscript should be read as "father." We have added *eru*$_2$ to Holmberg's list of eleven terms, giving twelve in all. There is a general cover term for both sexes of spouse, *eosonda* (Schermair 1958: 286–87).

The final preliminary observation: Priest (1964: 1151) reports that a person's parents "call him *eco*, or if a son *tiiri-nje*." This suggests that *tiiri-nje* is a special term for "son." Schermair, however, reports *tiiri* as a simple phonetic variant of *riiri*, "child," and Priest's *-nje* appears to correspond to Schermair's *-te* or *-nte* (see above, p. 43). It would seem from this that the two sexes of *edidi* (Schermair's *e-rriri*) are not distinguished, except perhaps by the addition of the masculine or feminine suffix.

The first step in analysis is to establish the focal referents of each term. These are the kintypes that fall within the ranges of the terms when used in their primary senses, and in the case of some of the terms we know that the use of the terms in these senses may be marked by the suffixes *-te*, *-tuti*, or *-aeae*, "true" or "proper," while their use in extended senses may be marked by any one of several other terms. Schermair specifically reports this mode of distinguishing between primary versus extended senses for the parent, child, and sibling terms; it is not reported for the grandparent, grandchild, niece, nephew, or potential spouse terms. If this difference between these two sets of terms is a real one, and we have no reason to suppose it is not, it suggests a fundamental distinction not simply between the focal as opposed to derived members of certain categories but also a distinction between kintypes belonging to the nuclear or elementary family as opposed to all other types of kin. If this marking of the parent, child, and sibling terms has this dual function, it is not to be expected in the contexts of the grandparent, grandchild, niece, nephew, and potential spouse terms (*ami, ari, ake, akwani, akwanindu, yande*).

It should be noted, however, that Schermair reports that Siriono speak of a man's actual wife as his *enindisi-te* and of another woman with whom he is having extramarital sexual relations as his *enindisi-tyono* or *enindisi-ramey*, i.e., his "pseudowife" (1958: 270). Similarly, a woman's actual husband is her *eru-te* (1958: 349). The fact that these distinctions may be made in the context of the spouse terms does not contradict the hypothesis that they serve to distinguish kintypes belonging to the nuclear or elementary family as opposed to all other types. We show in due course that any Siriono's marital choices are not restricted to kinswomen of any particular type or category, or to kinswomen as such. It follows from this that ego's actual spouse is not presumed to be his or her kinsman of any particular type or even a kinsman at all. Thus, the spouse terms are not, strictly speaking, kinship terms in the first place; they do not belong to the same natural set as the ten other terms, because they have no reference to any presumed genealogical connections, but only to marital (and marital-like) connections. Although they are subject to metaphorical extension, this extension is not genealogically based (note that they are not extended to siblings-in-law). Therefore, when -*te* is used with either of these terms it cannot be to distinguish between primary as opposed to derived kintype denotata; the distinction is rather between one's actual spouse and another person with whom he or she is having an extramarital affair. The extension, in the case of the spouse terms, is metaphorical and based on social, not genealogical relationships. All that -*te* versus -*tyono*, etc. does is to distinguish between literal and nonliteral usage; in and of itself it does not tell us anything about the nature of the simple extension or the metaphor.

The fact that the primary and extended applications of the grandparent, grandchild, nephew, niece, and potential spouse terms are not lexically marked as they are in the case of the parent, child, and sibling terms does not indicate that no such distinctions are made in the case of the former terms. The primary denotata of these terms are readily describable by relative products of the parent, child, and sibling terms, and their extended ranges are describable by relative products of the parent, child, and sibling terms in their extended senses. Furthermore, such distinctions *are* made in the case of the parent, child, and sibling terms, and since the grandparent, grandchild, niece, nephew, and potential spouse terms belong to the same natural set, we must assume that the same semantic distinction is made for them, though it would appear that it is not verbally expressed in the same way.

The foci of the parent, child, and sibling terms are immediately obvious and require no further comment. As for the other terms, we assume (on general principles) that the focal types are the genealogically closest kintype or types in each class. For purposes of computing closeness, parent–child ties take priority over sibling ties, inasmuch as the latter are products of the former. For example, in the *ari* class we find FM, MM, and FZ, as well as several other more distant kintypes (e.g., MMZ, FZD, etc.). Of these, we identify FM and MM as the focal types. We designate both of these as focal types for the *ari* class because they are the closest types, they are equally close, and we have no reason to assume that one is regarded as focal to the exclusion of the other. On the basis of these foci, we may gloss *ari* as "grandmother." FZ is not included as a focal type since such a person is also FFD or FMD, or both, and we take FF and MF to be logically and genealogically prior to FFD and FMD. We think it would make no sense to speak of FM and MM as being included in a FZ or a "paternal aunt" class, for this would be to define FM's status as a kinswoman by reference to that of her daughter, and MM's by reference to that of her daughter's husband's sister. We have found it unproductive to assume that the sibling link is regarded as equivalent to the parent–child link for purposes of kin classification (i.e., to assume that siblings, like parents, are "first-degree kin").

The focal referents of Siriono kin terms are readily identifiable, at least on a preliminary basis (see Table 2).

Table 2

PRIMARY RANGES OF SIRIONO KINSHIP TERMS

Term	Focal Type(s)	Gloss
1. *ami*	FF, MF	grandfather
2. *ari*	FM, MM	grandmother
3. *eru*	F	father
4. *ezi*	M	mother
5. *anongge*	B, Z	sibling
6. *yande*	♂ MBD, ♀ FZS	potential spouse*
7. *edidi*	S, D	child
8. *akwani*	♂ ZD, ♀ BD	niece
9. *akwanindu*	♂ ZS, ♀ BS	nephew
10. *ake*	SS, SD, DS, DD	grandchild
11. *nininizi*	W	wife
12. *eru₂*	H	husband

*From Holmberg (1950: 54).

The next step is to establish componential definitions of the terms at these posited primary ranges of denotation. Note, however, that the foci of *akwani* and *akwanindu* (Numbers 8 and 9) are without reciprocals in Table 2. Their reciprocals (MB and FZ) do not appear as the foci of any terminological class. All other terms and their foci are arranged in reciprocal sets, as follows:

1. $$\frac{ami \text{ (FF, MF)} + ari \text{ (FM, MM)}}{ake \text{ (SS, SD, DS, DD)}} = \frac{\text{"grandfather"} + \text{"grandmother"}}{\text{"grandchild"}}$$

2. $$\frac{eru \text{ (F)} + ezi \text{ (M)}}{edidi \text{ (S, D)}} = \frac{\text{"father"} + \text{"mother"}}{\text{"child"}}$$

3. $$\frac{anongge \text{ (B, Z)}}{anongge \text{ (B, Z)}} = \frac{\text{"sibling"}}{\text{"sibling"}}$$

4. $$\frac{yande \text{ (♂ MBD)}}{yande \text{ (♀ FZS)}} = \frac{\text{"potential spouse"}}{\text{"potential spouse"}}$$

5. $$\frac{eru_2 \text{ (H)}}{nininizi \text{ (W)}} = \frac{\text{"husband"}}{\text{"wife"}}$$

MB and FZ, however, are members of the *ami* and *ari* classes—nonfocal members by our criteria. *Akwani* and *akwanindu*, therefore, have the same reciprocals as *ake*, viz., *ami* and *ari*. This arrangement must be clarified before componential definitions can be assigned to these terms at their primary ranges. It is not an unusual arrangement; ample precedent is found in other well-documented kinship terminologies (see e.g., Lounsbury 1964*a*: 364–65). Presumably the solution for the Siriono case will be similar.

Ami and *ari* taken together—including all of their referent kintypes, not just the focal types—constitute a superclass, the reciprocal of which is another superclass consisting of all of the referents of *ake, akwani,* and *akwanindu*. The most convenient English labels for these hypothetical superclasses (neither of which has, so far as we know, any single covering term in the Siriono language) are GRANDPARENT and GRAND-CHILD.[1] It must be understood, however, that these terms can apply literally only to the focal members of the two superclasses and must be taken in extended senses (Siriono-type extensions) when they refer to the totality of these superclasses. Under this interpretation, *akwani* and *akwanindu* are subclasses of a verbally unrealized superclass that also includes the subclass *ake* (just as *eru* and *ezi* must be presumed to be subclasses of the perhaps verbally unrealized superclass PARENT). The terminological distinction is on the subclass level and is not reflected in any analogous terminological distinction among the reciprocals (*ami* and *ari*).

It appears, moreover, that the words *akwani* and *akwanindu* are etymologically derived from *ake*. Thus, on both etymological and structural grounds,[2] we may say that *akwani* and *akwanindu* are special kinds of *ake*, and the GRANDCHILD superclass may be designated by the apparent common root *AK-*. The focal referents of *AK-* are the same as those of *ake* (SS, SD, DS, DD). The focal referents of the special subclasses *akwani* and *akwanindu* (the children of ego's opposite-sex siblings) are of a lower and derivative order. This will be apparent again when we come to apply the reduction rules that must be posited for this system. *The foci of any derivative subclass* ("subfoci" as we shall call them) *are*

---

[1] Hypothetical superclasses are indicated in capital letters. The use of capital letters in distinctive features of componential definitions and their abbreviations is somewhat different (see text pp. 101, 102). For further discussion of superclasses in semantic analysis, see Lounsbury (1964*a*: 364–65, 368–69, 375), Kay (1966), and Berlin, Breedlove, and Raven (1968).

[2] The Roman case is similar (see Lounsbury 1964*a*: 375). In some cases, however, morphology offers little or no evidence for the existence of super- and subclasses, and these have to be recognized on structural grounds alone (as in Lounsbury 1964*a*: 366). See also the Hopi case (Eggan 1950: 20–21), where the FZ category is a subcategory of the "grandmother" category, but this is not evident from the morphology.

not invariant to such rules, in contrast to the foci of the principal or nonderivative classes.

The relations in this subset of terms may now be diagrammed as:

$$\frac{ami\text{ (FF, MF)} + ari\text{ (FM, MM)}}{AK\text{- (SS, SD, DS, DD)}} + \frac{\text{GRANDPARENT}}{\text{GRANDCHILD}}$$

Again, *AK-* represents a hypothetical superclass from which are derived the subclasses *akwani* and *akwanindu* and the residue class *ake*. The derivative subfoci of *akwani* and *akwanindu* must be presumed to relate to the foci of *AK-* (and of *ake*, since they are the same) by the same equivalence rules as govern the whole system. (These rules are developed in Chapter 5.) The total GRANDPARENT class consists then of the focal kintypes of *ami* and *ari* together with all of the other kintypes that, by the rules of the system, are "equivalent" to these. The total GRANDCHILD class consists of the focal kintypes of *AK-* (the same as those of *ake*) together with all of the other kintypes that, by the same rules, are "equivalent" to these. These include both those classed as *ake* and those placed in the related derivative classes *akwani* and *akwanindu*. The *ake* are kintypes literally of second or lower descending generation. The *akwani* and *akwanindu* are kintypes of "other generations" (ego's generation and first descending generation) that the rules and reciprocal relations determine as "equivalent" (in some sense critical to the system) to second or lower descending generation kintypes; but not being literally of those generations, they are singled out of the *AK-* class and given separate designations.

These latter terms, it will be noted, are differentiated also for sex: *-ndu* appears to be a suffix signifying "male." *Akwanindu* is thus also a derivative term, derived from *akwani* by the addition of a suffix. We are justified, as far as the evidence goes, in regarding *akwanindu* as the marked term in this opposition (*akwanindu* are in effect simply "male *akwani*"), in which case we must posit also a superclass *AKWANI-* within the *AK-* superclass.

We may now phrase the situation in this way. There is a verbally unrealized superclass which may be represented by the symbol *AK-*; this superclass consists of all kintypes that are literally of second or lower descending generation plus certain other kintypes that are attributed this generational feature by extensions (of *ake*) governed by equivalence rules. However, the terminology recognizes the distinction between the actual and attributed (or classificatory) generational status, and differentiates the various kinds of *AK-* as *ake*, *akwani*, and *akwanindu*. The *ake* are kintypes that are actually of second or lower descending generation; these are opposed to classificatory *ake* (the hypothetical cover term for these is *AKWANI-*) which are verbally realized as *akwani* and *akwanindu*.

In order to realize the full implications of this we must also consider the term *yande* (Number 6 in Table 2) whose situation is similar. *Yande* is the term by which a man denotes his MBD and a woman her FZS, and which Holmberg glosses as "potential spouse." Note, however, that the kintype FZS classified as *yande* by a female ego is classified as *ami* by a male ego. A woman's "potential spouse" is her brother's GRANDFA-THER (classificatory "grandfather"). In all other cases, however (as we should expect to be the case in any kinship system), male ego and female ego employ the same distribution of senior consanguineal terms over the kintypes to which these apply. That is to say, siblings of opposite sex—in any kinship system—normally apply *senior* consanguineal terms in the same way; differences for sex of ego are usually found only in the dis-tribution of the junior terms within the consanguineal domain (see Tax 1955*b*: 19–20; Greenberg 1966: 100–111). Here in the Siriono classification of FZS we seem to have an exception to this "rule" (which is, of course, only an empirical generalization). But this is only an apparent and spurious exception. If one accepts the "rule" just stated (and we have no reason whatsoever—on the basis of our more or less extensive comparative studies of kinship terminologies so far—to doubt its validity), then it only proves that *yande* is *not simply* a consanguineal[3] term. This, of course, we should have known—and did know—from the beginning: Holmberg's gloss is "potential spouse."

The various sociological facts that probably account for Holmberg's gloss of *yande* are fully discussed in Chapter 8. Here it will be sufficient to anticipate the results of that discussion by noting that the ethnography offers strong reasons to suppose that each man has the right to claim his MBD in marriage; conversely, it must be the duty of each woman to marry her FZS if he chooses to claim her. This jural relationship is con-noted by the term *yande*. However, the ethnography also offers good reasons to believe that *yande* may be used to denote women other than a man's MBD without at the same time implying that the speaker has the right to claim such women as wives or that such women are obliged to marry him if he asks one of them to do so. A man has privileged sexual access to all women he calls *yande* (Holmberg 1950: 57), but his right to claim women as wives is limited to MBD. In other words, *yande* appears

---

[3] We trust our usage of "consanguineal" in this context will not be taken as naïve. As previously indicated, we are aware of the fact that many peoples, including perhaps the Siriono, have no concept of "consanguinity" in the literal sense. "Consanguineal term" is here employed as a convenient, brief designation for "term designating a genealogically established category or categories." The phrase has been so used by anthropologists for many years.

to have two status connotations for each sex of ego. For these reasons, we attribute a specific and a general connotation to *yande*. The specific connotation we gloss as "rightful spouse," the general connotation as "potential spouse." This latter gloss is not meant to imply that men may marry only women they call *yande*—the ethnographic evidence is all to the contrary. It is rather that by virtue of their specification as *yande*, certain kinswomen (and kinsmen) are considered to be available, and some of them particularly appropriate as marital partners.

To return to *yande* as a category of kin, it is evident that a man who is *yande* to a woman is a special kind of *ami*, not just any *ami*, but a special one who can be singled out only by a descriptive (genealogical) specification in a three-term relative product: "a male *edidi* of a female *anongge* of the *eru*" of said woman, i.e., "a male child of a female sibling of her father." This special *ami* is marked ("prescribed") by the conventions of the society as her most appropriate or proper "husband-to-be"—and as a man with whom she is free to have sexual relations whether or not she is married to him or to anyone else (see Holmberg 1950: 57).

The same point can be made by considering the reciprocal kintypes. We have considered FZS from the point of view of both male and female ego. The reciprocal kintypes are a man's MBS and MBD. A man classifies his MBS as *akwanindu*, but he classifies the sister of this man as *yande* (rather than *akwani*). His MBS is a kind of *AK-* (GRANDCHILD) to him—viz., the "nephew" kind—but this person's sister is his "rightful spouse." Junior consanguineal terms, if distinguished at all for sex of kinsman—in any kinship system—normally come in pairs: male and female. Otherwise, a single term serves for both sexes of designated kinsman (e.g., *edidi*, "child"; and *ake*, "grandchild"), The regular match for *akwanindu* is *akwani*. A man's MBS is his *akwanindu*, but his MBD is his *yande*, not his *akwani*. The apparent exception is again only spurious. It only establishes the fact that *yande* is not only a consanguineal term but also an affinal one, insofar as it has "affinal" connotations. One who is *yande* to a man is a special kind of *akwani*; not just any *akwani*, but a special one who can be singled out only by means of a descriptive (genealogical) specification: "a female *edidi* of a male *anongge* of the e*zi*" of a male ego, i.e., "a female child of a male sibling of his mother." Again, this special *akwani* is, by virtue of her specification as *yande*, a man's most appropriate "wife-to-be," his "rightful spouse," and he is freely permitted to have sexual relations with her whether or not he is married to her or to anyone else—though pragmatically the jealousy of her actual spouse, or his, may interfere with his freedom in this respect (see Holmberg 1950: 50).

If *yande* is an "affinal" term in that it connotes jural statuses having to do with privileged sexual and prescribed potential marital relationships, this raises the question of whether it is correct to specify the kintypes ♂ MBD and ♀ FZS as the foci of the *yande* class (as we did in Table 2), for these are consanguineal (or kin) types—an apparent contradiction. But again, the contradiction is only apparent.

Although "consanguineal relatives" and "affinal relatives" may be opposed *categories* in any culture, it should not be forgotten that the categories are *relational* and deal not with "whole persons" but with *types of relationships* presumed to exist between persons. Thus, if a society does not forbid marriages between kin as such, though it may forbid marriages between particular kintypes or categories of kintypes, then it will be possible for one and the same person to be both consanguineally and affinally related to another. He may then classify the other in either way, provided, of course, that the culture has no rules regulating the appropriateness of one or the other classification in such a circumstance.[4]

Moreover, a culture may specify certain kintypes as appropriate spouses, and it may, *for purposes of classification*, assume that each person marries a person of the appropriate kintype or types. The culture thereby marks a particular kintype as one with whom ego has a relationship of "prescribed" affinity. Now where a particular consanguineal relationship is prerequisite to such an affinal relationship, and it is mandatory to express this relationship in the application of an equivalence rule equating the appropriate kintype (or types) with a person's spouse, then all affinal relations may be structurally equivalent to types of consanguineal relations (i.e., kintypes). The categories of such a system have kintypes as their foci and are therefore kin categories, but by virtue of certain classificatory principles of the system (equivalence rules) they contain affinal types as derivative members. The affinal types are derivative members (just as some kintypes may be) because their categorizations are determined by equivalence rules which "equate" them with the kintype foci of their respective categories. This is not to say that all systems of kin classification featuring rules of structural equivalence between certain kin and affinal types have no affinal categories, i.e., categories with affinal types as their foci. Nor is it to say that there are no systems in which some kintypes are classified as though they were affines. It is only to say that there are some systems with no affinal categories (see Chapter 9 for further discussion of these variations).

Thus, despite its "affinal" connotations, *yande* may be regarded as designating a kin category if it can be shown that the kintypes posited as

---

[4] The Miwok system provides a case in point (See Scheffler 1970c).

its foci in Table 2 are probably its foci. We shall continue to treat them provisionally as such, until we show (in Chapter 5) that the hypothesis is confirmed by our analysis of the system as a whole.

It would appear, then, that a set of rights and duties, conveniently described as "affinal" because they pertain to marriage, has been overlaid on certain kintypes. Persons of those kintypes are therefore (so far as we know) not specifiable by the terms *akwani* and *ami*, whose paired terms *akwani* and *ari* are used to denote their siblings, but form a separate subclass (or subclasses) designated by the term *yande*. The kintypes denoted by *yande* are, as it were, "taken out of" the *akwani* and *ami* classes. Therefore, it is necessary to posit the further hypothetical (not verbally realized) superclasses *AKWANI* and *AMI* representing these classes *before* this subtraction. The *ami* and *akwani* actually listed in Holmberg's diagrams and tables represent these classes *after* the subtraction. (Compare our *AKWANI-*, which merely distinguishes *AK-* that are not of the second descending generation from those that are.)

We have seen that the kintypes designated by *yande* are readily specifiable by means of three-term relative products of kinship terms. Each of these terms, however, has a dual range of denotation (i.e., two ranges for each sex of ego). It designates first the one-member class (i.e., single kintype) covered by the specification "opposite-sex *parent's* opposite-sex *sibling's* opposite-sex *child*," and second the broader class consisting of any other kintypes describable by a specification employing the same terms but understood in their broader senses. The latter range encompasses any more distant kintypes that by the equivalence rules of this system reduce to the kintypes specified by the former.

The precise composition of this broader *yande* category (or these broader *yande* categories, if we distinguish between the ranges for female and male ego) is not ascertainable from the data presented by Holmberg. There are no data on the classifications of second-cousin kintypes, e.g. FFZDD, etc. Yet Holmberg does write in several places of "second cross cousins" and "classificatory cross cousins," and the contexts leave little room to doubt that he was referring to persons of kintypes *other than* a man's MBD and a woman's FZS who are also called *yande* (1950: 81–83). We can infer that some second-cousin kintypes fall within the range of the specifications, man's "mother's brother's daughter" and woman's "father's sister's son," when the constituent terms of these expressions are taken in their extended senses, but we cannot infer which ones these are without introducing an element of circularity in the analysis. (Inferences may be drawn, however, about the classifications of types whose reciprocals are reported. For example, FZH is reported as *ami*, but the reciprocals WBS and WBD are not reported. We may assume that the latter are classified as *akwanindu* and *akwani*.)[5] Because of these lacunae in the available data, the possibility exists that with fuller data, the analysis might have to be modified. We note later (in Chapter 6) the points at which modifications might be required, depending on the nature of the second-cousin classifications.

It follows from these observations that it would be an error to argue that, in the Siriono view, the kintypes man's MBD and woman's FZS are affinal types rather than kintypes, or in other words, that a man's MBD is an affine to him rather than a kinswoman. She is a kinswoman with whom he has a special type of social relationship that is conveniently described as an affinal one. Similarly, it would be an error to argue that a man's MB is an affine to him rather than a kinsman.[6] The term *ami* (by which the kintype MB is denoted) may be said to have an "affinal content" insofar as it may be used (by extension) to denote certain kinds of affinal relatives, e.g., W.F, and insofar as it may have certain affinal or marital connotations.[7] But in its primary (kinship) sense, it is simply a

[5] We may assume this on the basis of the general principle of consistency of reciprocals. In any kinship terminology there must be a consistent relationship between pairs or subsets of terms such that the terms employed by any ego for his various kin are predictable from those employed by those persons in respect of ego (and vice versa). In the simplest case, if ego calls alter X, alter responds with Y and any relative called X responds with Y (or at least should do so if the parties concerned are employing the same classificatory criteria). Not all cases are so simple, however, and X may have more than one reciprocal which it may share with other terms, as in the case of Siriono *ami* and *ari* (see also Greenberg 1966: 104–5). As we have seen, this arrangement is readily comprehensible once the super- and subclass structure of the system has been understood. Goodenough (1967) notes the heuristic value of the assumption of consistency of reciprocals, but maintains that there is at least one kinship terminology, the Kalmuk Mongol, in which "ego's way of labeling his various relatives [has] little or no correspondence with the way they label him." Goodenough does not indicate whether in his yet-to-be-published analysis of this system he considered the possibility of super- and subcategorical distinctions which may or may not be evident in the morphology of the terms. In any event, it is difficult to conceive how any kinship terminology could constitute a *system* unless it did, perhaps in some relatively complex way, maintain the consistency of reciprocals.

[6] Compare Fison (1880: 76–90) and Dumont (1953a; 1953b), who deal with Dravidian-type systems. For criticism of the Fison-Dumont argument, see Radcliffe-Brown (1953), Schneider (1967), and Scheffler (1970b).

[7] According to Dumont (1957: 25), ". . . in societies where there are (positive) marriage regulations . . . there is likely to an affinal content in terms which are generally considered [by anthropologists] to connote consanguinity or 'genealogical' relationships (such as 'mother's brother,' etc.)." However, in the same paper (p. 28), Dumont argues that the mother's brother (in Dravidian systems) "is an affine pure and simple." But the father's sister is strangely described as "to some extent kin" and "less clearly and unambiguously an affine than the mother's brother." It is difficult to see how the principles that are alleged to result in the classification of the kintype MB as an "affine" do not also and inevitably apply to the kintype FZ (see Radcliffe-Brown 1953; Dumont 1953b). The truth of the matter appears to be that in many but by no means all Dravidian systems, FZ and MB are kin who stand in potential affinal rela-

kinship term. It must be that *ami* denotes WF because a WF is normally a MB, or a more distant kinsman who is terminologically equivalent to a MB, and WF is thereby attributed the terminological status (though not necessarily the jural status) of MB. Thus it is mistaken, because it imposes a wholly irrelevant distinction on the system, to speak of MB or of any other kintype as a "classificatory" affine in the Siriono system (cf. Needham 1961: 247). Surely, one of the distinctive characteristics of this system is that it posits no affinal *categories* (other than "spouse"), and a system without affinal categories can hardly be said to contain "classificatory affines."

Finally, on the subject of *yande*, we must deal with the appropriateness of the gloss, "potential spouse." This is an adequate gloss of what we have argued is the general connotative sense of *yande*, and "rightful spouse" is an adequate gloss of its specific connotative sense (though other glosses, such as "spouse designate," would perhaps do just as well). But what of its significata? Without entering into a detailed discussion of the matter, it seems to us that the only satisfactory English gloss is "man's mother's brother's daughter" and "woman's father's sister's son." Glosses such as "cross cousin" and "matrilateral cross cousin" (for male ego) seem wholly inappropriate, for the system features no opposed categories whose labels may appropriately be glossed as "cousin," "parallel cousin," or "patrilateral cross cousin" (for male ego). At least glosses such as "woman's father's sister's son" and "man's mother's brother's daughter" are directly translatable into Siriono, and are thus possible paraphrases of *yande*, whereas glosses such as "matrilateral cross cousin" are not.

The spouse terms, like *yande*, also connote affinal statuses, but "actual husband" and "actual wife" rather than "rightful spouse" or "potential spouse." However, a consanguineal relationship is *not* prerequisite to "actual spouse" status; a male ego is not limited to MBD or "MBD" (classificatory MBD) in his choice of a spouse. This is evident in the fact, among others (see Chapter 8), that a man *may* marry a "nonrelative in the band" or a woman of another band (Holmberg 1950: 81). We are not told what the terminological procedures are when marriage to a nonkinsman does occur. By analogy with other societies (see Sternberg 1933 [1964]; Leach 1954: 305) where certain kintypes are singled out as special potential spouses and this is reflected in the system of kin classification, we presume that one's spouse would then be called *nininizi* or eru_2 and his or her kinsmen would be classified as though they were the appropriate kin of ego (e.g. WF would be classified as though he were MB, *ami*). This may

---

tionships in respect of ego. The terms for these types of kin designate kin categories and may or may not connote jural statuses having to do with marriage (i.e., affinity). Note that Dumont's "connote" is equivalent to our "signify" and that Dumont does not distinguish between what we describe as signification and connotation.

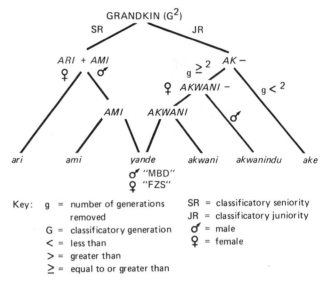

Figure 6. Grandkin Superclass

well be the case since Siriono apparently lack any terms for affinal relatives who are not also ego's kin. Such an arrangement would follow from the convention which, we have already seen, is surely employed by this terminological system, i.e., that a man is presumed to have married his MBD (and a woman her FZS) whether or not he actually did so. In any event, some actual spouses are special kinds of *yande*, those with whom the jural status of prescribed potential affinity has been realized by marriage, but others are not (or were not) *yande* to begin with.

The hierarchical relations of inclusion that have been established between the various classes, superclasses, and subclasses of GRANDKIN (GRANDPARENTS + GRANDCHILDREN) can best be portrayed in the form of a semantic tree (Figure 6). In this "tree" we summarize the matters thus far discussed that pertain to these classes, *taking them in their total ranges of denotation*, but without as yet having specified the rules of equivalence that account for their extensions from their focal referents to these total ranges. Moreover, we have yet to specify the definitions of these terms at their primary ranges (though certain notations on the "tree" anticipate these definitions). Before discussing this GRANDKIN category any further, we should note the other category that is structurally opposed to it, for these categories can be understood only in relation to one another.

It is fairly obvious that the terms *ami, ari, ake, akwani, akwanindu*, and *yande*, all taken at their broadest extensions, form a subset in this system, and this subset is structurally opposed to one consisting of *eru, ezi, anongge*, and *edidi*, all taken at their broadest extensions. This latter

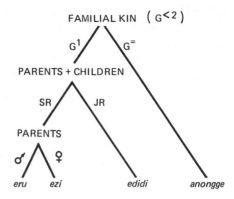

Figure 7. Familial Kin Superclass

subset may be described as FAMILIAL KIN (see Figure 7). Although, so far as we know, neither of these broad categories has a label in the Siriono language, we have seen that the lesser categories of which they are composed are treated as two distinct sets of categories. The terms of the FAMILIAL KIN set have their primary and derived significata distinguished by means of the suffixed forms -te, etc. versus -avarea, etc.; the terms of the GRANDKIN set do not. That is, although the two sets are not simply distinguished by means of two directly opposed cover terms, they are nonetheless indirectly distinguished in other ways. Taken together, the two sets comprise the inclusive set labeled tiesenda, "relatives" or "kin.".

We may now turn to the task of formulating componential definitions for these various classes.

The primary senses of eru, ezi, and edidi are, we have seen (Chapter 2), "genitor," "genetrix," and "offspring," and we have supposed that these are the "core" terms and relationships of this classificatory system. These glosses constitute adequate definitions of these terms in their primary senses. We have not treated anongge as one of the core terms of the system, because the relationship it signifies is a relative product of the relationships signified by the parent and child terms. But we have seen in this chapter that anongge is a member of a set composed of eru, ezi, edidi, and anongge, and we have called that set FAMILIAL KIN. We must suppose that this is a higher-order set of terms, those which designate categories of kin within any ego's nuclear family (and which are extended to kin who are not members of ego's nuclear family). Obviously, by "nuclear family" we here mean "any ego's genitor and genetrix plus those persons who share their genitor and genetrix with him or her." The opposition (Number 1) between familial kin versus nonfamilial kin is what distinguishes the kintypes F, M, S, D, B, and Z from all other kintypes; and, thus, the root feature common to the definitions of the terms eru, *ezi, edidi,* and *anongge,* when considered as a subset of the totality of Siriono kinship terms, is "familial kinsman."[8] This feature we signify by "f", and its contrary by "∼f."

Within the FAMILIAL KIN category, focal types of the various classes are distinguished from one another by the additional contrasts:

2. lineal (i.e., direct ascendant or descendant) vs. collateral relationship (1 vs. c); the latter includes co-lineal (co-1) relationship as a special case (see below)
3. one generation removed vs. same generation as ego (g^1 vs. $g^=$)
4. senior generation vs. junior generation (sr. vs. jr)
5. male vs. female (♂ vs. ♀)

Given these dimensions of contrast the focal types of the several FAMILIAL KIN classes may be defined componentially as in Table 3.

Our use of the component co-lineal requires some comment. We assume that half-siblings are not among the foci of *anongge;* a "sibling" in this, as probably in most kinship systems, is the parents' child, not just *a* parent's child. A full sibling is a special kind of first-degree collateral kinsman, viz., one with whom ego shares both of his or her parents and therefore all of his or her ancestors. This special subclass of kin of the first degree of collaterality may be described as *co-lineal kin.* (cf. Wallace and Atkins 1960: 61). Half-siblings constitute a residual subclass of first-degree collateral kin of ego's own generation, i.e., those with whom ego shares only one parent. In some kinship systems one or more types of half-sibling are given separate designations as special kinds of classificatory siblings (Henderson 1967); but here, as is most often the case, half-siblings are terminologically identified with full siblings (see the discussion of the half-sibling merging rule, Chapter 5).

The focal types of the principal nonderivative GRANDKIN classes *ami, ari,* and *ake* are of course nonfamilial kin, and the definitions of these terms all share the component ∼f. But they must share certain additional components or features which distinguish them from all other nonfamilial kin. The apparently relevant dimensions of contrast are Number 2 (above) and:

6. two generations removed versus less than two generations removed (g^2 vs. $g^{<2}$)

Within the GRANDKIN category, the focal types of the various principal categories are distinguished from one another by means of contrasts 4

---

[8] This excludes ego because we are dealing with ego's kin, and ego's relation to himself is one of identity, not one of kinship (cf. Romney and D'Andrade 1964; Pelto 1966); but it includes the relationship of parent to child as well as that of child to parent since the former is nothing more than the converse of the latter (cf. Tyler 1969).

Table 3

PRINCIPAL SIRIONO KIN CLASSES: NARROWEST RANGES

Term	Focal Type(s)	Componential Definition of Primary Sense
FAMILIAL KIN		
eru	F	$f \cdot 1 \cdot g^1 \cdot sr \cdot$ ♂
ezi	M	$f \cdot 1 \cdot g^1 \cdot sr \cdot$ ♀
edidi	S, D	$f \cdot 1 \cdot g^1 \cdot jr$
anongge	B, Z	$f \cdot co\text{-}1 \cdot g^=$
GRANDKIN		
ami	FF, MF	$\sim f \cdot 1 \cdot g^2 \cdot sr \cdot$ ♂
ari	FM, MM	$\sim f \cdot 1 \cdot g^2 \cdot sr \cdot$ ♀
ake	SS, SD, DS, DD	$\sim f \cdot 1 \cdot g^2 \cdot jr$

and 5 (listed above). The appropriate definitions are presented in Table 3.

The next step is to convert these limited definitions, valid for focal types only, into general definitions, valid for the corresponding total classes. (Note that at this point we are considering only the principal and nonderivative classes; we will turn to the subclasses that focus on noninvariant subfoci shortly.)

It is easy to see that it is not actual or natural generational standing (relative to ego, of course) that determines the classification of kintypes *other* than the focal ones. The classificatory generational (and hence terminological) status of other kintypes is determined by certain principles of extension which our equivalence rules must express. We can call such classificatory status "classificatory generation." In the ensuing componential definitions of total classes, "G" will be used to symbolize classificatory generation and "g" (as previously) to symbolize actual generation. For the ultimate focal types, to which the principal classes are anchored, classificatory generation is not different from literal generation. This being the case, general definitions of total classes can be expressed in terms of classificatory generation and still be applicable to the ultimate foci that are, of course, included within the larger classes. The general definitions of the total classes imply the previously stated definitions of class foci as special cases. Of course, as the concept "generation" is extended, the FAMILIAL KIN terms are extended beyond the confines of ego's nuclear family, necessarily to various collateral kinsmen. (The term, however, points to their locus of origin.) Similarly, the GRANDKIN terms are extended beyond the range of lineal kinsmen, again, necessarily to collateral kinsmen. Therefore, the genealogical distinctions represented by the contrasts between familial versus nonfamilial and lineal versus collateral (including co-lineal) kin are not represented in the broadened definitions of the terms.

Having introduced the notion of classificatory generation, we may now say that what distinguishes GRANDKIN from FAMILIAL KIN, this time as total categories, is the opposition:

> 6'. two or more classificatory generations removed vs. less than two classificatory generations removed ($G^{\geqslant 2}$ vs. $G^{<2}$)

A kintype is of senior classificatory generation (SENIOR GENERATION) if, by the equivalence rules of the system, it reduces to one of the senior focal types. The kintype itself may or may not be actually of senior generation. Thus, for example, FZS, a $g^{=}$ kintype, will be shown to be classificatorily of senior generation (G^{+2}). FZS reduces to (i.e., under the equivalence rules of the system, is equivalent to) FF, and like FF, FZS is *ami* (or *AMI* and *yande* for a female ego). Thus, for purposes of defining *total* classes we must use a modification of our seniority opposition:

> 4'. classificatorily senior (SENIOR) vs. classificatorily junior (JUNIOR) (SR vs. JR).

As with classificatory generation, so with classificatory seniority and juniority, capital letters are employed in the symbols used to distinguish them from the literal meanings of these terms.

The broadest ranges of the principal Siriono kin classes may now be defined componentially as in Table 4. Only the subclasses *akwani* and *akwanindu* remain to be dealt with. *Yande*, as we have already seen, has its ranges defined by three-term relative products of class labels, stated first in narrow and then in broader senses.

Table 4

PRINCIPAL SIRIONO KIN CLASSES: BROADEST RANGES

Term	Focal Type(s)	Componential Definitions of Broadest Ranges
CLOSE KIN		
eru	F	$G^1 \cdot SR \cdot ☝$
ezi	M	$G^1 \cdot SR \cdot ♀$
edidi	S, D	$G^1 \cdot JR$
anongge	B, Z	$G^{=}$
GRANDKIN		
AMI	FF, MF	$G^2 \cdot SR \cdot ☝$
ari	FM, MM	$G^2 \cdot SR \cdot ♀$
AK-	SS, SD, DS, DD	$G^2 \cdot JR$

Note: *AMI* and *AK-* are here considered *before* subtraction of the subclasses *akwanindu*, *akwani*, and *yande*.

As noted above, in the cases of the irreducible foci (to which the principal classes are anchored), classificatory generation and literal generation are necessarily identical. For the subfocal types (about which the subclasses are formed) this is not necessarily so, for such subfoci are by the nature of the case susceptible to further reduction. Nevertheless, literal generation may be called upon to describe the subclassification affected by the terms *akwani* and *akwanindu* once the superclass structure has been recognized for what it is. As Figure 6 indicates, these subclasses at their broadest extension may be defined componentially as:

$$akwani \quad : \quad ♀ \cdot JR \cdot G^2 \cdot g^{<2} \cdot (\text{not male ego's "MBD"})$$
$$akwanindu : \quad ⚥ \cdot JR \cdot G^2 \cdot g^{<2}$$

These definitions may be read:

> *akwani*   :   A female who is classificatorily junior, two classi-ficatory generations removed, but less than two actual generations removed, and not a male ego's "mother's brother's daughter."
>
> *akwanindu* :   A male who is classificatorily junior, two classi-ficatory generations removed, but less than two actual generations removed.

The broad range of *akwani* might also be defined disjunctively by employing a separate definition for each sex of ego, as follows:

$$akwani: \quad ⚥ \ ego \cdot ♀ \cdot JR \cdot G^2 \cdot g^1, \ or$$
$$♀ \ ego \cdot ♀ \cdot JR \cdot G^2 \cdot g^{<2.}$$

As far as the available data go, these two ways of defining *akwani* are equivalent; the second differs from the first only in that it expresses somewhat differently the fact that for male ego the category is less inclusive than it is for female ego.

Even though *akwani* and *akwanindu* are subclass labels, like *yande* they may still be said to have foci. That is, these terms also may be said to have two distinct senses, one designating the foci of the respective subclasses and another designating their total ranges. The foci of the subclasses may be called *subfoci*. As noted earlier, they have a derivative status; they are not of the same structural order as the foci of the principal classes. In order to describe these subfoci and to relate them to the principal classes, we must introduce a further dimension of opposition:

> 7.   linking kinsman of the same vs. opposite sex, i.e., "parallel" vs. "cross" (|| vs. x).

The terms may be defined as follows:

$$akwani \quad : \quad {\sim}f \cdot c^1 \cdot g^1 \cdot jr \cdot x \cdot ♀$$
$$akwanindu \quad : \quad {\sim}f \cdot c^1 \cdot g^1 \cdot jr \cdot x \cdot ♂$$

The opposed "parallel" category consisting of the children of ego's same-sex siblings is encompassed by the "child" term, *edidi*, in its extended sense indicated in Table 4.

Our findings thus far are summarized in Table 5 which illustrates as much of the structure of this system as may be represented in terms of two sets of componential definitions. What remains to be done now is to describe the logic of the extensions noted above. This takes us to the task of formulating the equivalence or extension rules that underlie this system.

Table 5

SIRIONO KINSHIP TERMS

Term	Foci or Subfoci	Primary Sense	Broadest Sense
ami	FF, MF	${\sim}f \cdot 1 \cdot g^2 \cdot sr \cdot ♂$	$G^2 \cdot SR \cdot ♂ {\sim} ♀$ "FZS"
yande	♀ FZS	♀ FZS	♀ "FZS"
ari	FM, MM	${\sim}f \cdot 1 \cdot g^2 \cdot sr \cdot ♀$	$G^2 \cdot SR \cdot ♀$
eru	F	$f \cdot 1 \cdot g^1 \cdot sr \cdot ♂$	$G^1 \cdot SR \cdot ♂$
ezi	M	$f \cdot 1 \cdot g^1 \cdot sr \cdot ♂$	$G^1 \cdot SR \cdot ♀$
anongge	B, Z	$f \cdot co \cdot 1 \cdot g^=$	$G^=$
edidi	S, D,	$f \cdot 1 \cdot g^1 \cdot jr$	$G^1 \cdot JR$
ake	SS, SD, DS, DD	${\sim}f \cdot 1 \cdot g^2 \cdot jr$	$G^2 \cdot JR \cdot g^2$
akwani	♀ BD, ♂ ZD	${\sim}f \cdot c^1 \cdot g^1 \cdot jr \cdot x\ ♀$	$G^2 \cdot JR \cdot g^{<2} \cdot ♀ \cdot {\sim} ♂$ "MBD"
yande	♂ MBD	♂ MBD	♂ "MBD"
akwanindu	♀ BS, ♂ ZS	${\sim}f \cdot c^1 \cdot g^1 \cdot jr \cdot x\ ♂$	$G^2 \cdot JR \cdot g^{<2} \cdot ♂$

5 Siriono Kinship Terms: Extension Rules

The rules for specifying the ranges of Siriono kinship terms are of two sorts: defining rules and extension rules.

Defining Rules

A defining rule is a statement of the referent (or referents) of a term. Such a rule may be stated by listing the referents or by stating a componential definition that describes them in terms of distinctive features drawn from concurrently applicable dimensions of opposition. Of course, these are not simply equivalent means of defining the terms: one consists of a mere list of denotata, the other of a semantically informative statement of the criteria, and relations between the criteria, for distinguishing the denotata and among the various classes of them. Merely to list the denotata would be to leave an important part of the structure of the system undescribed (as in Coult 1967).

In any system, there are at least as many defining rules as there are terms of relationship. However, as we saw in previous chapters, since Siriono kinship terms are polysemic, it is necessary to formulate at least two defining rules (or more simply, definitions) for each term and to relate the narrower (primary) and broader (extended) definitions of each term by means of certain extension rules. In general, kintypes subject to primary defining rules (those stating the primary senses of the terms) are not subject to reduction under the extension or equivalence rules of a system (though, of course, they are subject to the same rules when treated as expansion rules, in order to derive the more distant from the primary or focal members of kin classes). However, the foci of subclasses are exceptional in this respect: they are subject to reduction under the operation of equivalence rules. These subfoci reduce to the ultimate and invariant foci of their respective superclasses (that is, the foci of *akwani* and *akwani-*

ndu, for example, reduce to SS, SD, DS, or DD, thus indicating in another way that *akwani* and *akwanindu* are indeed subclasses of the *AK-* superclass.) In other words, if we are to identify a particular kintype as a member of a particular kin class, subclass, or superclass, that kintype must reduce to one of the foci of that class, subclass, or superclass. This means that kintypes belonging to subclasses will reduce first to the foci of those subclasses (i.e., to subfoci) and then to foci of the relevant superclasses (i.e., to ultimate foci). Thus, we may think of subfoci as *labeled nodes in pathways of reduction* leading to the ultimate foci of superclasses. When the operations required by equivalence rules have taken us to one of these nodes, we are able to give it a terminological classification, thus determining the verbally realized classification of the kintype in question; but we may allow the rules to carry us further, to the foci of the relevant superclass, thus determining the superclass of the kintype in question.

Extension Rules

An extension rule is one that specifies the conceptual operations whereby the broad or extended sense (or senses) of a term is (or are) derived from its most narrow or primary sense. In dealing with systems of kin classification, these may also be described as "equivalence rules" since they specify either an overt or a covert structural equivalence of two or more kintypes (cf. Lounsbury 1965: 151). The "equivalence" of which we speak (whether overt or covert) is purely terminological. The ethnography offers no reason to assume that the various kintypes that form a single terminological category are all entitled to the same right- and duty-status with respect to ego, or vice versa. Assumptions of this sort about the social (or psychological) significance of kin categories have fared rather badly in the past, and there is no reason to assume that they would do any better in this study. As noted earlier, we must hold open the possibility that extensive terminological equivalences between close and distant kintypes may be merely the cumulative end result of the repeated operation of a few, perhaps more significant, equivalences of much more limited scope. The latter we formulate as "equivalence rules." Something of the variety of such rules necessary to account for the kintype classifications of certain Crow- and Omaha-type systems has been illustrated in previous publications. Some of the equivalence rules required for the Siriono system are similar, but others are novel in comparison with those discussed in earlier studies (Lounsbury 1964*a*; 1965; Henderson 1967).

The analytical process by which such rules are discovered is laborious and time consuming, but not mysterious. It is a relatively simple matter of trial and error based on "educated guesses" that are in turn based on successful analyses of other systems. There is nothing more to it than formulating and testing hypotheses that are suggested by one's previous experience with similar systems. However, previous experience is not an infallible guide and may lead one astray. For reasons of economy, the numerous blind alleys we traversed before arriving at the analysis presented here cannot be rehearsed in detail, but we should note a few of the observations that eventually led us to discover the perhaps least obvious and certainly the most distinctive equivalence rule of this system.

On the basis of little more than the isolated terminological equations of FZD with FZ and female ego's MBC with her BC, the Siriono system has often been described as "Crow" in type (Holmberg 1950: 54; Murdock 1949: 234; Eyde and Postal 1961), although it differs in many respects from other so-called Crow-type systems and does not conform to Murdock's more stringent definition of the type (see Murdock 1949: 102, 166; but see also p. 224 where the definition is considerably weakened). Moreover, as suggested elsewhere (Lounsbury 1964a), the conventional category "Crow-type systems" is somewhat heterogeneous if we attend to the structural or classificatory principles that must be presumed to underly the diverse terminological equations and distinctions of the systems that have been so classified. Much of the diversity among Crow-type systems, as defined by Spier (1925) and Murdock (1949), can be accounted for by means of equivalence rule analyses of these various systems; from a structural perspective, there is not one but there are several kinds of Crow-type systems.

One of the several equivalence rules required for many, but not all, of Murdock's Crow-type systems is a rule that equates specific collateral kintypes in one generation with specific collateral kintypes in a generation above or below that generation. The effect of such a rule, when consistently applied, is to skew the relationship between the classificatory generations (as given by the application of kinship terms) and the actual generations of the various kintypes. Hence the rule in question has been called a "skewing rule." These various skewing rules are quite similar to one another in that each operates on the opposite-sex sibling relationship in one or another genealogical context to equate a woman's son with her brother. Thus, the rules are of a single, logical type, and for this reason we may describe them all as *Crow-type skewing rules* and stipulatively define a Crow-type system as one that employs this type of skewing rule. Something of the variety among such rules has been dealt with in other papers (Lounsbury 1964a; 1965; also Lamb 1965; Hammel 1965d).

But the total variation within the conventional Crow category cannot be accounted for by means of the various Crow-type skewing rules, or even by means of relatively simple permutations of them (as in Lounsbury 1965; Henderson 1967). The category "Crow-type systems" as

defined by equivalence rules *is not coextensive with* the category of the
same name defined by reference to little more than the isolated terminological equation of FZD with FZ (cf. Buchler 1964). It would appear then
that the equation FZD = FZ (or even FZD = FZ = FM, see below p.
180) cannot be regarded as structurally diagnostic, since it may derive
from rules other than Crow-type skewing rules, as in the Siriono case.

That the Siriono system differs markedly from Crow-type systems
(in the equivalence rules sense) is readily demonstrated.

In systems that utilize Crow-type skewing rules, a uterine *line* of
female kin descended from the FZ, and sometimes from the FM as well,
is merged into one terminological category: a uterine *line* of males collateral to these female kin are merged into another such category. In other
words, insofar as Crow-type skewing rules are concerned, the most reliable equations are: FZ = FZD = FZDD, etc., and F = FZS = FZDS,
etc., and their reciprocals. These terminological mergings, and many
others, follow logically from a few underlying postulates that characterize
a Crow-type system and generate the extended references of the terms of
such a system.[1]

In the Siriono data we do indeed find a part of this, but only a very
small part. Ego's FZD receives the same designation as his (or her) FZ,
which is the same as that given to the "grandmothers" FM and MM
(viz., *ari*). But this is as far as the equation extends in this line. The term
ari is not extended further down this "matriline" as, by definition, is the
case in a Crow-type system. The next kintype in the line belongs to a
"niece" category, which is a subclass both structurally and etymologically
of the GRANDCHILD class of this system. Even more un-Crow-like is
the fact that for the corresponding male kin there is no "matrilineal"
transmission of kin-class status at all. Although FB = F (these being of
the same generation, and this equation being common to a great variety
of kinship systems), none of the other distinctive Crow-type equations
are found. For Siriono, F and FB are *eru*, "father"; but a man's FZS is
ami, "grandfather"; his FZDS is *akwanindu*, "nephew"; and in the next
generation we find only *ake*, "grandchild." In other words, the Siriono
system does not align these crucial male relationships "matrilineally" or
equate them categorically. There is no "matrilineal" transmission of kin-
class status indicated among males! Therefore, Crow-type equivalence
rules will not generate (i.e., cannot account for) the references of Siriono

---

[1] However, as we show below (*p.* 180), similar patterns of terminological equations
and distinctions of kintypes may also follow from somewhat different principles of
terminological extension. Therefore, it is an unreliable procedure to compare and contrast systems, and certainly to "type" systems, on the basis of some (or even a large
number) of the terminological equations and distinctions of kintypes that they may or
may not share. Comparison and classification *must* be based on the underlying structural
principles that different systems share with one another.

kinship terms. If a system fails in all of these regards, it can hardly be considered Crow-type, if a Crow-type system is defined in structural semantic terms. *Nor can a terminology be taken as indicative of matrilineal descent when it evidences no matrilineal alignments of male kin* (cf. Needham 1961; 1963: 195; 1964*a*). The most that can be said is that this terminology sometimes aligns one of ego's kins*women* with her *mother*.

If the Siriono terminology is not Crow, and if it is not indicative of "matrilineality," then what is it? Curiously, one might have made out almost as good a case for its being "Omaha" as for its being "Crow," for it also contains several Omaha-like equations, e.g., MB = MF, that show agnatic (i.e., father–son) cross-generation continuity in the assignment of kintypes to kin classes. But these are also limited, and an Omaha hypothesis would have fared no better than the Crow. However, it is interesting to note in these equations that *while the identifiable uterine equivalences concern only females, the identifiable agnatic continuities concern only males.* This makes it just as difficult to speak of patrilineal descent as it is to speak of matrilineal descent as a criterion of Siriono kin class member-ship. But we can say, without going beyond what is descriptively neces-sary and accurate, that the terminology identifies some of ego's kins*women* with their *mothers* and some of ego's kins*men* with their *fathers*.

What we may have here, then, is a kind of terminology not recognized in our traditional typologies, and probably of rather rare occurrence. While it is superficially similar to both Crow- and Omaha-type systems, it is in fact very different in its structure because it evidences no identi-fications of "matrilineally" related males and no identifications of "patri-lineally" related females. For purposes of ethnographic description, then, the terms "matrilineal" and "patrilineal" are irrelevant.

So far, it would appear (and we may treat it as a hypothesis) that in this system certain female kin-class statuses (but perhaps not any right- and duty-statuses) are transmitted from mother to daughter, and the corresponding male kin-class statuses are transmitted from father to son. Thus, for example, the hypothesis is that FZ is terminologically identified with FM *not* because ego's father's "matriline" is treated as unitary (with further differentiation for sex of alter), or because of a principle of genea-logical structural equivalence between certain "matrilineally" related kin-types, but because: (1) FM is one of the foci of *ari*; (2) FZ is her daughter (FMD); and (3) in certain specified genealogical contexts kins*women* take their kin-class statuses from their *mothers*. Similarly, the hypothesis is that MB = MF (*ami*) because: (1) MF is one of the foci of *ami*; (2) MB is his son (MFS); and (3) in certain specified genealogical contexts kins*men* take the kin-class statuses of their *fathers*. On this hypothesis, the problem is to specify the genealogical contexts in which these identifications are made. Obviously, the equivalence rule governing these identifications is not the only equivalence rule of the system, and we must also formulate the rules complementary to this one.

We may now proceed to a statement of the equivalence rules that may be posited for this system.

The two most distinctive equivalence rules of Siriono kinship terminology may be called (1) the *parallel-transmission rule* and (2) the *MBD-FZS–spouse equation rule*. (Occasionally, we refer to these as the "transmission rule" and the "spouse equation rule," but, it should kept in mind that the latter is a rule of kin classification, not of individual marital arrangements.) In addition, the system features three more common rules: (3) the *same-sex sibling merging rule;* (4) the *half-sibling rule;* and (5) the *step-kin rule.* These three rules are shared with a great many other kinship terminologies (e.g., the great majority of those that utilize Crow- and Omaha-type skewing rules). There are also "auxiliary rules" that must be stated in a complete formalization, but these are not so much additional *principles* as they are statements of *operations* which permit the use of other rules (especially the transmission rule). Because of the auxiliary nature of some of the rules and because of the super- and subclass structure of this system, the several equivalence rules must be *ordered* in relation to one another. That is, where a particular kintype simultaneously presents several possibilities for reduction, one of these possibilities will have to be allowed to take precedence over the others, and the order of precedence will always be the same. This ordering is discussed below.

Now to the rules themselves.

1. The Parallel-Transmission Rule

This rule states that kinsmen succeed to the kin-class statuses of their fathers and kinswomen to those of their mothers (relative to ego). Stated in this way, and without the necessary additional context restrictions, the rule may be written:

$$(\dots \male\; S \longrightarrow \dots \male) \equiv (\male\; F \dots \longrightarrow \male \dots)$$
$$(\dots \female\; D \longrightarrow \dots \female) \equiv (\female\; M \dots \longrightarrow \female \dots)$$

> **Or:** Let a linking relative's child of the same sex as himself or herself be regarded as structurally equivalent to ($\longrightarrow$) that linking relative himself or herself; and, conversely ($\equiv$), let any person's parent of the same sex as himself or herself, when as a link to some other relative, be regarded as equivalent to that person himself or herself.

It will be noted that this rule is already somewhat restricted in its range of effectiveness by the requirement that, e.g., a man's son is to be equated with that man himself only where that man is a linking kinsman; ego does not identify himself with his son in any genealogical contexts, but he does identify himself with his father in certain genealogical contexts, e.g., when his father is being considered as a linking kinsman. It should be obvious that ego does not always identify himself with his father even when his father is being considered as a linking kinsman, for if he did he would have to classify, e.g., his FB as *anongge*, "brother." But he classifies his FB as *eru*, "father." This indicates that other rules, yet to be noted, must take precedence over the transmission rule.

Our choice of the label *parallel-transmission rule* is quite deliberate. We have attempted to describe the phenomenon under consideration as simply and as accurately as possible, and we do not wish to suggest the existence of anything more (in Siriono culture) than we have already established. It is for the latter reason, especially, that we would reject any attempt to describe the phenomenon we are concerned with here as "parallel descent." The term "descent," in social anthropological discourse, has come to have such a variety of connotations and theoretical associations that it cannot be used casually without danger of completely obfuscating a discussion or description. (See Scheffler 1966 and 1967*b* for discussion of some usages of descent.) In particular, we should draw attention to the difference between "parallel transmission of kin-class status" and the phenomenon described by Maybury-Lewis (1960) as "parallel descent."

Maybury-Lewis uses "descent" to designate "the recognition of a *social* relationship between a child and one or both of its parents" (1960: 191, italics added). By "recognition of a social relationship," he refers not to "recognition" (or rather postulation) of parent–child relationships *per se* (i.e., genealogical relationships) but to a distribution of rights and duties with reference to one's parentage. Thus, he describes the Apinaye *kiye* system as a "system of parallel descent" because, according to Nimuendaju (1939), the rule of affiliation with these exogamous ceremonial units is that a man belongs to the *kiye* of his father and a woman to the *kiye* of her mother. Maybury-Lewis therefore describes *kiye* affiliation as "patrilineal for males" and "matrilineal for females."

While it seems to us that it is neither necessary nor useful to employ the terms "descent," "patrilineal," and "matrilineal" in the description of Apinaye *kiye*—surely it suffices to speak of the same-sex parent–child relationship as the criterion of *kiye* affiliation—it is important that for Maybury-Lewis "descent" designates the distribution of *rights and duties* by means of genealogical criteria. This usage has often led to considerable confusion in the anthropological literature, for "descent" is also commonly (though variously) used to describe genealogical connections *per se*. In order to avoid confusion of genealogical connections *per se* with such connections considered as criteria for the allocation of rights and duties, and because the term would add nothing to our description, we prefer not to employ the term "descent." The important thing to remember is that "parallel transmission of kin-class status" refers to nothing more than a characteristic of the Siriono system of kin classification; it is meant to imply nothing whatsoever about the distribution of rights and duties among and between kinsmen. We are concerned here with the significata (i.e., the category references) of Siriono kinship terms. We are necessarily concerned with parent–child relationships *per se* because these are the primitive elements of any kinship system. There may or may not be distinctive sets of rights and duties associated with each of the categorically distinguished concatenations of parent–child relationships, but, if there are, such "social relationships" have nothing to do with the category definitions *per se*. They are *implications* of category membership, and they constitute some of the social significance of category membership, but they are not criteria for the definitions of the categories. This is true even in the case of *yande*. Certainly, all persons whom ego calls *yande* do comprise a category of persons having certain rights and duties with respect to him or her. But these persons belong to the category and have these right and duties with respect to ego because they are genealogically related to ego in a specific way, or because, by virtue of certain rules of genealogical structural equivalence, they are treated as if they were so related.

We may turn now to the other most distinctive equivalence rule of this system.

2. The MBD-FZS—Spouse Equation Rule

This rule may be written, again without the necessary genealogical context restrictions, as:

$$(\male \text{ MBD} \rightarrow \male \text{ W}) \equiv (\female \text{ FZS} \rightarrow \female \text{ H})$$

> **Or:** Let a man's mother's brother's daughter be regarded as structurally equivalent to his wife; and, conversely, let a woman's father's sister's son be regarded as equivalent to her husband.

So expressed, the rule is of course inconsistent with our hypothesis that the kintypes man's MBD and woman's FZS are the foci of the *yande* category. It is also inconsistent with the fact that actual spouses are designated as *nininizi* or eru_2. It is inconsistent because, to write the rule in this way, we would have to treat the affinal types W and H as the foci of the *yande* class. It would seem from Holmberg's account that actual spouses are not denoted by *yande* and potential spouses are not denoted by *nininizi* or eru_2. It must be noted, however, that according to Schermair (1958: 115), *yande* (his *iande*) is the term by which a man denotes his wife until she has children for him; Schermair derives *nininizi* (his *nindisi*) from *eriiri + esi*, "mother + child," and translates it as "mother of one's child" or "wife" (1958: 269). It appears from this that Siriono, like some other peoples, do not regard a marriage as fully established until children have been born of the couple concerned; a man's *yande* retains her premarital kin-class status in relation to him until such time as she has borne children for him, when she becomes his *nininizi*, "the mother of his children." Presumably, if she marries someone else, she remains *yande* to ego, but her children are nevertheless treated terminologically as ego's children, but only in a "classificatory" sense. In other words, a man's MBD as such is his *yande*, but *as a linking kinswoman* she is treated as though she were his wife, whether or not she is in fact his wife. If she is his wife and a linking kinswoman, by virtue of being the mother of his children, then she is his *nininizi*.

Therefore, we must assume that the relationships man's MBD and woman's FZS on the one hand and the relationships W and H on the other are terminologically distinct even though a man may, after he has married her, denote his MBD by *nininizi*. We must assume that the structural equivalence between a man's MBD and his W and between a woman's FZS and her H is *covert* and restricted to certain genealogical contexts. It is tempting to assume that a man's MBD is structurally equivalent to his W and a woman's FZS to her H in all genealogical contexts *other than* male ego's MBD as a designated kinswoman and female ego's FZS as a designated kinsman, because this is the most general expression of the rule consistent with the terminological facts noted above—but not quite! We know that some second-cousin kintypes are classified as *yande*, but we do not know which ones, and if we were to write the rule as just stated we would in effect make definite predictions about the classifications of certain second-cousin kintypes. To be properly cautious we should write the rule in a more restricted form, i.e.,

$$(. \; ♂ \; MBD \ldots \rightarrow . \; ♂ \; W \ldots) \equiv (\ldots \; ♀ \; FZS . \; \rightarrow \; \ldots \; ♀ \; H .)$$
$$(. \; ♀ \; FZS \ldots \rightarrow . \; ♀ \; H \ldots) \; \equiv (\ldots \; ♂ \; MBD . \rightarrow \; \ldots \; ♂ \; W .)$$

Or: Let male ego's mother's brother's daughter when as a link to a more distant relative be regarded as structurally equivalent to male ego's wife when as a link to a more distant relative; conversely, let a female linking relative's father's sister's son as a designated relative be regarded as structurally equivalent to that woman's husband as a designated relative. Also, let a female ego's father's sister's son when as a link to a more distant relative be regarded as structurally equivalent to female ego's husband as a link to a more distant relative; conversely, let a male linking relative's mother's brother's daughter as a designated relative be regarded as structurally equivalent to that man's wife as a designated relative.

Note that although this rule states that certain kintypes and affinal types are to be regarded as "equivalent," *the rule has a directionality*; it requires the substitution of, e.g., ♂ W for ♂ MBD in specified contexts and not vise versa. This directionality is structurally necessary. Of course, the rule could be written in the expansion (rather than the reduction) form, in which case we would have to write the other rules of the system in the same form. But to do so would not imply a reversal of the structural relationship between the focal and derived members of the categories. As noted earlier, expansion rules "generate" the extended kintype referents of terms from their focal referents; reduction rules operate on more distant kintypes and "generate" their class foci from them. An analysis using expansion rules logically implies an analysis using reduction rules, and vice versa, and both require the hypothesis that the focal types are indeed focal to the categories. The case of marriage to a nonrelative is dealt with by means of corollaries to the spouse-equation rule.

A number of corollaries—i.e., logically equivalent restatements of the rule in yet other genealogical contexts, and in relation to other kin types—will have to be stated in the complete formalization. One example of these is (♂ WF → ♂ MB), or, let any man's wife's father be regarded as structurally equivalent to that man's mother's brother. Other such corollaries are discussed below, where appropriate, and all are listed in Table 6, p. 127. It should be kept in mind that these are merely corollaries, not wholly different rules. All of them express exactly the same terminological convention or structural principle and they are implications of the spouse-equation rule itself. That there are many such corollaries is a matter for little concern; their number is not a measure of the complexity of the system—structurally, the system is really quite simple—but merely reflects the pervasiveness of the fundamental principle. In addition to the corollaries, there are also two auxiliaries to the spouse-equation rule. These deal with equivalences that are not logically entailed by the spouse-equation rule itself, and so they cannot be described as corollaries of that rule. (These auxiliary rules are discussed below, pp. 123–24.)

Of the three rules that this system shares with many others, we may consider first the same-sex sibling merging rule.

3. The Same-Sex Sibling Merging Rule

This rule expresses the principle of terminological equivalence between siblings of the same sex (e.g., FB and F, FFB and FF). Holmberg describes the same-sex sibling relationship as *socially* the most solidary of all kin relationships (1950: 57). Here we are concerned with a classificatory phenomenon which may or may not be a reflection of this social situation. The rule may be written:

$$(\male B \ldots \rightarrow \male \ldots) \equiv (\ldots \male B \rightarrow \ldots \male)$$
$$(\female Z \ldots \rightarrow \female \ldots) \equiv (\ldots \female Z \rightarrow \ldots \female)$$

Or: Let any person's sibling of the same sex, when as a link to some more distant relative, be regarded as equivalent to that person himself or herself as if directly linked to said relative; and, conversely, let a linking relative's sibling of the same sex as himself or herself be regarded as equivalent to that linking relative himself or herself; each of which statements implies the other.

4. The Half-Sibling Rule

$$(FS \rightarrow B; MS \rightarrow B; FD \rightarrow Z; MD \rightarrow Z)$$

Or: Let a half-sibling be regarded as structurally equivalent to a full sibling.

This rule is necessitated by the report (Holmberg 1950: 52) that half-siblings are terminologically equivalent to full siblings (all are classified as *anongge*). We assume that full siblings are the proper *anongge* (just as in English only persons who share the same father *and* mother are fully "brother" and "sister" to one another). There may be some societies in which the focal members of sibling categories are half-siblings or only certain half-siblings, and there are some in which certain types of half-siblings are foci of subclasses of the general sibling class (see Henderson 1967: 22–23). But these are rare and exceptional arrangements, and we know of nothing to suggest that Siriono is among the exceptional cases.

5. The Step-Kin Rule

$$(FW \rightarrow M) \equiv (\female HC \rightarrow \female C)$$
$$(MH \rightarrow F) \equiv (\male WC \rightarrow \male C)$$

Or: Let any person's parent's spouse (who is not also that person's parent) be regarded as equivalent to that person's parent; conversely, let any person's spouse's child (who is not also that person's child) be regarded as equivalent to that person's child.

This is a common feature of kinship terminologies, though, again, there are exceptions. In some societies (e.g., Seneca Iroquois), step-parents and step-children are not merged terminologically with parents and children but are assigned to categories which are also separate from the parent-in-law and child-in-law categories. Similarly (in the Seneca system), the spouses of parents' siblings are not merged with parents' siblings (and then parents, in the case of same-sex siblings), though such terminological mergings are one of the more general features of systems of kin classification. In general, the spouses of parents (who are not themselves ego's parents), or the spouses of collateral kin of the parental generation, are *not* classified as though they were parents-in-law (i.e., as structurally equivalent to WF, WM, etc.).[2]

The common anthropological practice of describing all "relatives by marriage" as "affines" is therefore somewhat misleading, and it has been the source of considerable analytical confusion. The simple analytic dual division between "kin" and "affines" tends to place the spouses of generationally senior kin in the latter category, whereas in most kinship systems they are classified as though they were kinds of kin, and in the remainder they are assigned to special categories. Therefore, it is necessary to distinguish analytically between two categories of "relatives by marriage." One of these may be called *step-kin*: it consists, in the first instance, of spouses of generationally senior familial kin (i.e., spouses of one's parents) and, conversely, the junior familial kin of one's spouse (i.e., one's spouse's children who are not also one's own children). More broadly, since the spouses of parents' siblings and, conversely, the children of one's spouse's siblings usually are terminologically identified either with parents' siblings and siblings' children or with step-parents and step-children, these too may be described as step-kin. Moreover, where parents' spouses are merged terminologically with parents, their children (i.e., FWC, MHC, English "step-siblings") usually are merged with siblings, but there are a few cases in which they are not (see Keesing 1968), due to a simple context restriction on the step-kin merging rule.

The other category of "relatives by marriage" may be described as *affines* (or in-laws): it consists, in the first instance, of one's spouse's familial kin of the spouse's generation and of generations senior to the spouse (i.e., of spouse's parents and siblings) and, conversely, of the spouses of ego's familial kin in ego's own and descending generations (i.e., of the spouses of ego's siblings and children). In most systems of kin classification, these relatives are placed in several special categories which we may

---

[2] The case of modern French may be exceptional, but the Trobriand system is not. Malinowski maintained that Trobrianders regard themselves as "affinally" related to their fathers, i.e., as wives' children and mothers' husbands: "a son is not a kinsman but simply a relative-in-law of his father." However, Malinowski added: "Not that sons would ever be spoken of as relatives-in-law, but their relation to the father is only through the wife" (1935, I: 474). In other words, Trobriand men do not *classify* their children (or step-children) as in-laws, nor do they *classify* their fathers (or step-fathers) as in-laws. *Tama* is not an "affinal" (*veivaisi*) category.

call "affinal categories" because their class foci are affinal types (as defined above). But some or all affines may be merged into consanguineal categories, often as the result of a rule of kin classification like the MBD-FZS–spouse equation noted above. However, not all such mergings are due to spouse-equation rules. For example, in many societies, parents-in-law and children-in-law may be referred to or addressed as "mother," "father," and "child," or as "grandparent" and "grandchild," and these extensions have nothing to do with any marriage rules (see Scheffler 1970a and 1970b for further discussion of this point). Of course, many types of relatives in addition to those noted above (e.g. spouse's parents' siblings, etc.) are commonly denoted by affinal terms; but their inclusion in the relevant categories is, again, by extension, and so the category "affinal relative" itself need not be defined to include them. Probably in most systems the rules of extension for affinal terms are the same as the rules of extension for consanguineal terms, but this need not necessarily be the case. Finally, it should be noted that, by this definition of the category "affines," ego's own spouse is not an affinal relative, though of course related to ego "by marriage." Just as the category "familial kin" is defined by reference to ego but does not include ego, so the category "affinal relatives" is defined by reference to one's own spouse, but does not include one's spouse.[3]

We may now consider the rules that are auxiliary to the parallel-transmission rule. These rules and something of their derivation may be illustrated by considering the kintype ♂ FZS and its reciprocal ♂ MBS. Consider the question, Why (or how) is it that ♂ FZS is classified as *ami*, "grandfather," and ♂ MBS as *akwanindu*, "nephew," a subclass of *AK-*, GRANDCHILD?

First, it should be noted that ♂ FZS is treated, terminologically at least, as a SENIOR kintype, and ♂ MBS is treated, reciprocally, as a JUNIOR kintype, whereas both are in fact of ego's own generation and are naturally neither senior nor junior to ego in generational status. It would appear that Siriono have arbitrarily assigned the children of father's sisters to the status SENIOR and, conversely, the children of mother's brothers to the status JUNIOR. (Again, the "status" referred to is a terminological one and not necessarily a jural one.) However, we will see that this assignment is necessitated by the parallel-transmission rule (though it might be equally possible to assign mother's brother's children

---

[3] Although anthropologists often describe spouses as "affines," we know of little or no precise ethnographic or linguistic data that would support the practice. What evidence we know of suggests that the observation of one of Schneider's American informants is more generally relevant. An elderly woman was asked to list all of her relatives. When she finished, she was asked: "I notice that you did not mention your husband. Do you consider him a relative?" To which she replied: "My husband? A lover, Yes! A relative, No!" (Schneider 1968a: 38).

to the status SENIOR, etc.). The necessity is a general structural one and has to do with consistency of reciprocals.

Note that in Crow- and Omaha-type systems, where categories also extend across natural generational lines, the skewing rules move some kintypes up one (or more) generations and their corollaries move the reciprocal kintypes down one (or more) generations, thus giving each kintype concerned a GENERATIONAL status complementary to that of its reciprocal. The range of these skewing rules may be rather broad, but it is usually restrained or confined by the nature of the rule itself. In some such systems the range of the rule is further confined by a spouse-equation rule similar to that we have already noted for the Siriono system. The spouse-equation rule of the Siriono system takes priority over the parallel-transmission rule (and all other rules, for that matter), and thus limits the range of effectiveness of that rule. But if this were the only restraint, the transmission rule would tend to move *all* kintypes *up* in generational status: a man's FZS *and* his MBS would be placed in the "grandfather" category, so that *ami* would have to be a self-reciprocal term. But this is not the case: the reciprocal of *ami* is always *ake*, or *akwanindu* or *akwani*. This consistency of reciprocals can only be maintained by arbitrarily assigning to one side of ego's genealogical tree, in his own generation, SENIOR GENERATIONAL status and to the other side JUNIOR GENERATIONAL status.

The relevant rule is best stated in ordinary language as the *seniority rule*.

6. The Seniority Rule

Let ego's father's sister's children as designated kinsmen be regarded as having SENIOR GENERATIONAL status, and, conversely, let ego's mother's brother's children as designated kinsmen be regarded as having JUNIOR GENERATIONAL status.

Having stated this rule, we are now in a position to consider a further restriction that must be imposed on the parallel-transmission rule. It should be obvious that consistency of reciprocals requires that if the kin-class status of a particular male kintype (e.g., MB) is to be the same as that of the kintype representing his parent of the same sex (e.g., MF), then the kin-class status of the reciprocal kintype (e.g., ♂ ZS) will be determined by ego taking the genealogical position of his (or her) parent of the same sex (e.g., ♂ F). Also, only SENIOR (including senior) kintypes can have the same classificatory statuses as their parents of the same sex; JUNIOR kintypes must have the same classificatory status for ego as they have for ego's parent of the same sex. (This is true of course

only in cases where the transmission rule applies.) Thus, the rule
(... ♂ S → ... ♂) and (... ♀ D → ... ♀) applies only to SENIOR
kintypes, and the corollary (♂ F ... → ♂ ...) and (♀ M ... → ♀ ...)
applies only to JUNIOR kintypes. This restriction may be indicated by
suffixing the symbol + for SENIOR and − for JUNIOR to the relevant
protions of the transmission rule. The rule must now be written:

$$1'. \quad (\ldots ♂\ S \rightarrow \ldots ♂)^+ \equiv (♂\ F \ldots \rightarrow ♂ \ldots)^-$$
$$(\ldots ♀\ D \rightarrow \ldots ♀)^+ \equiv (♀\ M \ldots \rightarrow ♀ \ldots)^-$$

Or: In the context of a SENIOR kintype, let any linking relative's
child of the same sex as himself or herself be regarded as equivalent
to that linking relative himself or herself; and, conversely, in the
context of a JUNIOR kintype, let any person's parent of the same
sex as himself or herself when as a link to some more distant relative
be regarded as equivalent to that person himself or herself when
as a link to that more distant relative.

To return now to why or how it is that ♂ FZS is classified as *ami*,
we see that part of the reason is that he is SENIOR in generational status
and is the son of an *ami* (FZH). Conversely, ♂ MBS is an *akwanindu*
because he is JUNIOR and therefore has the classificatory status assigned
to him by ego's father, i.e., that of ♂ WBS, which must be *akwanindu*.
This, however, is merely to raise another question: How is it that ♂ FZH
is classified as *ami* and ♂ WBS as *akwanindu*? What are the rules governing these classifications?

First let us note that the situation of ♂ FZH is readily explicable in
terms of general principles, i.e., classificatory principles that are not in
the least peculiar to this system. As we noted in Chapter 4, kinship terms
often come in pairs, as do *akwani* and *akwanindu*, each of which denotes
a male or female member of a sibling set, such that if a woman is denoted by *akwani*, her brother will be noted by *akwanindu*, and vise versa.
(The case of *yande*, we saw, is a spurious exception.) The same is true,
very often, of *spouse* sets. In most kinship terminologies, if a man is classified as, say, "father," then his wife is classified as "mother," and if a man
is classified as "grandfather," then his wife is classified as "grandmother"
(and so, too, for "uncle-aunt" as in English). The Siriono system appears
nonexceptional in this respect. The logic of this "pairing" seems relatively
obvious: "father-mother," "grandfather-grandmother," etc., are "natural
pairings" insofar as normally one's FFW or MFW is one's FM or MM,
and whether or not the women actually married to one's grandfathers are
one's grandmothers, they may be classified as such because that is the way
things naturally go together (note our discussion of the step-kin merging
rule). This is exactly analogous to the fact that English speakers address

their step-fathers as "father," and so it might be supposed that in the identification of ♂ FZH as *ami* we have an example of the merging or step-kin with consanguineals.

Perhaps, then, the reduction of ♂ FZH proceeds, via parallel transmission, in this way:

$$\text{♂ FZH} \rightarrow \text{♂ FMDH} \rightarrow \text{♂ FMH} \rightarrow \text{♂ FF, therefore } ami$$

But the reduction cannot proceed in exactly this way, as will be obvious on consideration of the reciprocal type WBS. WBS must be classified as *akwanindu* because WBS must be equivalent to the kintype ♂ MBSS. This is certainly correct, but it must be noted also that the foci of *akwanindu* (subfoci of *AK*-) are ♂ ZS and ♀ BS, so that ♂ WBS and ♂ MBSS must therefore reduce to one or the other of these and eventually to one of the foci of *AK*- itself (in this case, ♂ DS or ♀ SS). In other words, a man classifies the son of his wife's opposite-sex sibling in the same way as he classifies the son of his own opposite-sex sibling. To phrase the situation in this way, however, at least suggests that a man covertly equates his wife with his opposite-sex sibling, and for a number of reasons it seems best to avoid any such suggestion (e.g., the ethnography and the rest of the terminology make it clear that in general men's wives and sisters are radically opposed categories of relatives). In any event, it should be apparent that on the basis of the available evidence it might just as well be said that for purposes of classifying persons to whom male ego is related through his WB, he "follows" his wife (and, similarly, a female ego "follows" her husband in the classification of persons to whom she is related through his sister). The rule may be written:

7. $(. ♂ \text{ WB} \ldots \rightarrow . ♀ \text{ B} \ldots) \equiv (\ldots ♂ \text{ ZH} . \rightarrow \ldots ♂ \text{ Z} .)$
    $(. ♀ \text{ HZ} \ldots \rightarrow . ♂ \text{ Z} \ldots) \equiv (\ldots ♀ \text{ BW} . \rightarrow \ldots ♀ \text{ B} .)$

> **Or:** Let ego's spouse's opposite-sex sibling when as a link to some more distant relative be regarded as equivalent to the opposite-sex sibling of *the other sex of ego*; and, conversely, let a linking relative's opposite-sex sibling's spouse as a designated relative be regarded as equivalent to that linking relative's opposite-sex sibling as a designated relative. (Note again, that the single prefixed dot or period indicates restriction of the rule to the locus of ego, and a single postfixed dot or period indicates restriction of the rule to the locus of the designated relative.)

At first glance, this rule may seem peculiar, for it appears to require the reduction of FZH to proceed in this way:

$$\text{FZH} \rightarrow \text{FZ} \rightarrow \text{FMD} \rightarrow \text{FM, therefore } ari \text{ (sic.)}$$

The rule appears, that is, to equate a male kintype with a female kintype. Note, however, that it equates that male kintype with a female kintype in the category that is "paired" with the category we know it belongs to (*ami*). So there is in fact nothing peculiar about this rule at all: *It must be remembered that the sole function of the rule is to determine the classificatory generational status of nonfocal kintypes.* Thus, the rule must be taken as determining FHZ's GENERATIONAL status relative to ego and not as literally requiring that FZH be regarded as female rather than male sex. FZH is to be regarded as having the same GENERATIONAL status as FZ, whose status is that of FM (g^2 or G^2).

Note that this is precisely the sort of rule we might expect to find in a classificatory system with a spouse-equation rule of kin classification, and we may treat it as an auxiliary of the spouse-equation rule itself. In a society where people are expected, or have the right, to marry persons of particular kintypes, and especially where this expectation is built into the kinship terminology, competing possibilities for classification of certain kintypes are bound to arise. And the rule that spouses should "follow" the classifications employed by one another, especially for their junior consanguineals, seems a fairly obvious method of dealing with such situations. (This is, in effect, a hypothesis about how Siriono might go about reckoning certain classifications, and as such it would be easy to check in the field. But more significantly in the immediate context, this and other equivalence rules like it are formally necessary—and this, in the final analysis, is our justification for positing them.)

The kintype ♂ WBS may now be presumed to reduce as:

♂ WBS ⟶ ♀ BS, therefore *akwanindu*, (♀ BS ⟶ ♀ MSS ⟶ ♀ SS, therefore *AK-*)

So far we have passed without comment over the rule that permits (and requires) us to rewrite, e.g., FZ as FMD, and ♀ BS as ♀ MSS. These are examples of the operations we mentioned earlier, the preliminaries necessary to utilization of the transmission rule. The necessary auxiliary rules are:

8. The Opposite-Sex Sibling Rule

$$(\ldots ♀ \, B \longrightarrow \ldots ♀ \, FS)^+ \; \equiv (♂ \, Z \ldots \longrightarrow ♂ \, FD \ldots)^-$$
$$(\ldots ♂ \, Z \longrightarrow \ldots ♂ \, MD)^+ \equiv (♀ \, B \ldots \longrightarrow ♀ \, MS \ldots)^-$$

Or: In the context of a SENIOR kintype, let a linking relative's opposite-sex sibling be regarded as structurally equivalent to that linking relative's opposite-sex parent's same-sex child; and, conversely, in the context of a JUNIOR kintype, let an opposite-sex sibling when as a link to some other relative be regarded as structurally equivalent to a same-sex parent's opposite-sex child.

9. The Opposite-Sex Parent—Child Rule

$$(\ldots ♀\, S \longrightarrow \ldots ♀\, HS)^{+} \equiv (♂\, M \ldots \longrightarrow ♂\, FW \ldots)^{-}$$
$$(\ldots ♂\, D \longrightarrow \ldots ♂\, WD)^{+} \equiv (♀\, F \ldots \longrightarrow ♀\, MH \ldots)^{-}$$

Or: In the context of a SENIOR kintype, let a linking relative's opposite-sex child be regarded as structurally equivalent to that linking relative's spouse's child; and, conversely, in the context of a JUNIOR kintype, let an opposite-sex parent as a link to some more distant relative be regarded as structurally equivalent to a same-sex parent's spouse as a link to some more distant relative.

The reader will have noted that this latter rule is a limited version of a step-kin rule written as an expansion rule rather than as a reduction rule (note rule Number 5 above). Similarly, the opposite-sex sibling rule we have just written is a limited expansion rule version of the half-sibling rule (note Number 4 above). These auxiliaries of the transmission rule appear to require operations on kintypes that are precisely the opposite of the operations required by the step-kin merging and half-sibling merging rules, though in more limited genealogical contexts. However, auxiliaries of the transmission rule must have the same status in relation to other rules of the system as the transmission rule itself, and, as we noted earlier, other rules of this system must have priority over the transmission rule. In general, the simple step-kin merging and half-sibling merging rules take priority over the transmission rule and its auxiliaries. In other words, the auxiliaries of the transmission rule are to be utilized only in contexts where the transmission rule itself is applicable, and they will serve, as it were, only to "prepare" a kintype for the application of the transmission rule.

We may now write the reduction for the kin-type ♂ FZS, along with the appropriate equivalence rules, as follows:

1. ♂ FZS $\longrightarrow$ ♂ FZHS   :   SR, $(\ldots ♀\, S \longrightarrow \ldots ♀\, HS)^{+}$
2. ♂ FZHS $\longrightarrow$ ♂ FZH   : $(\ldots ♂\, S \longrightarrow \ldots ♂)^{+}$
3. ♂ FZH $\longrightarrow$ ♂ FZ(H)   : $(\ldots ♂\, ZH . \longrightarrow \ldots ♂\, Z .)$, i.e., let FZH have the G status of FZ
4. ♂ FZ(H) $\longrightarrow$ ♂ FMD(H)   : $(\ldots ♂\, Z \longrightarrow \ldots ♂\, MD)^{+}$, i.e., let FZH have the G status of FMDH

5. ♂ FMD(H) → ♂ FM(H) : (... ♀ D → ... ♀)⁺, i.e., let FZH have the G status of FMH

6. ♂ FM(H) → ♂ FF   : (MH → F), i.e., FZH has the G status of FF

7. ♂ FF i.e., ♂·SR·G²   : *ami* by definition.

For the reciprocal, ♂ MBS, the reduction is:

1. ♂ MBS → ♂ FWBS : JR, (♂ M ... → ♂ FW ...)⁻
2. ♂ FWBS → ♂ WBS : (♂ F ... → ♂ ...)⁻
3. ♂ WBS → ♀ BS   : (. ♂ WB ... → . ♀ B ...)
4. ♀ BS → ♂·jr·g¹·x : *akwanindu* by definition
5. (♀ BS → ♀ MSS) : (♀ B ... → MS ...)⁻
6. (♀ MSS → ♀ SS) : (♀ M ... → ♀ ...)⁻
7. (♀ SS i.e., JR·G²) : *AK-* by definition

The equivalence rules of this system have now been presented in full, except for some of the corollaries (all of which may be found in Table 6, p. 127) and one further auxiliary of the spouse-equation rule, and it remains only to note the latter and the necessary ordering among all the rules.

The equivalence rules so far formulated, when properly ordered in relation to one another, reduce nearly all kintypes for which we have classificatory data to the foci (or subfoci) of their respective classes. One set of exceptions consists of ♀ MBSS, ♀ MBSD, ♂ FZDS, ♂ FZDD, and the reciprocals FFZD and MMBS. The former are designated as *akwani* and *akwanindu*, and we have assumed that kintypes so classified reduce to the foci of *AK-* via the foci (or subfoci) of these subclasses. The simplest and most direct means of achieving this reduction is via an auxiliary of the spouse-equation rule that posits a limited covert equivalence between a man's FZD and his Z and, conversely, between a woman's MBS and her B. We should restrict this rule in the same way as we restricted the spouse-equation rule itself, because to do otherwise would, again, make predictions about the classifications of certain second-cousin kintypes.

10. An Auxiliary of the Spouse-Equation Rule

(. ♂ FZD ... → . ♂ Z ...) ≡ (... ♀ MBS . → ... ♀ B .)
(. ♀ MBS ... → . ♀ B ...) ≡ (... ♂ FZD . → ... ♂ Z .)

Or: Let a male ego's FZD when as a link to some more distant relative be regarded as structurally equivalent to a male ego's Z as a link to that more distant relative; conversely, let a female linking

relative's MBS as a terminus (i.e., as a designated relative) be regarded as structurally equivalent to that woman's B as a terminus;
etc.

This rule may be treated as an auxiliary of the spouse-equation rule because it appears to deal with problems of classification which are, in a
sense, created by the presence of that rule. This matter is discussed further
in Chapter 6. A not-strictly terminological reason for regarding this as
an appropriate rule is discussed in Chapter 8.

Another set of kintypes whose classifications are not accounted for
by the rules so far posited consists of the opposite-sex siblings of one's
grandparents and their reciprocals, the grandchildren of one's opposite-
sex siblings. These are classified as *ami*, *ari*, and *ake*, but the rules so far
posited will not reduce them to any of the foci of these classes, as these are
listed in Tables 3 and 5. The kintype MMB, for example, is made structurally equivalent to the kintype MMF by the rules so far posited, and
MMF is not listed as one of the foci of the *ami* class—though we have
stated (pp. 91, 102) that *ami*, *ari*, and *ake* consist of kintypes *two or more*
generations removed from ego. This requires further explanation.

It appears that in this system (as in many others) the principal
GRANDKIN terms are extended to all kintypes more than two generations removed from ego. Few if any Siriono are ever consociates of their
great grandparents, for few are consociates of their grandparents (Holmberg 1950: 85), but we may presume that if persons of third-ascending
generation status are ever referred to by kinship terms, those terms must
be *ami* and *ari*. Similarly, if persons of third-descending generation status
are ever referred to by a kinship term, that term must be *ake*. We know of
no other Siriono kinship terms that might be employed to this end, and the
nonkinship senses of *ari* and *ami*, "old woman" and "old man" (Holmberg 1950: 52), further suggest the possibility of such an extension of range
within the kinship or genealogical domain. Moreover, P. Priest (personal
communication, 1968) reports that the grandparent terms *ami* and *ari*
may be used in the sense of "ancestor" (see also Schermair 1958: 39,
297).

We may suppose, then, that Siriono do not distinguish terminologically between their grandparents and more remote ascendant lineal kin
but merge the latter with the former. This extension of the "grandparent"
(and, conversely, the "grandchild") category is accomplished by neutralization of the distinction between lineal kintypes *more than two* generations
removed and those who are *only two* generations removed from ego, when
the former are considered as designated kinsmen. Given the limitations of
the notational system we have found to be necessary so far, it is difficult

to express the ancestor rule in a kintype formula (though it could be done).

11. The Ancestor Rule

In the classification of lineal kin greater than two generations removed from ego, suspend the distinction between $G^{>2}$ and G^{2}, thus classifying lineal kin greater than two generations removed from ego as lineal kin only two generations removed from ego.

Since this rule governs extension of the "grandparent" and "grandchild" terms alone, it may be regarded as a "special" rule (see Lounsbury 1965: 151), though in this case, since there can be no conflict between this and the other equivalence rules of the system, there is no need to specify an order among this and those other rules.[4] This rule may also be regarded as determining what we may call *first-extended senses* of the Siriono "grandparent" and "grandchild" terms, which senses may be expressed componentially as:

ami : $k \cdot \sim f \cdot 1 \cdot g^{>2} \cdot sr \cdot$ ♂ (i.e., "ancestor")
ari : $k \cdot \sim f \cdot 1 \cdot g^{>2} \cdot sr \cdot$ ♀ (i.e., "ancestress")
ake : $k \cdot \sim f \cdot 1 \cdot g^{>2} \cdot jr$

As noted earlier, the equivalence rules of this system comprise an ordered set; some rules take precedence over others when a kintype offers simultaneously several possibilities for reduction. Consider, for example, the kintype FMBD. In the Siriono language this kintype is classified as "mother" (*ezi*). If we reduce this kintype without regard to the necessary order among the various rules, we may reduce it via the spouse-equation rule or via the transmission rule and its auxiliaries. If we choose the latter route, the reduction would be:

FMBD ⟶ FMBWD ⟶ FWBW ⟶ FMFSW ⟶ FMFW ⟶ FMM, therefore *ari*, in the first-extended sense of that term

However, FMBD is not classified as *ari*. Therefore, it must be that the spouse-equation rule takes precedence over the transmission rule and its auxiliaries.

[4] Note that in the Trobriand system (Lounsbury 1965: 150–52), as in the Fox (Bright and Minnick 1966: 383), there is an additional complication. In these systems collateral merging is somewhat stronger in the second ascending and descending generations than it is in the three medial generations, but even there it is subject to restrictions imposed by the Crow- or Omaha-skewing rule. To express these restrictions it seems necessary not only to distinguish between "general" and "special" rules but also to recognize an order among them.

For similar reasons, which the reader may explore for himself, the spouse-equation rule must also take precedence over the parallel-sibling merging, half-sibling, and step-kin rules; all of these rules must take precedence over the transmission rule and its auxiliaries; and the transmission rule itself must take precedence over its auxiliaries. This means that the rules are, in effect, divided into three sets, as illustrated in Table 6. Note that rule Number 11, the "ancestor rule," does not appear in Table 6, largely for this reason: This is a special rule which applies only to the "grandparent" and "grandchild" terms, and it is so restricted that it cannot conflict with any other equivalence rules. Thus, despite the fact that it is no less an equivalence rule than the others, it has a rather special status in the system as a whole. This status is intermediary to the primary defining rules and the other equivalence rules, as is reflected in the fact that it is not necessary to assign it a place within any of the three subsets of rules specified in Table 6.

The procedure to be followed in employing the rules is simple enough:

> Scan a kintype to determine whether any part of the spouse-equation rule may be applied to it. If applicable, exhaust all possible applications of the spouse-equation rule before turning to any other rule. If not applicable, determine whether the parallel-sibling, the half-sibling, or the step-kin merging rules are applicable. If applicable, exhaust all possible applications of these rules before turning to any other rule—with the exception that if at any point in the reduction process it proves possible to apply any part of the spouse-equation rule, then that rule must be applied. Finally, if no other rules are applicable, then the transmission rule or its auxiliaries may be applied, whichever is appropriate. When an auxiliary of the transmission rule has been applied, it will be possible then to apply the transmission rule itself, *and it must be applied.*

Following this simple procedure, all kintypes for which we have data and which are not themselves foci of principal categories may be reduced to the foci of their respective classes, superclasses, and subclasses, or, in a few cases, to types which are the foci of first extended senses of the principal GRANDKIN terms (as illustrated in Table 7).

We do not suppose that this procedure for the reduction of kintypes is necessarily the procedure employed by Siriono in reckoning the classificatory status of kinsmen of the same kintypes. The concern here is with the structure of a well-formed cognitive system, *not* with the structure or operation of the cognitive processes whereby that system is put to use. However, on the basis of this analysis, hypothesis about cognitive processes may be formulated, and we propose such a hypothesis in Chapter 7.

Table 6

SIRIONO EQUIVALENCE RULES

I. 1. *The spouse-equation rule:*

   Rule: 1.1   (... ♂ MBD. → ... ♂ W.)   ≡ (. ♀ FZS ... → . ♀ H ...)
                  (... ♀ FZS . → ... ♀ H .)   ≡ (. ♂ MBD ... → . ♂ W ...)

   Corollary: 1.2   (... ♀ MBD . → ... ♀ BW) ≡ (. ♀ FZD ... → . ♀ HZ ...)
                  (... ♀ FZD . → ... ♀ HZ .) ≡ (. ♀ MBD ... → . ♀ BW ...)
         1.3   (... ♂ MBS . → ... ♂ WB .) ≡ (. ♂ FZS ... → . ♂ ZH ...)
                  (... ♂ FZS . → ... ♂ ZH .) ≡ (. ♂ MBS ... → . ♂ WB ...)
         1.4   (. ♂ WB . → . ♂ MBS .) ≡ (. ♂ ZH . → . ♂ FZS .)
         1.5   (. ♂ WZ . → . ♂ MBD .) ≡ (. ♀ ZH . → . ♀ FZS .)
         1.6   (. ♀ HB . → . ♀ FZS .) ≡ (. ♂ BW . → . ♂ MBD .)
         1.7   (. ♀ HZ . → . ♀ FZD .) ≡ (. ♀ BW . → . ♀ MBD .)
         1.8   (♀ BWB → ♀ MBS) ≡ (♂ ZHZ → ♂ FZD)
         1.9   (♂ SW → ♂ WBD) ≡ (♀ HF → ♀ FZH)
        1.10 (♀ SW → ♀ BD) ≡ (♀ HM → ♀ FZ)
        1.11 (♂ DH → ♂ ZS) ≡ (♂ WF → ♂ MB)
        1.12 (♀ DH → ♀ HZS) ≡ (♂ WM → ♂ MBW)

   Auxiliary: 1.13 (. ♀ WB ... → . ♀ B ...) ≡ (... ♂ ZH . → ... ♂ Z .)
                 (. ♂ HZ ... → . ♂ Z ...) ≡ (... ♀ BW . → ... ♀ B .)
        1.14 (. ♂ FZD ... → . ♂ Z ...) ≡ (... ♀ MBS . → ... ♀ B .)
                 (. ♀ MBS ... → . ♀ B ...) ≡ (... ♂ FZD . → ... ♂ Z .)

II. 2. *The same-sex sibling merging rule:*
         (♂ B ... → ♂ ...) ≡ (... ♂ B → ... ♂)
         (♀ Z ... → ♀ ...) ≡ (... ♀ Z → ... ♀)

    3. *The half-sibling merging rule:*
         (FS → B, MS → B, FD → Z, MD → Z)

    4. *The step-kin merging rule:*
         (FW → M) ≡ (♀ HC → ♀ C)
         (MH → F) ≡ (♂ WC → ♂ C)

III. 5. *The seniority rule:*
         Let ego's father's sister's children as designated kinsmen be regarded as
         having SENIOR GENERATIONAL status, and, conversely, let ego's
         mother's brother's children as designated kinsmen be regarded as having
         JUNIOR GENERATIONAL status.

    6. *The parallel-transmission rule:*
     Rule: 6.1   (... ♂ S → ... ♂)$^+$ ≡ (♂ F ... → ♂ ...)$^-$
                  (... ♀ D → ... ♀)$^+$ ≡ (♀ M ... → ♀ ...)$^-$
     Auxiliary: 6.2   (... ♀ B → ... ♀ FS)$^+$ ≡ (♂ Z ... → ♂ FD ...)$^-$
                  (... ♂ Z → ... ♂ MD)$^+$ ≡ (♀ B ... → ♀ MS ...)$^-$
         6.3   (... ♀ S → ... ♀ HS)$^+$ ≡ (♂ M ... → ♂ FW ...)$^-$
                  (... ♂ D → ... ♂ WD)$^+$ ≡ (♀ F ... → ♀ MH ...)$^-$

Table 7

REDUCTION OF KINTYPES TO FOCI OF SIRIONO KIN CATEGORIES

I. *Ami*, foci = FF, MF

1.	FFB	:	$2 \longrightarrow$ FF
2.	MFB	:	$2 \longrightarrow$ MF
3.	MB	:	$6.2 \longrightarrow$ MFS, $6.1 \longrightarrow$ MF
4.	MFBS	:	$2 \longrightarrow$ MFS, $3 \longrightarrow$ MB, *see* No. 3
5.	MMZS	:	$2 \longrightarrow$ MMS, $3 \longrightarrow$ MB, *see* No. 3
6.	FMBS	:	$1.3 \longrightarrow$ FWB, $4 \longrightarrow$ MB, *see* No. 3
7.	MMBS	:	$1.14 \longrightarrow$ MB, *see* No. 3
8.	FZH	:	$1.13 \longrightarrow$ FFZ(H), $6.2 \longrightarrow$ FMD(H), $6.1 \longrightarrow$ FM(H),
			$4 \longrightarrow$ FF
9.	FZS	:	SR., $6.3 \longrightarrow$ FZHS, $6.1 \longrightarrow$ FZH, *see* No. 8
10.	FFZS	:	$1.3 \longrightarrow$ FZH, *see* No. 8
11.	MMB	:	$6.2 \longrightarrow$ MMFS, $6.1 \longrightarrow$ MMF (first-extended sense of *ami*)
12.	FMB	:	$6.2 \longrightarrow$ FMFS, $6.1 \longrightarrow$ FMF (first-extended sense of *ami*)
13.	♂ WF	:	$1.11 \longrightarrow$ ♂ MB, *see* No. 3
14.	♂ ZH	:	$1.4 \longrightarrow$ ♂ FZS, *see* No. 9
15.	♀ HF	:	$1.9 \longrightarrow$ ♀ FZH, *see* No. 8
16.	♀ HFF	:	$1.9 \longrightarrow$ ♀ FZHF, $1.9 \longrightarrow$ FZFZH, axiom* $\longrightarrow$ FFZH,
			$1.13 \longrightarrow$ FFZ(H), $6.2 \longrightarrow$ FFMD(H), $6.1 \longrightarrow$ FFM(H),
			$4 \longrightarrow$ FFF (first-extended sense of *ami*)
17.	♀ HZH	:	$1.13 \longrightarrow$ ♂ ZH, $1.4 \longrightarrow$ ♂ FZS, *see* No. 9
18.	♂ WFF	:	$1.11 \longrightarrow$ ♂ MBF, axiom* $\longrightarrow$ ♂ MF

II. *Ari*, foci = FM, MM

1.	FMZ	:	$2 \longrightarrow$ FM
2.	MMZ	:	$2 \longrightarrow$ MM
3.	FZ	:	$6.2 \longrightarrow$ FMD, $6.1 \longrightarrow$ FM
4.	FMZD	:	$2 \longrightarrow$ FMD, $3 \longrightarrow$ FZ, *see* No. 3
5.	FFBD	:	$2 \longrightarrow$ FFD, $3 \longrightarrow$ FZ, *see* No. 3
6.	MFZD	:	$1.2 \longrightarrow$ MHZ, $4 \longrightarrow$ FZ, *see* No. 3
7.	FFZD	:	$1.14 \longrightarrow$ FZ, *see* No. 3
8.	FZD	:	SR., $6.1 \longrightarrow$ FZ, *see* No. 3
9.	FFZ	:	$6.2 \longrightarrow$ FFMD, $6.1 \longrightarrow$ FFM (first-extended sense of *ari*)
10.	MFZ	:	$6.2 \longrightarrow$ MFMD, $6.1 \longrightarrow$ MFM (first-extended sense of *ari*)
11.	MBW	:	$1.13 \longrightarrow$ MB(W), $6.2 \longrightarrow$ MFS(W), $6.1 \longrightarrow$ MF(W),
			$4 \longrightarrow$ MM
12.	MMBD	:	$1.2 \longrightarrow$ MBW, *see* No. 11
13.	♂ WM	:	$1.12 \longrightarrow$ ♂ MBW, *see* No. 11
14.	♀ HM	:	$1.10 \longrightarrow$ ♀ FZ, *see* No. 3
15.	♀ HZ	:	$1.7 \longrightarrow$ ♀ FZD, *see* No. 8
16.	♂ WMM	:	$1.12 \longrightarrow$ ♂ MBWM, $1.12 \longrightarrow$ MBMBW, axiom* $\longrightarrow$
			MMBW, $1.13 \longrightarrow$ MMB(W), $6.2 \longrightarrow$ MMFS(W),
			$6.1 \longrightarrow$ MMF(W), $4 \longrightarrow$ MMM
			(first-extended sense of *ari*)
17.	♀ HMM	:	$1.10 \longrightarrow$ ♀ FZM, axiom* $\longrightarrow$ ♀ FM

*It may be regarded as an axiom of all kinship systems we know of that, e.g., the parent of a sibling is a parent or step-parent, and, conversely, the sibling of a child is a child or step-child. Similarly, the sibling of a sibling is regarded as a sibling (which statement contains its own corollary). In equivalence rule analyses it is not always possible to avoid kintype notations such as FZFZH, perhaps especially where spouse-equation rules of kin classification are present. But the occasional necessity of such notations is not to be regarded as embarrassing to an analysis.

III. *Eru*, Focus = F

1.	FB	:	$2 \rightarrow F$
2.	FFBS	:	$2 \rightarrow FFS, 3 \rightarrow FB, 2 \rightarrow F$
3.	FMZS	:	$2 \rightarrow FMS, 3 \rightarrow FB, 2 \rightarrow F$
4.	MFZS	:	$1.1 \rightarrow MH, 4 \rightarrow F$
5.	MH	:	$4 \rightarrow F$
6.	MZH	:	$2 \rightarrow MH, 4 \rightarrow F$

IV. *Ezi*, focus = M

1.	MZ	:	$2 \rightarrow M$
2.	MMZD	:	$2 \rightarrow MMD, 3 \rightarrow MZ, 2 \rightarrow M$
3.	MFBD	:	$2 \rightarrow MFD, 3 \rightarrow MZ, 2 \rightarrow M$
4.	FMBD	:	$1.1 \rightarrow FW, 4 \rightarrow M$
5.	FW	:	$4 \rightarrow M$
6.	FBW	:	$2 \rightarrow FW, 4 \rightarrow M$

V. *Anongge*, foci = B, Z

1.	MS	:	$3 \rightarrow B$
2.	MD	:	$3 \rightarrow Z$
3.	FS	:	$3 \rightarrow B$
4.	FD	:	$3 \rightarrow Z$
5.	MZS	:	$2 \rightarrow MS, 3 \rightarrow B$
6.	MZD	:	$2 \rightarrow MD, 3 \rightarrow Z$
7.	FBS	:	$2 \rightarrow FS, 3 \rightarrow B$
8.	FBD	:	$2 \rightarrow FD, 3 \rightarrow Z$

VI. *Edidi*, foci = S, D

1.	WD	:	$4 \rightarrow D$
2.	HD	:	$4 \rightarrow D$
3.	WS	:	$4 \rightarrow S$
4.	HS	:	$4 \rightarrow S$
5.	♂ BS	:	$2 \rightarrow S$
6.	♂ BD	:	$2 \rightarrow D$
7.	♀ ZS	:	$2 \rightarrow S$
8.	♀ ZD	:	$2 \rightarrow D$
9.	♂ FBSS	:	$2 \rightarrow ♂ FSS, 3 \rightarrow ♂ BS, 2 \rightarrow S$
10.	♂ FBSD	:	$2 \rightarrow ♂ FSD, 3 \rightarrow ♂ BD, 2 \rightarrow D$
11.	♂ MZSS	:	$2 \rightarrow ♂ MSS, 3 \rightarrow ♂ BS, 2 \rightarrow S$
12.	♂ MZSD	:	$2 \rightarrow ♂ MSD, 3 \rightarrow ♂ BD, 2 \rightarrow D$
13.	♂ MBDS	:	$1.1 \rightarrow ♂ WS, 4 \rightarrow S$
14.	♂ MBDD	:	$1.1 \rightarrow ♂ WD, 4 \rightarrow D$
15.	♀ FBDD	:	$2 \rightarrow ♀ FDD, 3 \rightarrow ♀ ZD, 2 \rightarrow D$
16.	♀ FBDS	:	$2 \rightarrow ♀ FDS, 3 \rightarrow ♀ ZS, 2 \rightarrow S$
17.	♀ MZDD	:	$2 \rightarrow ♀ MDD, 3 \rightarrow ♀ ZD, 2 \rightarrow D$
18.	♀ MZDS	:	$2 \rightarrow ♀ MDS, 3 \rightarrow ♀ ZS, 2 \rightarrow S$
19.	♀ FZSD	:	$1.1 \rightarrow ♀ HS, 4 \rightarrow S$
20.	♀ FZSS	:	$1.1 \rightarrow ♀ HD, 4 \rightarrow D$

(continued)

Table 7 (continued)

VII. *Yande*, foci = ♂ MBD, ♀ FZS

    1. ♂ MBD   : subfocus, not invariant, JR, 6.3 ⟶ ♂ FWBD,
                         6.1 ⟶ ♂ WBD, 1.13 ⟶ ♀ BD, AKWANI,
                         6.2 ⟶ ♀ MSD, 6.1 ⟶ ♀ SD, AK-

    2. ♀ FZS   : subfocus, not invariant, SR, 6.3 ⟶ ♀ FZHS,
                         6.1 ⟶ ♀ FZH, 1.13 ⟶ ♀ FZ(H), 6.2 ⟶ ♀ FMD(H),
                         6.1 ⟶ ♀ FM(H), 4 ⟶ ♀ FF, AMI

    3. ♂ WZ   : 1.5 ⟶ ♂ MBD, *see* No. 1
    4. ♂ BW   : 1.6 ⟶ ♂ MBD, *see* No. 1
    5. ♀ HB   : 1.6 ⟶ ♀ FZS, *see* No. 2
    6. ♀ ZH   : 1.5 ⟶ ♀ FZS, *see* No. 2

VIII. *Akwani*, foci = ♂ ZD, ♀ BD

    1. ♂ ZD   : subfocus, not invariant, 6.2 ⟶ ♂ FDD, 6.1 ⟶ ♂ DD
    2. ♀ BD   : subfocus, not invariant, 6.2 ⟶ ♀ MSD, 6.1 ⟶ ♀ SD
    3. ♀ MBD   : JR., 6.1 ⟶ ♀ BD
    4. ♀ FBSD   : 2 ⟶ ♀ FSD, 3 ⟶ ♀ BD
    5. ♀ MBDD   : 1.2 ⟶ ♀ BWD, 4 ⟶ ♀ BD
    6. ♀ MBSD   : 1.14 ⟶ ♀ BD
    7. ♀ MZSD   : 2 ⟶ ♀ MSD, 3 ⟶ ♀ BD
    8. ♀ FZDD   : 1.2 ⟶ ♀ HZD, 1.13 ⟶ ♂ ZD
    9. ♂ MZDD   : 2 ⟶ ♂ MDD, 3 ⟶ ♂ ZD
    10. ♂ FBDD   : 2 ⟶ ♂ FDD, 3 ⟶ ♂ ZD
    11. ♂ FZSD   : 1.3 ⟶ ♂ ZHD, 4 ⟶ ♂ ZD
    12. ♂ FZDD   : 1.14 ⟶ ♂ ZD
    13. ♂ MBSD   : 1.3 ⟶ ♂ WBD, 1.13 ⟶ ♀ BD
    14. ♂ SW   : 1.9 ⟶ ♂ WBD, 1.13 ⟶ ♀ BD
    15. ♀ SW   : 1.10 ⟶ ♀ BD
    16. ♂ WBW   : 1.13 ⟶ ♀ BW, 1.7 ⟶ ♀ MBD, *see* No. 3

IX. *Akwanindu*, foci = ♂ ZS, ♀ BS

    1. ♂ ZS   : subfocus, not invariant, 6.2 ⟶ ♂ FDS, 6.1 ⟶ ♂ DS
    2. ♀ BS   : subfocus, not invariant, 6.2 ⟶ ♀ MSS, 6.1 ⟶ ♀ SS
    3. ♂ MBS   : JR, 6.2 ⟶ ♂ FWBS, 6.1 ⟶ ♂ WBS, 1.13 ⟶ ♀ BS
    4. ♂ FZDS   : 1.14 ⟶ ♂ ZS
    5. ♂ MZDS   : 2 ⟶ ♂ MDS, 3 ⟶ ♂ ZS
    6. ♂ FZSS   : 1.3 ⟶ ♂ ZHS, 4 ⟶ ♂ ZS
    7. ♂ FBDS   : 2 ⟶ ♂ FDS, 3 ⟶ ♂ ZS
    8. ♂ MBSS   : 1.3 ⟶ ♂ WBS, 1.13 ⟶ ♀ BS
    9. ♀ MBS   : JR, 6.1 ⟶ ♀ BS
    10. ♀ MBSS   : 1.14 ⟶ ♀ BS
    11. ♀ FZDS   : 1.2 ⟶ ♀ HZS, 1.14 ⟶ ♂ ZS
    12. ♀ MBDS   : 1.2 ⟶ ♀ BWS, 4 ⟶ ♀ BS
    13. ♀ MZSS   : 2 ⟶ ♀ MSS, 3 ⟶ ♀ BS
    14. ♀ FBSS   : 2 ⟶ ♀ FSS, 3 ⟶ ♀ BS
    15. ♂ WB   : 1.4 ⟶ ♂ MBS, *see* No. 3
    16. ♂ DH   : 1.11 ⟶ ♂ ZS
    17. ♀ DH   : 1.12 ⟶ ♀ HZS, 1.13 ⟶ ♂ ZS

X. *Ake*, foci = SS, SD, DS, DD
                        Includes all g^{-2} kintypes

6 Discussion of the Rules

Our analysis of the available data on kin classifications in the Siriono language is now complete. It constitutes a formally satisfactory theory of the structure of the system, insofar as the available data are capable of revealing that structure. However, the absence of data on second-cousin kintypes must raise some doubt about the advisability of asserting that the definitions and rules posited here are *the* definitions and rules of the system. The analysis as it now stands accounts for all of the available data, does so without difficulty, and within the framework of a general theory of kinship semantics which utilizes concepts that are commonly employed in lexico-semantic studies of natural languages. Yet we could fairly argue that the definitions and rules presented here are *the* definitions and rules of the system only if we had perfect control over the data. This we plainly do not have. Nevertheless, the available data are sufficient to reveal the principal morphological features of this system. We doubt very much that additional data would necessitate any substantial reappraisal of our identification of these as the MBD-FZS–spouse equation rule and the parallel-transmission rule.

Some additional comment is in order, however, on the precise phrasing of the spouse-equation rule. We have assumed, on the basis of Holmberg's occasional references to "second cross cousins" and "classificatory cross cousins," that some second-cousin kintypes are classified as *yande*, but because we do not know which ones they are, we restricted the spouse-equation rule and its auxiliaries so as to make no predictions about second-cousin classifications. We think we may be reasonably confident that ♂ MMBDD, ♂ MMZSD, ♂ FMBSD, and their reciprocals, ♀ MFZDS, ♀ FMZDS, ♀ FFZSS, are so classified. All of these certainly meet the specifications of the three-term relative product definitions we have attributed to *yande* in its broad sense—provided of course that the spouse-equation rule and its corollaries, and the half-sibling, same-sex sibling, and step-kin merging rules are applicable to these types, just as they are to the kintypes representing the parents of these types. The spouse-equation rule may be made applicable simply by relaxing some of the restrictions stated above so that it would apply to any man's MBD and any woman's FZS, *other than* male ego's MBD as a designated kinswoman (*yande*) and female ego's FZS as a designated kinsman (also *yande*). Thus, for example, ♂ MMBDD might be classified as a *yande* because this kin type is equivalent to ♂ MBWD by the spouse-equation rule corollary 1.3, and ♂ MBWD is equivalent to ♂ MBD by the step-kin merging rule.

We can be fairly confident, too, about the classifications of many other second-cousin kintypes—those whose classifications are presumably in no way affected by the spouse-equation rule and its corollaries or the parallel-transmission rule. These are, of course, the kintypes representing the children of parents' parallel cousins, e.g., FFBSS, FMZSS, and many others of the same sort, all of which probably reduce to B or Z (with the exception of MMZSC and FMZDC, which probably reduce to the cross-cousin types MBC and FZC and which probably are classified in the same ways as these).

The remaining third-degree collateral kintypes in ego's generation are MMBSC and the reciprocals FFZDC. Holmberg reports that WBW is classified as *akwani* and the reciprocal HZH as *ami*. These classifications were accounted for above as products of one of the auxiliaries (1.13) and one of the corollaries (1.7) of the spouse-equation rule, by means of which WBW was reckoned as equivalent to female ego's (male ego's wife's) MBD. That is, male ego was presumed to "follow his wife" in classifying this affine of his wife, whom she classifies according to the appropriate consanguineal status. Now if the presumption of MBD-FZS marriage-ability is a general one, a woman related (affinally) to ego as WBW might be assumed, in the general case, to be also his kinswoman of some specific (consanguineal) type. That type would be ♂ MMBSD; this would follow from the assumption that ego's WB is ego's MBS who in turn has married his MBD. Therefore, WBW may be assumed to be also ♂ MMBSD, and HZH may be assumed to be also ♂ FFZDS. If so, these kintypes would be classified as *akwani* and *ami*, respectively. Since the brothers of *akwani* are normally *akwanindu* and the sisters of *ami* are normally *ari*, the remaining classifications may be:

♂ MMBSS	akwanindu	♂ FFZDS	ami
♀ MMBSS	akwanindu	♂ FFZDD	ari
♀ MMBSD	akwani	♀ FFZDD	ari

If these classifications are actually made by Siriono, the analysis presented in Chapters 4 and 5 may be readily adapted to account for them, though the alteration that would be required has to do with the generality of the seniority rule (Table 6, number 5), not the spouse-equation rule.

Note that the seniority rule as stated above is restricted to determining the classificatory statuses of ego's FZC and MBC as designated kinsmen. If the restrictions on this rule are removed so that it determines the classificatory statuses of any person's FZC and MBC as *linking* as well as designated kin, it may be applied to reductions of the kintypes in question here. Consider, for example, the case of ♂ MMBSD. Rule 1.14 as written in Table 6 does not apply here. Nor do any other rules, unless we release the restrictions on the seniority rule, in which case the parallel-transmission rule will apply. If these restrictions are released, ♂ MMBSD may be reduced to ♀ BD, the apparent appropriate subfocus of the *akwani* class, as follows:

♂ MMBSD :   JR, since alter's parent is JR in relation to ego's parent who forms the link to alter; therefore, now apply rule 6.1

♂ MBSD   :   see Table 7, VIII, 13, where this kintype is shown to reduce to ♀ BD = *akwani* via WBD

It is not essential that the reduction of ♂ MMBSD should pass through WBW but rather that, inasmuch as these two relationships may be expected to coincide in the same individuals, the rules of the system should classify both relations in the same way. If the context restrictions on the seniority rule are released, the rules posited in Chapter 5 yield the (apparently) required result.

It must be emphasized that we do not know how any of these second-cousin kintypes are classified, and we cannot even be sure that they are in fact given designations under the terms of this system. There is, indeed, a bit of ethnographic data that leads us to suspect that some of them may not: Holmberg refers in three places (1950: 81) to the possibility of marrying "nonrelatives in the band." It is difficult to see, however, how there can be any nonrelatives *in* the band, except for the rare inmarried male, and such a man would be married already rather than looking for a first wife. But Holmberg quite plainly states that men may and sometimes do marry unrelated females from the same band. How could this be? If a woman were the daughter of an inmarrying male, she would still be related to her husband through her mother (because women do not "marry out") —unless for some other reason she is considered to be "unrelated." That is, perhaps there are some kintypes that do not receive designations under the terms of this system, so that persons related to ego in those ways are "not kin," in the limited sense that they belong to no kin classes. Formal restrictions on the lateral range of kin-class inclusion are known in other cases (e.g., Goodenough 1956: 201; Hunt 1969: 39), and a *limited* restriction of the same sort could easily be imposed on this system. In this case it may be that third-degree collaterals (i.e., second cousins) who cannot be reckoned as first- or second-degree collaterals (i.e., as siblings or as first cousins), or in some other way (e.g. WBW) are accorded no kin-class statuses, so that, in a sense, they are "not kin," i.e., not members of any kin classes. If so, the necessary formal restriction is already given in the seniority rule (Table 6, Number 5); for, if this rule is so restricted, the kintypes MMBSC and FFZDC are simply unclassifiable under the rules of this system. A kintype such as ♂ MMBSD, for example, would be a member of no kin class and thus a marriageable woman, unless she were related in some other way because of an "unorthodox" (i.e., non-*yande*) marriage or as the W of one's WB, in which case she would be an *akwani*.

It was no mean feat for Holmberg to collect the kintype data reported in his monograph, and it is conceivable that he did obtain all the data of that sort that could have been gotten by any ethnographer. That is to say, there may be good ethnographic reasons for the fact that he reports no data on the classifications of second-cousin kintypes. The small scale and effective endogamy of the band (see Chapter 8) makes it highly probable that each Siriono is related genealogically to most other members of his band in more than one way. Moreover, the bands are so small (94 and 58 persons for the two reported) that, given the terminological convention that every man is presumed to have married his MBD (and every woman her FZS), it is probable that Siriono seldom if ever have to reckon kin classifications through second-cousin types. (A man need not worry about whether another man called *anongge* by his mother is his mother's actual brother or her classificatory brother in order to know that man's daughter is his *yande*.) The children of parents' opposite-sex, but unmarriageable, cross cousins (i.e., FFZD's children and MMBS's children) might be exceptional in this respect, but these may also be the descendants or spouses of other kin and therefore classifiable by reference to other relationships—or, as we noted above, they may not be classified at all.

Thus it may well be that an *extensive* and *infinitely* ramifying genealogical tree would not properly represent the scale of a Siriono's universe of kinsmen. Genealogical data of the scale presented by Holmberg, encompassing over 100 kintypes for each sex of ego, may represent the scale of that universe as accurately as possible. If so, this system would not be suited to a larger society (cf. Needham 1964a: 237). The Siriono system of classifying kin may be workable only in the circumstances of Siriono demography and effective band endogamy.

In conclusion, the analysis presented here accounts for the available data on Siriono kin classification in terms of a straightforward and well-known body of linguistic concepts that have a much broader relevance. Beyond this, it points precisely to the additional data that might confirm or disconfirm aspects of it. We must now consider the question if its cognitive or psychological validity.

Addendum

After our analysis was completed, we wrote to Perry N. Priest, who has done linguistic work among the Siriono and published a number of papers and brief monographs on the Siriono language. We inquired whether or not he had any further information on Siriono kinship terminology. He kindly replied that he could add little to Holmberg's report and that Holmberg's data are, so far as he knows, generally correct: "He did a very thorough piece of work." We specifically inquired about the classifications of second cousins. Mr. Priest replied, "There are no terms for second cousins. Second cousins are not considered by the Siriono to be related." This appears to contradict Holmberg's report that some second cousins are classified as *yande*, but we suspect that the contradiction is only apparent. As noted above, it is highly probable that most people in the band can be classified *as though* they were related within sibling or first-cousin range, as the great majority would be anyway. It is conceivable, however, that there would remain a few second cousins who could not be so regarded, and they might be regarded as "not related" in the limited sense that they can receive no designations under the terms of the system. It seems relatively improbable that they would be regarded as *literally* unrelated, since their parents clearly are regarded as kin and classified as such. It seems equally unlikely that Holmberg was mistaken when he reported that *yande* is applied to women other than MBD, WZ, and BW, some of whom, he must have had reason to believe, were kinswomen of more distant degrees.

7 The Question of Cognitive Validity

Formal semantic analyses of systems of kin classification have encountered a good deal of resistance on the part of many anthropologists because, it is argued, they do not represent the true cognitive reality for the objects of description, but are only an apparatus invented by the analyst that by some stroke of ingenuity (or luck) enables him—irrelevant though it may be—to make it appear that he has captured the essence of the system. In Chapter 3 we noted that some "formalists" have replied that their analyses are useful for the purposes of other-than-cognitive studies, whether or not the resulting models closely approximate the content and structure of the classificatory (and cognitive) systems in question. So far as we have been able to determine, this argument was first presented by Wallace and Atkins (1960: 75–79) who distinguished between a "psychologically real" and a "structurally real" description of a cultural system such as a system of kin classification.

For Wallace and Atkins a "psychologically real" description of a cultural system "is a description which approximately reproduces in an observer the world of meanings of the native users of that culture." In contrast, "structural reality . . . is a world of meanings, as applied to a given society or individual, which is real to the ethnographer, but is not *necessarily* the world which constitutes the mazeway of any other individual or individuals" (1960: 75). (On the concept "mazeway," see Wallace 1961.) As they see it, the proponents of "psychologically real" models argue that the classificatory criteria posited in their models are the same as those employed by the peoples who utilize the classificatory systems in question; the proponents of merely "structurally real" models claim only that their models replicate, and can be used to predict accurately, the classifications effected by those who utilize the systems, but who may or may not utilize the criteria posited in the models. The important thing for the latter is that their models enable them to "account" for how types of kin are classified, and the fact that the posited criteria may or may not be those employed by the people who use the terms is regarded as a matter of minor importance for the analyst's (perhaps sociological) interests. Wallace (1965: 232) characterizes Lounsbury's Crow-Omaha study (1964a) as one concerned with "structural" rather than "psychological reality," but we do not subscribe to that restriction.

Wallace and Atkins (1960) described models that make no pretensions to being "psychologically real," as well as those that do, as "semantic" models, whereas it seems what they are really attempting to distinguish between are analyses that *are* and analyses that *are not* concerned with questions of semantics. Wallace has since acknowledged this (1965: 230), but he has continued to argue as though it is possible to do sociologically useful "componential" analyses without committing oneself to "the production of psychologically valid semantic descriptions" (1965: 232). As we see it, this is a misleading argument.

The aim of any kind of structural analysis is to isolate and describe the *inherent* properties of the object of analysis. The aim is to establish valid existential propositions about the very nature of the object of analysis. In the case of a descriptive or structural semantic analysis, a model purporting to account for the distribution of kin terms over kin-types is valid (or structurally valid) only to the extent that it replicates the cognitive discriminations made by those who use the system in their daily lives, for this is precisely what a *semantic* analysis attempts to determine. The criterion of parsimony must be invoked not only because it is a general canon of scientific method, but also because it is required in the light of well-established principles of cognitive psychology (see Kintsch 1970, especially Chapter 8). We find it extremely difficult to imagine how a truly satisfactory and parsimonious model of the distribution of kin terms over kintypes could help but be anything other than a satisfactory or adequate model of the structure of the cognitive system in question. Furthermore, we find it difficult to imagine how such a model could provide a basis for accurate prediction of usage (given, of course, the necessary limits on the kinds of usage that it may be called upon to predict) unless it were "psychologically" or "cognitively real." And finally, we cannot even begin to imagine what kind of sociological utility a psychologically or cognitively "unreal" model could have. In short, it seems to us a complete contradiction in terms to speak of "structural reality" without at the same time speaking of "psychological" or "cognitive reality."

Much of the anthropological doubt about the "reality" of structural semantic analyses of systems of kin classification is based on the much more fundamental doubt that the systems in question *are* systems of kin classification, i.e., that the words in question are in fact kinship terms, and that one of the things about them that *has* to be accounted for is their distribution over kintypes. It has been based also on largely intuitive feelings that many if not most of the componential analyses so far published are unrealistic, as indeed they are because most of them have failed to take the phenomena of extension and polysemy into account. These doubts have been reinforced by the apparent "generic indeterminacy" (Wallace and Atkins 1960: 76–78) of formal semantic analyses of systems of kin classification. Wallace and Atkins note that for any particular system it may prove possible to construct several different paradigmatic representations, each of which provides a somewhat different set of definitions for some or all of the terms of the system, but each of which may appear to account equally satisfactorily for the distribution of terms over kintypes (for some examples see Goodenough 1956; Elkins 1968). They argue that "there is, in fact, an indeterminate number of equivalent significata, both conjunctive and disjunctive, which will with equal extensional validity define any given terms" (1960: 77). They note but reject K. Romney's argument (in an unpublished paper) that the "indeterminacy" is only apparent and is a product of certain analytical procedures, not a property of the systems themselves.

There can be no doubt, however, that Romney's judgment is essentially correct. Goodenough's (1956) analysis of Truk kinship terminology, to which Romney, and Wallace and Atkins refer, is a genuine landmark in the study of structural or descriptive semantics. However, in spite of its recognition and its incisive treatment of certain problems of polysemy (Goodenough 1956: 206–8), it stops short of pursuit of the polysemy of the Trukese terms *into their specifically kinship domains*, and this is responsible for the apparent indeterminacy of the analysis. Once the polysemy of the Trukese sibling and sibling-in-law terms is recognized, it is apparent that none of the three "alternative" paradigms offered by Goodenough (1956; 206, 212) provides an adequate representation of the meanings and the relations among the meanings of the terms. While the definitions presented in Goodenough's paradigm 1 (1956: 206) do adequately describe the total ranges of the terms, these definitions only appear to satisfy his criterion of simplicity (1956: 212) better than the definitions presented in paradigms 3 and 4 (1956: 212), for they are in fact disjunctive definitions. Their disjunctiveness is obscured and the terms are made to appear monosemic by use of a disjunctively defined dimension of opposition (see Goodenough 1956: 205 on the Trukese "concept of generation"). It follows that the analysis presented in Goodenough's paradigms 1 and 2 is only partially satisfactory; the definitions are satisfactory only as statements of the broadest ranges of the terms. This is true also of Lounsbury's analysis of the Pawnee (1956) and Seneca-Iroquois (1964a) systems, which are similarly deficient (note the pertinent comment by Fischer, in Lounsbury 1964a: 1092).

Elkins (1968) presents three analytic models of a simple Eskimo-type system from the Philippines. One of the models is in the form of a matrix display, another is a conventional componential analysis, and the third is an equivalence rules analysis. Elkins does not argue that the three models are formally equivalent or equally satisfactory, although in Wallace and Atkins' terms they are of "equal extensional validity," insofar as each model accounts for the distribution of terms over kintypes. But as Elkins notes, only the equivalence rules analysis takes account of the fact that certain denotata (of the terms for collateral kin) are structurally primary, and are lexically marked as the "real" denotata of the terms, whereas the others are structurally derivative (1968: 188). In other words, many of the terms of this system are polysemic; neither the "matrix display" nor the "componential analysis" takes that fact into consideration.[1]

Similarly, none of the several published analyses of "American kinship terminology" (for a list see Burling 1970) take the phenomena of extension and polysemy sufficiently into account and, thus, not one is at all adequate.[2]

In short, the alleged "indeterminacy" of structural semantic analyses of systems of kin classification probably is an artifact of the use of inadequate semantic theory.

Wallace and Atkins also argue that the "exclusion of 'connotative' dimensions" is a "major source of indeterminacy" in semantic analyses (1960: 76–77), but they can only mean that, insofar as connotative meaning is not considered, an analysis cannot claim to provide an account of *all* usage. Once it has been conceded that "definitive meaning" (i.e., signification) (Wallace and Atkins 1960: 67–68) and connotative meaning are two different though related things, it has to be conceded, too, that they must be analyzed separately, signification before connotation. The category-designating senses (i.e., significata) of kinship terms comprise a natural subset of the total set of meanings associated with any kinship terminology, and the structure of the categories themselves may be and must be analyzed independently of the structure of any social-status system

---

[1] It should be noted that Elkins' statement of the appropriate equivalence rules may be simplified and considerably improved. Since this is a simple Eskimo-type system, the extensions of its terms may be accounted for by specifying that the terms for non-familial lineal and first-degree collateral kin shall be extended to kin of all degrees of collaterality and of the appropriate generations. This requires one simple neutralization rule, rather than the five reduction rules posited by Elkins (1968: 181–82), one of which (2a and b) is unnecessary in any event.

[2] The analysis presented by Bock (1968) is nonexceptional. Bock presents a so-called generative rules analysis which posits no less than 30 ordered rules. (Bock does not distinguish between defining and extension rules.) All of this is quite unnecessary since the extensions of terms for kinds of first- and second-degree collateral kin depend on nothing more than one simple extension or neutralization rule (see Chapter 1, pp. 11–12).

that *may be* associated with those categories. A limited analysis of a natural and structurally prior subset of meanings can provide a complete account of the content and structure *of that domain,* provided of course that data belonging to that domain are not arbitrarily excluded from consideration.

Formal analysis of the category-designating senses of kinship terms may be called upon to predict who (or persons of which kintypes) may *appropriately* be called or referred to by those terms *on genealogical grounds.* Such information is essential to any broader synthesis of semantic data which might aim to predict all usage. Such a synthesis would have to consider not only the designata and significata of kinship terms and their associated status connotations (if any) but also the cultural rules permitting the assumption of partial kin statuses or kin-like statuses by non-kinsmen, and thus the metaphoric use of kinship terms. It is obvious that social anthropology is a long way from being able to achieve such a synthesis, especially on the basis of the ethnographic data generally available in published literature. Meanwhile, formalists and their critics will have to be content with something less than the perfection of being able to say the final word about the meanings and rules of usage of any set of kinship terms.

In summary, there has not yet been any adequate demonstration that several equally sufficient and parsimonious formal models may be offered for the same system of kin classification. The apparent ability to do so has rested on the use of inadequate semantic theory and on casual analytic methods. Inasmuch as one and only one truly adequate and parsimonious model can be offered for a given system, the psychological or cognitive "reality" of the model is not particularly problematic.

It has to be noted, however, that few if any informants ever offer statements about the meanings of their kinship terms which correspond more or less exactly (allowing for problems of translation) to the statements of those definitions as expressed in componential analyses. Ordinary speakers of American English, for example, do not describe their cousins as "kin of second or further degree of collaterality," although this is a satisfactory componential definition of the broadest range of the term. If asked directly what the term "cousin" means, a competent informant is likely to respond with "my cousins are the children of my uncles and aunts," i.e., with a statement that describes the primary range of the term as a relative product of other kin classes. From our experience and that of other ethnographers (see Nayacakalou 1955), we know that in general this is the way in which other peoples typically respond to direct questions about the "meanings" of their kinship terms. It is important to consider the relevance of such statements for the kind of analysis presented in the preceding chapters, for this has been the subject of considerable misunderstanding among anthropologists, some of whom appear to think that such statements reflect negatively on the ethnographic value, and especially the "psychological reality," of componential and extension rule analyses (see Wallace and Atkins 1960: 74; Coult 1967; Ridington 1969; Burling 1970).

As we see it, such statements by informants are to be expected. But they are not to be taken as sufficient guides to the "psychological reality" of kinship concepts. It is hardly to be supposed that an individual should be capable of expressing accurately, in ready verbalizations, the ground structure and implicit premises that underlie his discriminations and give shape to his "world of meanings." This limitation applies as surely to the semantic structure of lexicon—including that of kinship—as it does to one's knowledge of the grammar of his language or the organization of his personality. Yet, to deny "psychological reality" to features of one's behavior that one cannot immediately verbalize by oneself would be to place a most peculiar interpretation on the notion of what "psychology" is supposed to be about. It would certainly be at variance with an older view and tradition in anthropology—stemming in part from Boas, and exemplified especially in the work of Sapir and his successors—that emphasized the "unconscious" character of the underlying premises and the structures of cultural and linguistic behavior, as well as of individual personality. Rather, and in line with this older view, we would attribute psychological and cognitive reality to such implicit premises and inherent structures. That these are often not immediately verbalizable, and that analysis is required to bring them out, is only due to the fact that these are not themselves ordinary topics of discourse in everyday life. They are— as it used to be said—part of the "unconscious background."

It is probable that most people learn how to classify (i.e., what to call) many of their kinsmen and other relatives before they are aware of genealogical connections or the meaning of such connections. They are simply told by their parents and other older and more experienced persons what the proper terms are for specific relatives, without being told anything about the types of genealogical connections involved. In time, however, they learn that there are certain regular relationships among kin categories as such, so that if they know how one or the other of their parents classifies a specific kinsman, or how they themselves classify the father or mother of that kinsman, then they can apply to that person a term that other people will agree is the correct one. For example, a person from a society with an Iroquois-type kinship terminology may deduce from a number of examples with which he has been provided that any man whom his father calls either "brother" or "cousin" (i.e., cross cousin) is to be called "father " and the son of any man he calls "father" is to be called "brother." (Of course, he may not have to deduce these "rules" for himself; they may be generally known and communicated to him as such.) Thus, when he encounters a man whose father is (or was) called "brother" or "cousin" by his father, he knows that man is his "father" (or rather his "classificatory father") and he knows that man's son is his "brother" (or rather his "classificatory brother"). He need not inquire into whether the former is his father's long-lost brother, or his father's FBS, or his father's FZS, etc., in order to know how to classify him, though he may want to know which he is for other reasons.[3]

A large part of what any native user of a system of kin classification usually needs to "know" in order to use that system effectively is a set of rules composed largely of rules having the form of relative product statements rather like those noted above. Some of these are *primary defining rules*, as in the case of English "a cousin is the child of an uncle and aunt"; others, however, are *extension rules*, as in the case of "the children of my great uncles, great aunts, and cousins are also my cousins." Of course, not all primary sense definitions of kinship terms can be stated in this fashion; relative product definitions are possible only in the cases of those terms whose foci are themselves relative products of kintypes which are the foci of other terms. That is to say, the primary senses of parent and child terms are not so definable (but those for siblings are); their primary senses may be expressed as class products (i.e., in componential definitions), or alternatively, since they designate the primitive relationships of any kinship system, they may be treated as the primitive elements of the system. Thus, native speakers usually define these terms discursively, e.g., "my 'mother' is the woman who have birth to me." This difference does not imply any basic logical difference between the structures of the significata of these two kinds of terms, for, as Wallace and Atkins (1960: 74) have noted, terms whose definitions may be stated as relative products of other terms may also have their primary meanings defined as class

---

[3] Many ethnographers have noted this and similar facts about pragmatic kin-class reckoning and have drawn the conclusion that such reckoning is not genealogically based. It would have been more appropriate to conclude that the relations between kin categories (narrow and broad) are such that partial genealogical knowledge suffices for their proper use. The classifications and extensions established in previous generations may be built upon without knowledge of precisely how they came to be, and this may be done without any difficulty, even though the users of the system may not be accustomed to speaking or "thinking" in the abstract of lengthy genealogical chains, e.g., of father's father's brother's son's sons, etc. (see Epling 1967).

products. That native speakers do not usually (if ever) offer class product definitions for such terms is presumably to be explained by the fact that these are at a more abstract level, beyond the level at which people normally express their thoughts verbally. It is not that such definitions are not part of the culture, but they may express highly abstract features of the culture,[4] features that are not normally subject to immediate verbal report.

Now if we limit the ethnographic task to determining what, at the most superficial phenomenological level, a person has to "know" in order to classify his kinsmen in the culturally appropriate fashion, it will often be sufficient and relatively easy to compile a list of relative product type statements supplied by informants, some of which would constitute primary sense definitions and others extension rules. Indeed, anthropologists have often compiled such lists (see Morgan 1871; Fison 1880; Tax 1955b; Gilbert 1955; Burling 1970) though usually they have deduced the statements themselves from data gathered by "the genealogical method" or in other ways, and they have usually overlooked the factor of polysemy in the process (but see Burling 1965; Wallace 1965). But whether such lists are compiled from the statements of informants or represent the deductions of anthropologists from other data, it is hardly fitting to describe these as "analyses," and it is seriously misleading to suggest that they are, in any profound sense, more psychologically or cognitively "real" than other symbolically more elaborate treatments of systems of kin classification. They are little more than simple ethnographic statements, a "little more" only because no informant is ever likely to volunteer such a list *in toto*, but only one or a few statements at a time. Many of these are likely to be only partially adequate: they are correct as far as they go, but they do not go nearly far enough toward providing a full statement of the range of the term or terms in question.

We do not intend to belittle this kind of ethnographic data; indeed, it seems to us that anthropologists can and should make a great deal more use of the kinds of definitional rules and extension rules that their infor-

---

[4] That is, if they are truly adequate. As Burling (1970: 23) notes, "we need no fancy notions like 'ablineal' . . ." in order to state adequate componential definitions of American English kinship terms. One good reason for not using such notions, as Burling suggests, is that they are quite alien to the thinking and speaking of native users of American English; but another good reason is that they fail to provide part of the basis for a formally satisfactory structural semantic analysis. However, concepts such as "generation," "collaterality," and "degrees of genealogical distance" (variously defined) are necessary and do have a reasonably well known place in American culture, albeit largely in the technical language of the legal profession. As for "co-lineal," while the term is not employed by native speakers the concept it designates is well known to them and so there is no serious objection to our use of the term.

mants volunteer. It seems to us that one of the uses to which they may be put is to validate[5] a formal semantic analysis, for if an analysis is valid it should turn out that its posited definitional and extension rules can be paraphrased in terms of the rules volunteered by informants. Let us consider this possibility in the Siriono case.

The set of local language rules we envision here as a possible paraphrase of our analysis will comprise rules similar to that rule already noted for *yande*. It will be recalled that the primary range of *yande* may be defined by means of a three-term relative product of the parent, child, and sibling terms of the language understood in their narrow or primary senses. Similarly, the broad range of *yande* is definable by means of the same three-term relative product, this time taking the parent, child, and sibling terms of the language in their broadest senses. The primary and derived ranges of all Siriono kinship terms (except the parent and child terms) can be represented in the same general way.

In what follows we take the liberty of putting words in the mouths of Siriono, but we assume only a limited privilege in this respect. We first list definitions for each of the ten Siriono kinship terms (omitting consideration of *nininizi* and *eru$_2$*), employing only English words for which we may reasonably expect to find a simple Siriono language equivalent. For the most part these are merely the English glosses we have given to the Siriono terms, but "brother" and "sister" are employed to avoid forms such as "male sibling." In our experience, the complexity of these statements does not exceed that of many which anthropologists frequently encounter in the field. Of course, informants seldom volunteer such sets of statements *in toto*, but they often volunteer one or two at a time, and it is precisely the anthropologist's task to record and then order them into a workable and coherent whole. Having formulated such a set of rules, he may present them to his informants for verification or refutation. Unfortunately, we have no Siriono handy to whom the following could be submitted, and so we offer it only as a sample of what we think might be done by way of confronting the cognitive validity issue.

The narrow ranges of Siriono kinship terms may be stated quite simply as a set of "rules" phrased in terms of genealogical definitions of the nuclear terms *eru*, *ezi* and *edidi* and their relative products, as follows:

---

[5] We do not think of this as a matter of choosing between alternative analyses (see Burling 1970: 15), for as previously noted, it has not yet been demonstrated that two or more different analyses of the same system are all equally acceptable on formal grounds. The kind of validation we have in mind is more a matter of seeing whether or not the results of analysis can be translated back into natural language and, if not, how the statement of the results might be modified so as to be more readily expressible in natural language.

1. The woman who bore me is my *mother* (*ezi*).
2. The man who engendered me is my *father* (*eru*).
3. I am their *child* (*edidi*).
4. The child of my father and mother is my *sibling* (*anongge*).
5. The father of my father or of my mother is my *grandfather* (*ami*).
6. The mother of my father or of my mother is my *grandmother* (*ari*).
7. The child of my child is my *grandchild* (*ake*).
8.-9. If I am a man, the child of my sister is my *niece* (*akwani*) or my *nephew* (*akwanindu*), but if I am a woman, the child of my brother is my *niece* (*akwani*) or my *nephew* (*akwanindu*).
10. If I am a man, my mother's brother's daughter is my *potential spouse*, but if I am a woman, my father's sister's son is my *potential spouse*.

The *extended ranges* of the terms of the FAMILIAL KIN set are also statable in terms of simple relative product definitions:

1. *Ezi:* My mother's sisters (her female *anongge*) and my father's potential spouses (his *yande*) (who tend to be the same persons) are also my "mothers."
2. *Eru:* My father's brothers and my mother's potential spouses (who tend to be the same persons) are also my "fathers."
3. *Edidi:* If I am a man, the children of my brothers and the children of my potential spouses are also my "children"; if I am a woman, the children of my sisters and the children of my potential spouses are also my "children."
4. *Anongge:* The "child" of anyone I call father or mother is my "sibling."

These four definitions are simple and exhaustive; so far as we know, they encompass all kintypes denotable by these terms. Note that they express the same thing as our parallel-sibling merging, step-kin, and spouse-equation rules. However, when we apply the same principles of extension to the terms of the GRANDKIN set, the result is a set of definitions which is not exhaustive. This is only to be expected: parallel transmission of kin-class status occurs in this domain, but not in the FAMILIAL KIN domain, and we have yet to consider a possible Siriono paraphrase of that rule. The extended ranges of the GRANDKIN terms are subject to the same rules as the extended ranges of the FAMILIAL KIN terms and to additional rules as well. Let us first note how far parallel-sibling, half-sibling, step-kin, and spouse-equation rule principles will take us in accounting for the extensions of the GRANDKIN terms:

5. *Ami:* The "father" of anyone I call "father" or "mother" is my "grandfather," and so too is the "brother" of anyone I call "grandfather" or "grandmother," *provided that he is not my potential spouse.* Moreover, the potential spouses of my "grandmother" are my "grandfathers," *provided that they are not my "brothers."*

6. *Ari:* The "mother" of anyone I call "father" or "mother" is my "grandmother," and so too is the "sister" of anyone I call "grandmother" or "grandfather." In addition, the potential spouses of my "grandfathers" are my "grandmothers."

7. *Ake:* The "child" of anyone I call "child" is my "grandchild." The "children" of my "nephews" and "nieces" are also my "grandchildren," *unless they are entitled to be called "nephew" and "niece" themselves.* That is, in order to avoid tangles, if my potential spouse calls someone "nephew" or "niece," then I follow his (or her) usage. Thus, for reasons that I will explain in a moment, I call my mother's brother's son my "nephew," and I call his son my "nephew," too, because he is the "nephew" of my potential spouse.

8. *Akwani:* If I am a man, the "daughter" of any woman I call "sister" is my "niece," but if I am a woman my "niece" is the daughter of any man I call "brother." The "nieces" of my potential spouses are also my "nieces."

6. *Akwanindu:* If I am a man, the "son" of any woman I call "sister" is my "nephew," but if I am a woman, my "nephew" is the "son" of any man I call "brother." The "nephews" of my potential spouses are also my "nephews."

10. *Yande:* If I am a man, the "daughter" of any man called "brother" by any woman I call "mother" is my "potential spouse"; but if I am a woman, the "son" of any woman called "sister" by any man I call "father" is my "potential spouse."

Now in addition to all of this I call my father's sisters (and "sisters") my "grandmothers," and I call my mother's brothers (and "brothers") my "grandfathers," the same as I call their mothers and fathers. ([*In response to a query*]: I do not know why we Siriono do this—it is just our custom.) That means that they should call me their "grandchild," for if they are like my "grandfather" and "grandmother" then I am like their "grandchild." But I am also their potential spouse's "nephew" (or "niece"), and that means they must call me "nephew" (or "niece," as the case may be). Anyway, "nephews" (and "nieces") are like "grandchildren"—you might say that they are sorts of "grandchildren" in that they are "grandchildren" who are not so far away—so it is straight either way. You have noticed that if I am a man I call my father's sister's son "grandfather" and I call my father's sister's daughter "grandmother." (That "grandfather" is my sister's potential spouse.) In other words, I call these people the same thing that I call their father and mother. In fact, I call them "grandfather" and "grandmother" because that is what I call their father and mother.

[*Query*]: But you do not always do this; that is, not all "sons" of "grandfathers" are your "grandfathers." For example, you do not call your mother's brother's son "grandfather" but he is the "son" of a "grandfather." Why is that?

[*Reply*]: Well, you see, it cannot work both ways or things would not be straight. If I called my father's sister's son, or my father's "sister's" son, "grandfather" and he called me "grandfather" too, that would not be right. If I call a man "grandfather," he must call me "grandchild" or "nephew," or "niece" if I am a woman. So it is only the "sons" of "grandfathers" on the father's side that we call "grandfather"—and the same is true of the "daughters" of "grandmothers" on the father's side. Also, I call the "son" of a "grandfather" my "grandfather" too, only if I cannot call him something else. For example, if he is my father's "brother" then I would not call him "grandfather" but I would call him "father."

This, then, is the kind of thing one might expect to hear from a Siriono about "how the system works." There is, as we have already noted, no reason to expect that any Siriono would be able to volunteer such a *set* of statements *in toto*. Indeed, Holmberg (1950: 3) observed that Siriono were not voluble informants who readily engaged in abstract discussions of their culture or social organization. This, however, does not mean that an intelligent Siriono could not volunteer similar statements of a limited scope, especially in response to carefully calculated, but not leading, questions, which would add up to a set such as that presented above. The construction and presentation of such sets of data are precisely the ethnographic task, and they are not more misleading or ethnographically misrepresentative than well-constructed grammars or models of social structure.

It should be obvious from the preceding that no Siriono needs to "know" anything about componential definitions of terms in narrow or broad senses, or anything about equivalence rules, as we have posited them in order to employ this terminology properly. All he has to "know" are the proper primary applications of the terms, a few simple rules of interclass relationships, and a few terminological priorities. Moreover, he need know nothing about the genealogical connections between himself and others *beyond first-cousin range*, for beyond that point he can go on his knowledge of interclass relationships, provided he knows what a given distant kinsman is already called by one or more less distant kinsmen.

Does this mean that our formal semantic analysis is farfetched, that it has no cognitive validity, and no ethnographic value? If the system is simply and satisfactorily described by the above statements, why bother with our analysis in Chapters 4 and 5? Perhaps needless to say, we think that analysis is not farfetched, that it has cognitive relevance and ethnographic value, and that it offers anthropological dividends that the list of relative product statements does not.

To begin with, the list of "Siriono statements" is in fact nothing more than a paraphrase of the formal semantic analysis, though the paraphrase features a degree of particularity and redundancy that is not characteristic of the other. For example, the statements that mother's sisters are also "mothers" and that fathers' brothers are also "fathers," and the corollaries of these statements, that the children of my brothers are my "children" (male ego speaking) and that the children of my sisters are my "children" (female ego speaking), are all exemplifications or special cases of the same-sex sibling merging rule. And the fact that the "child" of anyone called "father" or "mother" is called "sibling" is likewise dependent on the rule of same-sex sibling merging. Any analysis that does not point out this fact—that does not reduce a series of highly specific rules to the more general rule that underlies them all—is simply incomplete; it has not yet revealed the fundamental underlying principles of the system. Although a Siriono may not volunteer any remark to the effect that the several specific rules are in fact but special cases of a more general rule, the general rule is as much a part of Siriono culture, and of Siriono cognitive psychology, as is the set of more specific rules.

Second, our formal analysis led us to the discovery of a way in which the structure of the system might be phrased "more simply" (i.e., in ordinary language), and in which persons not familiar with the concepts and methods of structural semantics—people like ordinary Siriono, for example—could understand it. Anthropological skeptics might suppose that had we tried harder or had we been more clever or had we been less concerned with appearing to be clever (see Coult 1967), we could have discovered the "simpler" statement without the aid of our formal methods. Or they might note that the discovery procedure could have worked the other way round, with the formal analysis being formulated after the "simpler" statement was formulated. As for the first possibility, we can only observe that heretofore the structure of Siriono kinship terminology was an anthropological mystery. There have been several published and unpublished attempts to account for the system (for example, Shapiro 1968), but no successful ones. If we have had to solve the problem the hard way, so be it; at least the effort has paid dividends.

But we do not think we have done it the hard way, and we do not think that the so-called Siriono paraphrase is in fact any simpler than our formal analysis. The two statements are formally equivalent, and that is the major point of the discussion in this chapter. Our Siriono paraphrase *is* a paraphrase of our formal analysis, but, similarly, our formal analysis

THE QUESTION OF COGNITIVE VALIDITY 149

may be seen as a paraphrase of the Siriono language statement. Thus, of course, the discovery procedure could have worked the other way around. But while the two statements are formally equivalent, and thus have the same descriptive value, the componential and equivalence rule statement has a definite value that the other statements lack.

In order to be intelligible to anyone other than a Siriono or an ethnographer who may speak Siriono, a Siriono statement has to be translated into a more widely known language. We have already done that, and so our ordinary language paraphrase of the formal analysis is, in effect, an English language paraphrase too. Now fairly simple English language paraphrases of other peoples' kinship terminologies, such as that presented above for Siriono, are common enough in the ethnographic literature, and there are even some elegant ones formulated by scholars sophisticated in logic (see Fison 1880: 76–90). All too often, however, they account only partially for the distribution of terms over kintypes, or fail to reveal certain structurally significant relations among kin classes, or make use of unanalyzed relations among kin classes or unanalyzed constructs. Such attempts to explicate the structures of kinship terminologies have failed most notably where the systems exhibit skewing, that is, where terms extend over natural generational lines. Aside from their inadequacies (which may not be inherent in the method itself), such analyses simply fail to carry the analytic process far enough to make the results of several such analyses readily comparable with one another. Yet kinship terminologies constitute a natural class of classificatory systems, all of which share the same primitive elements, but which differ largely in the ways in which concatenations of those elements are segmented into culturally constituted categories. Therefore, although it is legitimate to argue that an ethnographic analysis has reached its end when it has shown how a particular system segments genealogical space, that analysis has ethnological, or comparative, or theoretical relevance only insofar as it is capable of revealing precisely how and where that particular system is similar to and different from yet other kinship systems. It seems to us that English language paraphrases of kinship terminologies and their rules of extension (if they have any) are hardly adequate to this task, but componential and equivalence rules analyses are.

Our argument is simply this: A simple English language paraphrase of the definitions and other rules of a vernacular kinship terminology may be valuable, but "translation" must be carried further if it is to be of any comparative and theoretical utility. It seems to us that to restrict analysis of systems of kin classification to a list of discursive and relative product statements such as those which informants can readily volunteer would be comparable to restricting structural or descriptive linguistic analysis to the reporting of folk grammars; linguists have long recognized that these are inadequate, not because they are necessarily "wrong" but because their rules are typically only partially valid generalizations which are "correct" as far as they go (within narrow but usually unstated limits) but which, as generalizations beyond a case in hand, may be more wrong than right.

The psychological or cognitive status of the definitional and equivalence rules posited in Chapters 4 and 5 should now be fairly clear; it is highly probable that they are general structural principles underlying and relating a number of more specific relationships between terms and the kin classes they designate. Siriono are probably quite aware of and habitually make use of their knowledge of these more specific relationships, but at the same time they make use of or apply the more general structural principles just as they speak their language without being fully aware of the rules of its grammar. If, by some definition of "psychological" or "cognitive" (e.g., one that restricts psychological or cognitive phenomena to perceptual discriminations subject to immediate verbal report), we must reject our definitional and equivalence rules as "psychologically" or "cognitively unreal," then we must at the same time reject a great deal more, e.g., any structural linguistic analysis that goes beyond reporting folk grammars. This we are not prepared to do.

8

On the Social Structural Correlates of Siriono Kin Classification

In this chapter we consider some of the possible social structural correlates of the Siriono system of kin classification. We do not attempt to explain *why* the Siriono system of kin classification has the structure that it has; rather we attempt only to show that the system of kin classification is at least logically and functionally consistent with certain other aspects of the Siriono social order. We must consider also the more general question of the relationship between structural semantic and sociological analyses of systems of kin classification.

Let us deal with the more general question first, since our exclusion of sociological considerations from the preceding discussion of Siriono kin classification[1] was motivated in part by the way in which we think this relationship (between structural semantic and sociological analyses) ought to be conceived.

Structural Semantics and Sociology

Had we chosen to define this purely as a linguistic study, and solely as an investigation into the structure of the *significata* of Siriono kinship terms, there would be no objection to treating the analysis presented in Chapters 4 and 5 as an end in itself (cf. Leach 1970: 97), or as but one of many such analyses designed to contribute to a general theory of systems of kin classification as linguistic and semantic systems, or even, eventually, as an analysis that would contribute to a theory of systems of classification in general (again, as linguistic and semantic systems). But, of course, one could hope to go beyond even these broad ends and, eventually, to develop a theory that would account for the widespread (if not universal) occurrence of systems of kin classification and for the differential distri-

[1] Except in the case of *yande*, where sociological considerations were admitted in order to clarify Holmberg's gloss, "potential spouse," and to establish that this, too, is a "consanguineal" or kin term.

bution of the various "types" of such systems, however such "types" might be defined on the basis of structural semantic analyses. Such a theory would be likely to include reference to a variety of social structural and other kinds of cultural variables, hypothesized as important determinants of the structures in question. And certainly, in order to account for the general existence of systems of kin classification, it would have to deal with certain very general conditions of human social experience and the general attributes of the human "mind" which interprets that experience (cf. Leach 1970: 95).

The formulation of such a broad theory has been one of the aims of anthropologists at least since the publication of L. H. Morgan's *Systems of Consangunity and Affinity of the Human Family* in 1871. But a number of misconceptions have impeded the development of such a theory, only two of which need to be considered here.

First, the attempts of Morgan and later scholars to develop a general structural typology of systems of kin classification have not been successful, largely we think because none of them has taken sufficient account of the factors of extension and polysemy.[2] Thus a great deal of effort has been expended in attempts to explain the existence of features which these systems do not possess, and features which they do possess have often gone unnoted or misunderstood (see Scheffler 1970*d*).

Second, and most relevant to the topic of this chapter, it has been assumed almost universally that terminological distinctions between different kinds or classes of kin are always socially motivated, that, in particular, co-classification implies similarity of jural status, and that, conversely, classification under different terms implies dissimilarity of jural status. It has been widely regarded as a well established empirical generalization, and therefore as a reliable principle of interpretation, that terminological equations and distinctions of kintypes *follow from* equivalence and nonequivalence, respectively, of social status, or that both terminological and jural status are dependent "on the group structure of the society" (Firth 1968: 31–32).

Now it may be true in some cases that co-classification does correlate with similarity or identity of status and that, conversely, classification

---

[2] Lowie (1929), following Kroeber's (1909) lead, recognized the need to distinguish structural semantic from sociological analysis and the need to consider the various classificatory principles of a system separately when attempting to explain the system sociologically (which is what Kroeber seems to have been getting at when he argued that a kinship terminology is not "a logically coherent whole" but must be resolved into the several "categories," i.e., principles of classification, that it "recognizes"). But Kroeber and Lowie were misled in their identifications of the relevant classificatory principles by their common failure to take the factors of extension and polysemy into account (for an interesting exception see Lowie 1935: 19–20).

under different kinship terms implies dissimilarity of status, but this is far from being a nonexceptionable arrangement (see Lowie 1929; Opler 1937; Murdock 1949: 107; Tax 1955a; Goodenough 1965a). It is sometimes the case that jural (or right- and duty-) statuses ascribed in the first instance between kinds of familial kin are extended in attenuated form to some nonfamilial kin designated by the same terms, but not necessarily to all such kin. In other cases, the statuses associated with kin relationships beyond the nuclear family are differentiated hardly at all, so that inclusion in different classes implies little or nothing about differences in jural status. And in yet other cases, statuses are ascribed between sets of kin that receive no single lexemic designation, and the sets in question are composed of kintypes which belong to several different lexically marked categories. Moreover, most ethnographic reports of a neat and simple correlation between terminological and jural statuses rest on little more than casual observation, not on rigorous independent structural analyses of the terminological and jural status systems, and so it may be that the correlation is less common than a superficial examination of the ethnographic literature might suggest.

In any event, the assumption that such a correlation exists must be treated heuristically, as pointing to an arrangement known (or at least reported) to exist in some cases and to be looked for as a possibility in others. It must not be treated, as it often has been, as a principal tenet of analysis and used as an excuse for shortcutting the analytical process by failing to provide first a satisfactory structural analysis of the system of classification as such. The two systems (the system of kin classification and the system of social statuses) must not be fused *a priori* into a single system; they must be analyzed independently and their structures then compared to determine whether and to what extent, they are isomorphic. Otherwise, the analyst runs the risk of purporting to demonstrate (anecdotally) nothing more than what he assumed had to be the case to begin with.

Further still, the anthropological preoccupation with this mode of sociological analysis of systems of kin classification has led to failure to develop yet other and perhaps complementary modes of interpretation, again to be regarded heuristically, i.e., as pointing to an arrangement known (or hypothesized) to occur in some cases and to be looked for as a possibility in others. The necessity to reckon with the factors of extension and polysemy suggests at least one such mode of interpretation, viz., that the extension rules employed in a particular system reflect or express the structure of rules governing the transmission of (or succession to) various other (i.e., nonterminological) kinds of statuses within the same society (see also Lounsbury 1964a: 382–86; 1965: 175–81).

Of course, this idea is not new. It corresponds to the way in which at least some peoples explain why they classify kin as they do. For example, Fortes writes of the Ashanti:

> The critical element in the relation of mother's brother and sister's son is the latter's status as the former's prospective heir. This comes out in the kinship terms used in addressing or referring to them by their nonlineage kin. Thus a man's children address his sister's son as father (*agya*) if they wish to show respect to him, since he might well step into their father's position some day. An honorable and conscientious man who inherits his mother's brother's property and position will treat the latter's children with the consideration due from a father (Fortes 1950: 270–71).

Fortes notes also that a man can address his MBW as "wife," "since he has the right to inherit her if his uncle dies," but he has no right of sexual access to her so long as she is the wife of his MB. In other words, a man may succeed to certain of his MB's statuses, both as a relative of other individuals (e.g. as a father and a husband) and as a property owner in his own right; this is expressed in the system of kin classification in the form of a Crow-skewing rule, a rule specifying a covert structural equivalence between a man and his sister's son. One consequence of this rule is that ego may address or refer to his FZS as "father," but this does not imply a corresponding extension of the status relationship ascribed between father and child. Fortes (1950: 278) notes that "the jural and affective relationships associated with the use of these terms in their primary contexts" (i.e., primary senses) are not so extended. Thus ego does not treat his FZS as a father (except terminologically), and conversely, a man does not treat his MBS as a child (again, except terminologically), unless ego's father is deceased and his FZS has succeeded to his father's statuses. To all appearances, prior to this the social relations of male cross cousins are governed only by the general principle of "kinship amity" (see Fortes 1950: 277).

So we may treat it as a hypothesis that rules of kin-class or terminological extension may reflect rules of *status succession*. Extensions of a kinship term, then, would define a class of potential legal successors—and successors to successors—to statuses held by one's nearer kinsman. This succession may be inter- or intragenerational, and the statuses involved may be of various sorts. As we have seen, in the Ashanti case they include both kinship and nonkinship statuses (since one's MB's status as a property holder is not a status that he holds in respect of any particular type or class of kin). They might also include such nonkinship statuses as head of family, other positions in the domestic group, headship of a lineage, hereditary political office, religious office, etc. The exact specifications may be different from case to case, and it is well to leave these open to empirical determination. The kinship terminology may follow one of these while ignoring or running counter to another.

It should be emphasized that we present this suggestion as a hypothesis. Our assumption is that rules of kin-class or terminological extension *may* reflect rules of status succession, not that they *necessarily* do so.[3] Indeed, we are reasonably sure that there are some cases in which they do not.

In a previous discussion of this hypothesis (Lounsbury 1964a: 383), it was noted that unilineal descent groups may provide excellent contexts for statuses important enough to have their succession reflected in kinship terminology, and so we might expect a certain correlation of Crow-type terminology (i.e., Crow-type skewing rules) with matrilineal descent groups and of Omaha-type terminology (i.e., Omaha-type skewing rules) with patrilineal descent groups (without the necessity, however, of assuming that it is descent-group categories that are being labeled by the kinship terms). However strong this correlation may be,[4] there are certain "deviant" cases that have to be considered. That is, in a few societies described by their respective ethnographers as "patrilineal"—largely because they feature patrilineal descent groups—we find not Omaha- but Crow-type systems of kin classification (see Meek 1931; Deacon 1934; Netting 1968). It was suggested (in Lounsbury 1964a: 383) that the existence of matrilineal succession to important offices in these societies might account for these cases that run counter to the expected association. In at least two of these cases, however, no such offices are reported, nor are any other forms of what we would term matrilineal succession or inheritance reported by the ethnographers (Deacon 1934; Netting 1968). While it is possible that such forms of succession or inheritance are present in these societies but were not detected by the ethnographers, it seems equally possible that

[3] Note Lévi-Strauss (1965: 14) who argues that "in human societies kinship has a much wider range than succession," and who suggests that "in order to make both fields coincide" Lounsbury (1964a: 384) finds it "necessary to pool status of every conceivable kind and fill up the remaining gaps with psychological affects such as 'uneasiness'." The "unease" hypothesized in the passage to which Lévi-Strauss refers was not invoked in order to save a dogmatically held conviction that extension rules necessarily reflect rules of status succession, but was intended merely as an allusion to the well known fact that jural relations are sometimes ambivalent and may well have affective consequences.

[4] Note that previous assessments of the correlation between Crow- and Omaha-type systems and matrilineal and patrilineal descent groups, respectively, have utilized different typological criteria than those suggested here. Since Murdock's (1949) sample of Crow- and Omaha-type systems includes some that do not employ Crow- and Omaha-type skewing rules, it may be that the correlation we would expect to find is even stronger than that found by Murdock.

they are simply absent. Therefore we must consider the possibility that in these cases the Crow-skewing rules do not reflect rules of matrilineal succession or inheritance.

What, then, might they reflect or express? This is not the place to enter into an extended discussion of these cases, and so we may note only that in both cases the Crow-skewing rule specifies a covert structural equivalence of MB and B; it may be that this covert identification of MB with B reflects or expresses a perhaps partial identification of the MB–ZS social relationship with the B–B social relationship. The essential point here is that the ethnographic evidence gives no reason to believe that in these cases the Crow-skewing rule reflects or expresses the structure of other rules of status transmission.[5]

We should add, too, that in our view the sociological interpretation of rules of terminological extension need not be confined to attempts to explain why a system employs the rules that it does. An alternative and complementary approach is to consider the possible social implications of using certain rules. That is to say, even though we may assume that in general the institutionalization of such a rule is socially motivated, the rule, once established as a conventional procedure, becomes a "social fact" in its own right and may be regarded as having certain consequences for social action. Consider, for example, the once popular explanation of Crow-type systems. It was noted that in some of these systems MBW is designated as "wife," and it was argued from this observation that this designation and the designation of MBC as "child" (by male ego) both result from a rule of MBW marriage (as a "secondary" form of marriage). The argument is unacceptable as a general sociological explanation of Crow-type systems because in many of them MBW is not designated as "wife"; and it is unacceptable as an explanation of those cases in which she is so designated, for in some of those societies she is not regarded as a potential wife. Furthermore, the argument fails to provide the basis for a satisfactory formal account of these systems of classification per se. Thus it must be supposed that the designation of MBW as "wife" is the result of extension of the Crow-skewing rule into the domain of step-kin (thus ♂ MBW ⟶ ♂ BW), and of extension of the same-sex sibling merging rule into the domain of affinal classification (thus ♂ BW ⟶ ♂ W). (Context restrictions placed on these rules prevent this classification in many Crow-type systems.) Where leviritic succession is also the rule, MBW may

---

[5] It should be noted in passing that the rules of status succession reflected in Crow- and Omaha-skewing rules are perhaps not necessarily rules of "lineal" succession, i.e., uniform for the two sexes, and so these extension rules are not necessarily to be construed as rules of "lineal" transmission of kin-class or terminological status. It is sufficient to note that they transmit such statuses intergenerationally, without describing this as "lineal" transmission and perhaps thereby suggesting that they are necessarily associated with the "lineal" transmission of nonterminological statuses.

therefore be regarded as a potential wife, along with BW. But the conclusion that since MBW is classified as "wife" she is therefore to be regarded as a potential wife, is not a necessary implication of the rules of kin classification (or of these rules coupled with the rule of leviritic succession); therefore, people using such a classification are free to draw this conclusion if they wish or to disregard it if they wish.[6]

Although we have confined our attention so far to consideration of possible sociological explanations of extension rules, we have not meant to suggest that primary defining rules are without sociological interest. Presumably, the distinctions made by a system at this level are equally the result of, and may also have consequences for, a people's social experience. Here it seems appropriate to assume that, in general, designation of two or more kintypes by the same term may imply some perhaps limited similarity in their respective right- and duty-statuses in relation to ego, and conversely, that distinctions between kintypes may imply a dissimilarity of status in relation to ego. But, again, one cannot assume that this has to be the case, and the absence of such a correlation in some or many cases would not necessarily require rejection of the hypothesis that terminological equations and distinctions are so motivated in other cases.

Furthermore, certain distinctions at this level may be motivated by considerations that have little to do with social relations between particular types of kin as such. For example, the various distinctions by sex, e.g. sex of ego, sex of alter, and relative sex, may be motivated by a general concern with sex as a criterion of social discrimination. Use of the criterion of relative age may be similarly motivated. And, as others have noted, the terminological "isolation" of familial kin that occurs in some so-called Eskimo-type systems may be motivated by the general social independence of the nuclear family that is reported for some of these societies.

Finally, at this level of the structure of any system we have to consider the fact that the empirical variation is subject to certain logical and psychological (i.e., cognitive) constraints. Some of the logical constraints are imposed by the very nature of the primitive elements or relationships of any kinship system. For example, there are a dozen logically possible ways in which parents might be classified and a much larger number of logically possible ways in which grandparents might be classified; but many of the logically possible combinations are logically and psychologically quite complex and, probably for that reason, are rare or do not occur in actual human societies.[7] It may be assumed, again heuristically, that the

[6] For extended discussion of a somewhat more complex case see Scheffler (1970d)
[7] For further discussion see Greenberg (1966: 105-11). Greenberg observes (p. 109) that there are 15 logically possible classifications of the four grandparent kin types, but this may be substantially increased if one considers the possible relevance of the dimension of sex of ego (as Greenberg does not).

empirical variation within this range is socially motivated, but the range of variation itself is a phenomenon that requires explanation. Again, that explanation will have to deal with certain very general conditions of human social experience and with the general attributes of the human "mind" which interprets that experience.

We may now return to the Siriono case itself and to consideration of some hypotheses about the social significance of Siriono rules of kin classification. It will be useful first to outline some of the principal features of Siriono society.

Siriono Society

The Siriono lived until recently in the tropical forests of northeastern Bolivia. In 1940–41, the period of Holmberg's field work, a few of them were still living under relatively unchanged or precontact conditions, but in 1950 most of the estimated 2,000 Siriono lived on or around the ranches, farms, and mission stations that have grown up in their area (Priest 1964). Holmberg describes their aboriginal condition as seminomadic; they are (we write henceforth in the ethnographic present) aggregated into bands, each of which lives in a single large house, and they roam the forests in search of wild food, mostly game, which they take with long bows. The bands range in size from 30 to 120 persons (Holmberg 1948: 451); the two bands Holmberg lived with numbered 58 and 94 individuals (see Table 8). Siriono bands have no clearly defined and conventionally bounded territories, only "hunting trails," which other bands avoid (1950: 51). Bands rarely come into contact with one another, and partly as a consequence

Table 8

SIRIONO BAND COMPOSITION*

	Band	
	Aciba-eoko	Eantandu
Total members	94	58
Adult males	27	17
Pre-adult males	18	10
Adult females	30	19
Pre-adult females	21	12
Extended families	5	4
(Average size)	18.8	14.5
Nuclear families	17	14
(Average size)	5.5	4.1
Polygynous families	4	4

*Data from Holmberg (1950: 51, 82–83).

of this tend to be effectively endogamous—that is, there is no rule of endogamy, but most marriages are within the band, and there seems to be an aversion to "marrying out" (1950: 81). As is commonly the case among peoples dependent on hunting and gathering, the band is cohesive during the wet season when travel is difficult. The Siriono then seek refuge on high spots in the forest. During the dry season, "the band is much more loosely organized," for at this time the families that compose a band disperse to hunt and collect over different areas for as much as a month at a time (1950: 6–7, 51). We are not told whether or not the people always reconstitute the same bands at the end of the dry season.

Postmarital residence is described as "matrilocal" (i.e., uxorilocal). When a man marries, he merely moves his hammock from his natal family's section of the band house to the section of his wife's natal family (or if he marries a woman from another band, he removes himself to that band). As a consequence, "groups of matrilineal relatives tend to cluster together in the house to form extended families" (1950: 50). Such a family is "made up of all females in a direct line of descent, plus their spouses and their unmarried children" (1950: 50). Holmberg states that the "primary function" of this unit is "economic." The women of an extended family, who are usually sisters, collect food together, and their husbands, who are frequently brothers, hunt together; the distribution of food rarely extends beyond the confines of this "group." These families are *not* corporate groups: they hold no properties in common; they engage in no activities *as units*; and they appear to have no specific names. Judging from the average size of the extended families in the two bands studied by Holmberg, extended families probably range in size from 10 to 25 persons.

What Holmberg intended to imply by the term "matrilineal" and whether his use of the term was justified have been topics of debate (see Needham 1964a), and so his use of the term requires close examination. It should be remembered that, in anthropological usage of the 1940s (when Holmberg's account was first written), the terms "matrilineal" and "patrilineal" usually were used in very broad and theoretically very weak senses; any genealogical or social relationship between mother and child, or between uterine descendants of the same woman, was often loosely described as "matrilineal," or as "matrilineal descent" (see also Fortes 1949: 31). Nowadays, however, the term is often more narrowly interpreted as signifying the presence of a specific kind of "rule of descent," i.e., an enunciated rule of membership in corporate groups, or the conceptualization of a special kind of genealogical relationship (one extending over at least three generations and in which the most senior party and all linking kin are females), a kind of genealogical relationship that usually is assigned a special normative value (see Fortes 1959; Barnes 1962; Scheffler 1966).

From the contexts in which Holmberg uses the term, it is evident that he meant to do no more than assert that the female members of Siriono extended families are most often related to one another as mother–daughter or sister–sister, or by some combination of such relationships. Holmberg nowhere speaks of a "rule of descent" (in the sense specified above), and he nowhere suggests that matrilineality is for Siriono a type of genealogical connection that is conceptualized, set off from other types of genealogical connection, and assigned a special normative value. Except for those instances in which he uses "matrilineal" as a virtual synonym for "matrilocal" (see his statement in Eyde and Postal 1963: 285), he uses the term to refer to a demographic arrangement, rather than to any concepts or rules intrinsic to Siriono culture.

We can find no evidence in the ethnography that any such concepts or rules are present in Siriono culture. Needham's suggestion (1964a: 233) that Siriono are "in some sense" matrilineal rests almost entirely on his interpretation of Siriono kin classification, and this, as we have seen, suffers from a number of serious defects. His suggestion (1964a: 234) that "the designation 'matrilineage' might be more appropriate" than Holmberg's "matrilineal extended family," rests, like Holmberg's designation, on the reported typical composition of these residential clusters. However, while the larger of these families may well be composed in part of women related to one another as classificatory sisters (e.g., as MZD or even MMZDD, *anongge* in the broad sense), this need not follow from, and cannot safely be taken as evidence for any "rule of descent." Needham does not argue that we may safely infer the normative structure of groups from their *de facto* genealogical composition, but he does assert that "it is in accord with these ethnographic facts" (Holmberg's report as to the composition of Siriono extended families) "to conclude that the Siriono have a matrilineal descent system," i.e., that they are organized into "matrilineal descent groups" (1964a: 234). The difficulty with this suggestion is that it is now generally conceded that, by whatever terms we may choose to describe them in the end, it is necessary to distinguish groups with formal genealogical charters or rules of affiliation from groups which lack such charters or rules, even though there may be no consistent differences in their respective composition. The failure to do so in the past has frequently led to comparisons of groups which are not strictly comparable from the point of view of the criteria which govern their composition and, perhaps more importantly, their internal organization. Thus, the fact that similar small groups have also been described as "lineage groups," often by ethnographers who have not been aware of these problems, is inadequate justification for describing the Siriono extended families as matrilineages or as matrilineal descent groups (cf. Needham 1964a: 234).

From the available data, the Siriono extended family appears to be little more than a residential cluster that derives its composition from the fact that sisters tend to remain together throughout life and are joined by their husbands, who are commonly brothers. If we wish to describe this arrangement by means of technical terms, it is sufficient to say that they are uxorilocal sororal extended families, i.e., families composed of sisters and/or "sisters," their husbands, and their offspring. This appears to be a fairly common feature of South American Indian societies, many of which have also been described as matrilineally organized (see Oberg 1955; Fock 1963: 203; Steward and Faron 1959; Martin 1969).

Within the band house, each monogamous nuclear family has two hammocks, one for the husband and one for the wife and children. Each nuclear family has its own hearth. In polygynous families, each wife has her own hammock and hearth (Holmberg 1950: 49).

Siriono have no real property to speak of, and private or movable property is meager, consisting entirely of tools, household furnishings, and ornaments, some of which are jointly held by husband and wife (1950: 21). Of Siriono inheritance, Holmberg writes:

> Actually, it hardly exists, for when a person dies most of the things with which he had intimate contact are placed with the body or thrown away. Thus one's pots, calabashes, pipes, and feather ornaments are left at the site where the body is abandoned. Exceptions include hammocks, necklaces, cotton strings, and sometimes a man's arrows, particularly if he has been a good hunter. These may pass to his son or to his brother, while the few possessions of a woman usually pass to a sister or a cowife, though they may also be inherited by a daughter. Thus inheritance of possessions may be either patrilineal or matrilineal, depending upon the objects and persons involved (1950: 21).

Now it may be that the acquisition by a man (or boy) of his father's properties, and by a woman (or girl) of her mother's, involves a right on the part of the heir to the possession of these properties. But if we conclude from this passage that such a right is acknowledged, we must also conclude that men are similarly entitled to the properties of their brothers and women to the properties of their sisters or co-wives (sisters or classificatory sisters). In the case of the women, it would seem that sisters and co-wives are more frequently heirs than are daughters, which possibly, though not necessarily, suggests that the rights of sisters (or classificatory sisters) take priority over the rights of daughters. But it is not at all clear from the evidence of this passage that any such rights are involved. The situation as described by Holmberg could also be summarized as follows: property, such as it is, is sex-linked, and passes, as it were, to the nearest of kin who is in a position to make use of it—presumably a man's brother takes his hammock and arrows if that man's son is not old enough to use them, and similarly for a woman's sister or co-wife if her daughter is not old enough to make use of her more valuable possessions.

Holmberg (1950: 21) reports that "succession to chieftainship . . . follows patrilineal lines." Elsewhere he explains more fully:

> Chieftainship is normally a hereditary office and passes patrilineally from father to eldest son, provided the latter is a good hunter, is mature, and possesses the personal qualities of leadership. In case an eligible son is lacking, the office may pass to the chief's brother. It so happens that the chiefs whom I knew had both inherited the office from their fathers. One of them told me, however, that were he to die the office would be inherited by his younger brother, because he had no eligible son to whom it could pass (1950: 60).

But "chief" is a rather grand title to bestow on the identity designated by the term *ererekwa*. The Siriono paraphrase as "big man" (Holmberg 1950: 60) seems more appropriate. An *ererekwa* is hardly an "official"; he is simply, as Holmberg notes, an unusually clever man who commands respect because of his talents, and there may be several such men in a band. Also, "if one asks a woman, 'Who is your *ererekwa*?' she will invariably reply, 'My husband'" (1950: 59). This accords with Schermair's (1958: 314) gloss of the term as *dueño*, "master." It may be, however, that the sons of men generally known as "big men" are entitled to expect that they, too, will be generally so designated, in which case, we think, it would be appropriate to speak of a Siriono *rule of succession*. But we see no advantage in describing this rule (if it is one) as "patrilineal"; it seems adequately described as a rule of filial (or alternatively fraternal) succession to a status which may be held only by males. Finally, we should not dismiss the possibility that no such rule exists and that the informants, some of whom were themselves "chiefs," were describing what generally happens (when they said sons succeed fathers) or were expressing their aspirations for their own sons or brothers.

At marriage, Holmberg reports, there are no ceremonies and no exchanges of property. Marriages are not arranged by parents, and when a couple wish to marry they merely notify the parents-in-law-to-be (presumably the woman's parents), and the man moves his hammock next to that of his wife's parents (1950: 82). Divorce is an equally simple matter; it is usually caused by "adultery," i.e., "too frequent intercourse with potential spouses to the neglect of the real spouse." "The men always divorce the women," who then commonly marry the men with whom they have been having sexual relations. Although husbands are said to "throw away" their wives, on divorce it is the husband who moves his hammock.

Children "always remain with the mother," but their father continues to supply them with food, at least until their mother remarries (1950: 83). Needless to say, however, parents and their children remain in the same band (i.e., in the same large house), perhaps even in the same extended family, and are never far removed from one another, either spatially or socially.

According to Holmberg, Siriono practice "preferential mating . . . of the asymmetrical cross-cousin type." The "preferred" marriage is that of a man to his MBD, and marriage to a FZD is forbidden. If a man has no eligible MBD, he may marry a "second cross cousin, a first cross cousin once removed, a classificatory cross cousin, or a nonrelative" (1950: 81). By "second cross cousin" and "classificatory cross cousin" Holmberg clearly means persons who are classified as *yande* but who are not male ego's MBD or female ego's FZS. In one place he asserts, "marriages do not occur outside of this type of relationship" (i.e., *yande*) (1948: 461), but elsewhere he gives at least two examples of marriages to women who were not *yande*. One of these was between a man and his FZDD (1950: 81), and the other was between a man and the widow of his MB (1950: 83). The former would have been an *akwani*, the latter an *ari*. But, we are told, "marriages of this kind are exceptional (secondary, etc.), . . . as attested by the fact that almost 50 percent" of the marriages (six out of fourteen in the Eantandu band) were between a man and his mother's brother's daughter (1950: 81). Holmberg does not report how many of the marriages were to *yande* other than MBD, but the remark that "marriages do not occur outside of this type of relationship" suggests that Holmberg found very few marriages to non-*yande*.

It would be unsafe, however, to conclude from the data cited so far that the general incidence of MBD-FZS marriage in Siriono society is about 50 percent. First, it is not certain that the fourteen marriages mentioned by Holmberg were all of the marriages in effect in the Eantandu band at the time, much less anything like a representative or random sample of Siriono marriages in general. Second, it is not clear whether Holmberg was describing fourteen wife-takings involving fewer than fourteen men, or the marriages contracted by fourteen men. The phrasing on page 81 (1950) suggests the former, but that on page 82 the latter. On page 82 Holmberg states, "Four of the fourteen marriages in the band of Eantandu were plural marriages, and three of these were sororal unions." The four "plural marriages" are then described as those contracted by four men to some twelve women.

We noted earlier than in at least one place Holmberg describes a man's MBD as his "rightful spouse," apparently distinguishing her from other *yande* who are merely potential spouses. He does this in the context of describing how, "when a young man reaches marriageable age, he may find that his first cross cousin has already been taken to wife, and he is forced to marry a classificatory cross cousin instead of his *rightful spouse*" (1950: 81, italics added). "Classificatory cross cousin" in this context can refer only to a woman who is a *yande* but who is not a man's MBD, and the whole statement may be taken to imply that while a man has rights of sexual access to all *yande*, he has a right to only one kind of *yande* in marriage, that kind being his MBD. Furthermore, "if a girl shows reluctance to marry with her potential spouse, she is chided by her *mother* for her shortcomings and is thus usually forced into the marriage by ridicule" (1950: 82, italics added). "Potential spouse" in this context must refer to a woman's FZS in particular, and not to *yande* in general, for the only other interpretation that can be placed on this statement is that a woman is obliged to marry any *yande* who wishes to claim her, regardless of her desires. But this is plainly not the case. A woman is not even obliged to have sexual intercourse with any and all *yande* (1950: 64), let alone marry them. Thus it must be that this latter passage refers to the case of a woman who was shirking her duty by refusing to marry a man who had a rightful claim over her, and such a man must have been a FZS. A woman who chides her daughter to marry a man who asserts his right to her is merely upholding the norms of the society; she is not bestowing her daughter, as neither parents nor mother's brothers have any rights of bestowal over women in marriage.

It would seem, then, that a man has a right in marriage over women of a particular kintype,[8] and if he chooses to assert that right it is the duty of the woman concerned to marry him. This is not to say that he cannot marry any other woman, for he most certainly can. He may marry other *yande*, his MBD's classificatory sisters, for example, if there are no other men actively asserting their rights to those women. And he may marry non-*yande* also. The ethnography offers no reason to suppose that these latter marriages are disapproved as illegitimate or "wrong," and we can be sure they are not regarded as "incestuous" (1950: 64). Holmberg says only that they are "exceptional" (i.e., infrequent) and "secondary," and apparently no stigma attaches to them. In order to understand why marriages to non-*yande* are infrequent, though not stigmatized, we must now consider the status connotations of Siriono kinship terms.

Holmberg reports that, "Generally speaking, there are no formalized, obligatory patterns of kinship behavior" among Siriono (1950: 56). Such dramatic and readily noticeable patterned social relationships as "brother–

---

[8] That such a right is a part of Siriono culture is further suggested by the following. In the context of his account of the meanings of *bi*, one of which he gives as "destined to be," Schermair (1958: 56–57) notes the expressions *enindisi-be te*, "destined to be his spouse; fiancee," and *se nindidi raambi a nde*, "she is destined to be (or is) my spouse or wife."

sister avoidance, parent-in-law taboos, joking relationships, etc., are lacking." Apparently, however, social relations between at least some kinds of kin are somewhat more definitely and normatively ordered than these general observations might lead one to expect. The most notable categories in this respect are *anongge* and *yande*.

In the case of *anongge*, subcategorical distinctions are of critical significance. Let us consider first the lexically unmarked subcategory, "opposite-sex *anongge*." There is an interdiction on sexual relations between opposite-sex *anongge*, and this interdiction extends across the total range of the term's denotata; it is not confined just to one's own siblings. Apparently, this is not a rule observed in the breach, for Holmberg reports that he heard of no case of "incest" among Siriono (1950: 64). Doubtlessly as a consequence of the interdiction on sexual relations between them, "a certain reserve can also be noted . . . between siblings of the opposite sex" (1950: 57).

A person is sexually forbidden if he (or she) is a sibling of the opposite sex or, by virtue of the rules of genealogical structural equivalence of this system, he (or she) has the same kin-class status as a sibling of the opposite sex. (This one-dimensional normative equivalence does not imply that the subcategory "*anongge* of the opposite sex" is jurally unitary in any other respects.) It cannot be that *anongge* designates the category "same generation member of my own extended family" (see Needham 1964a: 237) and that opposite-sex *anongge* are sexually forbidden because of their common extended family affiliations. The extended families lack specific names or any form of corporate possession that could give them an identifiable continuity independent of their more or less stable composition. Therefore, it seems that a man may identify and distinguish his natal extended family only as that unit containing his true sisters (or his mother, if still alive), and not vice versa.

Social relations between same-sex siblings (true siblings) are reported to be the most solidary in Siriono society, but it is not clear that same-sex siblings (or other same-sex *anongge*) have any specific rights and duties with respect to one another; their solidarity seems to be of a rather diffuse and informal nature (1950: 57). In any event, it is clear that same-sex siblings, not just any *anongge*, are in general socially substitutable for one another. They count one another's children as their own, at least terminologically, and they are also responsible for the rearing of those children should their parents die (1950: 49, 58). Brothers share the same rightful and potential wives (though they must also share the latter with their FBS and MZS); and sisters share the same potential husbands (whom they must share with their FBD and MZD). Brothers also have rightful first claims over one another's widows (1950: 81, 83). The jural equivalence of true brothers and of true sisters is further indicated by the following:

166 A STUDY IN STRUCTURAL SEMANTICS

Although men have privileged sexual access to all women they call *yande*, regardless of the marital status of either party,

> In actual practice, relations between a man and his own brothers' wives, and between a woman and her own sisters' husbands, occur frequently and without censure, but those with potential spouses more distantly related occur less often and are apt to result in quarrels or lead to divorce (1950: 64; also 57, 83).

The corollary of this is of course that women may freely indulge this privilege with their husbands' brothers, and men with their wives' sisters. This special privileged sexual access to the true siblings of spouses and, reciprocally, to the spouses of true siblings can only rest on the jural equivalence of same-sex siblings. It can have nothing to do with the degree of relationship between the *yande* concerned, for the spouse of ego's same-sex sibling is not necessarily ego's "true" *yande* or even ego's classificatory *yande*.

As already noted, *yande* appears to connote two jural statuses, one attributed to a man's MBD and a woman's FZS, the other to a man's "MBD" and a woman's "FZS" generally. We have seen that the second jural status varies with marital status; the privilege of sexual access to a given *yande* (true or classificatory) becomes attenuated if that *yande* is married to someone other than ego's true sibling or if ego is married to someone other than that *yande*'s sibling. However, insofar as privileges of sexual access are concerned, it would seem that the distinction between true and classificatory *yande* is inconsequential; the jural status of a *yande* in this respect varies with the genealogical propinquity of his (or her) spouse. In contrast, a man's *marriage rights*, and conversely, a woman's *marriage duties*, do vary with the attenuation of the genealogical relationship between them. A man has no marital rights over women who are not his *yande* or over his *yande* who are not his MBD.

Not all *yande*, then, are socially (or jurally) equivalent to one another. Social equivalence between various *yande* varies contextually with their genealogical propinquity to one another and to ego, and with their marital status, as well as with the genealogical propinquity of ego to the persons to whom they are married. So far as marriage rights are concerned, same-sex siblings, and certain parallel cousins, are jurally equivalent. Thus, conceivably, conflicts could arise among brothers or male maternal parallel cousins concerning which of them will marry a given MBD. Whether such conflicts do occur and, if so, how they are settled, is not reported; but it must be that the brothers or classificatory brothers would settle the issue among themselves, for as we have already noted, no one has the right to dispose of a woman in marriage.

The jural correlate of the MBD-FZS spouse-equation rule is not that a man is obliged to marry his MBD or even a woman he calls *yande*, but rather that it is his right to claim his MBD in marriage. The terminology, via the spouse-equation rule, assumes that he exercises that right, and the norms of the society allow him free sexual access to these women. As a consequence of this classificatory convention, and of the other definitional and equivalence rules of this system, certain other female kintypes are also designated as *yande*. But other men have marriage rights over those women and, thus, ego has no rights over them, at least insofar as marriage itself is concerned. This does not diminish their marriageability, when available, nor does it limit ego's right of sexual access to these women. However, ego's freedom to indulge in sexual relations with his or her *yande* is somewhat restricted by the fact of marriage of either party. The restriction does not consist in formal curtailment of the right of sexual relations between *yande* but derives informally from the rightful claims of spouses, with which this sexual freedom may interfere.

It is clear that rights over women in this society are wholly and solely rights *in personam* held by no persons other than their FZS. Women (or rights in respect of them) are not a class of "property" subject to certain types of transaction, as they are in some other societies. They are jurally free persons except to the extent that certain kinsmen have rights over them in marriage. The men hold those rights as individuals over individuals, not as members of corporate groups over members of corporate groups, or even as members of "categories" over members of "categories" (except insofar as the kintype ♂ MBD itself constitutes a single kintype category, which is a subcategory within a larger terminological category which also includes the kintype ♀ FZS).

The remaining Siriono kin categories appear to have relatively little jural significance as such. As in the case of *anongge*, there is an interdiction against sexual relations with all *eru*, *ezi*, and *edidi* regardless of the nature of the genealogical relationship concerned. In other words, all FAMILIAL KIN are categorically forbidden (1950: 64). In addition, sexual relations are also forbidden with "grandparent and grandchild, parent-in-law and child-in-law, uncle and niece [i.e., MB and ZD], aunt and nephew [i.e., FZ and BS], a woman and her mother's brother's son, and a man and his father's sister's daughter" (1950: 64). Since Holmberg quite explicitly states that "incest taboos are generalized to include non-family members who are designated by the same kinship terms as those used for members of the nuclear family" (1960: 64), we may presume that by "grandparents," "grandchildren," etc., he is in this context referring to specific kintypes and not to the various GRANDKIN categories as such. In other words, not all kin of the GRANDKIN categories are forbidden; it would appear that members of those categories *who are more distant than first cousins* are acceptable sexual and marital partners (cf. Shapiro 1968: 49). The two non-*yande* marriages specifically noted by Holmberg are of a man to an *akwani* (FZDD) or an *ari* (MBW), both of whom are more distant than first cousins (MBW is structurally equivalent to MMBD). Moreover, Holmberg (1950: 64) states that men "are constantly on the alert for a chance to approach a potential wife, or to carry on an affair with a *yukwaki* (young girl) who has passed through the rites of puberty." The phrasing suggests that men may and do "carry on affairs" with women who are not their *yande*, and since Holmberg also states that he "never heard of a case of incest occurring among the Siriono, even in mythology" (1950: 64) we may assume that these are affairs with *akwani* or *ari* or unrelated (i.e., unclassified?) women.

In addition, children are expected to show respect for their parents and grandparents. But apparently there is little respect for elderly parents or the aged as such: when parents "grow old and useless . . . little concern is shown for them" (1950: 57). We may presume that a child is taught to respect his parents' siblings and his parents' potential spouses (who are also his *eru* and *ezi*), for these persons are the parties most responsible for him in the event of his parents' death. Whether similar respect is extended to all *eru* and *ezi*, and to all *ami* and *ari*, is not reported. As previously noted, *ami* and *ari* have other than strictly kinship senses; they signify "old man" and "old woman" respectively (1950: 52), just as *ake* signifies "child" in the sense of an immature human being (1950: 54). Insofar as there is, apparently, no respect for the aged as such, it seems relatively unlikely that *ami* and *ari* are terms connoting deference on the part of ego.

These terms also denote parents-in-law, who are usually ego's kin as well. Here, too, they appear to lack jural connotations: "there are no taboos between parents-in-law and children-in-law" (1950: 57). Nevertheless, "the relationship between in-laws is usually polite . . ." (1950: 57). However, relations between particular in-laws may become strained due, for example, to a widow's demands for food from her son-in-law, for which she can offer nothing in return. To cope with this, the son-in-law avoids her if he can, but this may be difficult because his hammock may hang close to hers (1950: 57). Such difficulties are not confined to in-laws, however. Holmberg notes that drunken Siriono often fall to quarreling over lack of generosity in giving food to one another (1950: 36, 39). A man may then insult and even wrestle with his "cousin" (FZS), "brother, uncle, son-in-law, or even his father-in-law" (1950: 39). Needham (1961: 247) takes this as evidence that gifts of food are "conventional prestations between affines" because "presumably" FZH, FZS, MB, WF, B, and DH are the relatives involved in the reported incidents, and "all of these relatives except the brother are classificatory affines." We have already seen that the kinship system has no affinal categories and so there can be no such thing as "classificatory affines" in Siriono culture. It seems more reasonable to suppose that when Siriono insult one another and quarrel over lack of generosity with food they do so not as particular kinds of kin or affines but as close kin or family mates. It is quite clear from Holmberg's account that this is not a matter of "conventional prestations between affines" but rather one of economic responsibilities to one's family. And of course such responsibilities are altered by marriage. Holmberg has the following to say about this matter:

> Although matrilocal residence, in endogamous marriages, does not involve a very great spatial removal of a man from his relatives, it does produce a considerable change in his social obligations. After marriage, a man, instead of hunting for his parents, his sisters, and his unmarried brothers, must hunt for his wife's parents, for her sisters, and for her unmarried brothers. While these obligations are reciprocal, a man usually supplies more game to his in-laws than he receives in return. A man's relations with his own family, however, are not completely disrupted. Besides being related to his in-laws by blood, he continues to reside in the same house as his family. Moreover, his brother may be married to his wife's sister. If not, his brother is at least a potential husband of his own wife, with sex rights over her. Hence, brothers usually maintain close bonds after marriage. They may continue to hunt together especially, even though their game may be distributed in different ways (1950: 82).

The instances of complaint about food that Holmberg mentioned (e.g. "You never bring me meat with any fat on it"), which surfaced and led to aggression during intoxication, involved only types of relatives who are within the primary sphere of economic responsibility and cooperation, as outlined by Holmberg, specifically WF–DH, MB–ZS (= WF–DH), MBS–FZS (= WB–ZH), and B–B.[9] It is worth noting that in the case of "cousins" involved in such a quarrel it was the MBS whose complaint precipitated the quarrel with his FZS, and that the latter was reported as having "wives." His MBS was very probably a WB to him, and was reported as being a "chief" besides.

We may now consider why marriages to non-*yande* are infrequent though not stigmatized. It is obviously not a matter of men being *obliged* to marry *yande* and of some men being unable to find *yande* for demographic reasons and therefore marrying non-*yande* out of necessity (see Needham 1961: 245–46). But demographic factors probably do play a part:

---

[9] Note that FZH–WBC is not included in this list, though Needham (1961: 247) included it as one of the relationships "presumably" intended by Holmberg's use of the term "uncle." Although Holmberg's use of this term may be ambiguous, there is little apparent need to suppose that he intended to include FZH among those relatives whom a man may insult when intoxicated.

Only *yande* and distantly related *akwani* and *ari* are marriageable kin (for a man), and given the scale of Siriono bands there must be relatively few of the latter two. Also, other men have rights over those women and are likely to claim them as they become available for marriage. Thus, marriageable and available non-*yande* are likely to be few. But *yande* who are not MBD or FZS are relatively plentiful. According to Holmberg, "there may be as many as eight or ten potential spouses" in one's band, not counting one's "real spouse" (1950: 64). The number is perhaps larger for a married than an unmarried person, but only if he or she, or one of his or her same-sex *anongge*, has married a nonkinsman and thus extended the range of the *yande* category. We do not know whether or not a man's wife who is his FZDD, for example, is counted as a *yande* by his brothers (or "brothers"), for the effect of such marriages on the classification of kin is not reported.

The case of the marriage of a man to the widow of his MB is an interesting one. If Siriono society were ordered as a matrilineal asymmetric prescriptive alliance system, this marriage would be only to be expected. But Siriono society is not so ordered. The man concerned acquired his MB's widow as a wife partly because his MB left no brothers to claim her, as would have been their right (1950: 81, 83). There is no evidence, however, that failing the existence of a living brother the right passes to some other kinsman. It is probable, then, that this man took his MB's widow as his wife only because she was available and willing, and no other man had pressed or wished to press a rightful claim over her. It is not reported whether the man concerned was married to his own MBD or, if so, whether the widow was the mother of that woman. Nor is it reported whether a man may be married at the same time to a woman and her daughter, though it seems rather unlikely that this would be done, much less that it would be common and yet go unnoted by the ethnographer.

To summarize the analysis so far, it would appear that the basic structural unit of Siriono society is the same-sex sibling set and, by extension, the same-sex classificatory sibling set. In this light it is not surprising that "kinship" may be expressed idiomatically in terms of "siblingship" (Schermair 1958: 272). Sets of brothers tend to marry sets of sisters, who tend to remain together residentially throughout life, despite divorces and remarriages, and thus sisters (or "sisters") tend to form the nuclei of "extended families," which are nothing more than residential clusters within bands. The Siriono marriage rule, if it may be called a rule, is that each man has a right in marriage with respect to his MBD; he has privileged sexual access to all women he calls *yande*, and he may marry them; or he may marry women of the categories *akwani* and *ari* to whom he is not closely related, provided they are available. (*Yande* are themselves kinds of *akwani* for a man.) In marrying or having sexual relations with distant *akwani* or *ari*, a man is violating no rules, but such marriages are uncommon probably because such women are not generally available. Perhaps one reason they are not generally available is that Siriono men "prefer" to marry their MBDs, that is, they choose to claim their rightful spouses whenever possible.

Correlates of The Rules of Kin Classification

The jural correlates and the social structural concomitants of the MBD-FZS–spouse equation rule and of the parallel (or same-sex) sibling merging rule are obvious enough. But what of the parallel-transmission rule? We might expect such a rule to reflect some significant and striking jural equivalence between parents and their children of the same sex, but so far as the data permit us to determine, there are no such jural equivalences in Siriono society (and no reason to suspect that there might be some that were not noted by Holmberg). We might also expect this rule to reflect some aspect of a theory of reproduction or of inheritance of distinctive character traits, that is, for example, perhaps Siriono suppose that boys tend to look or act like their fathers and girls like their mothers (see Kaberry 1941: 245). But again, no such beliefs are reported. Or the classificatory rule might be expected to reflect rules of inheritance or of succession to some significant status within the society at large. While this may be so in the case of inheritance, as already noted, it is not clear from the available data that inheritance is governed by the principle of parallel transmission of property rights. Since the parallel-transmission rule governs the kin-class statuses of women as well as men, and since the status of *ererekwa* is available only to men, it seems unlikely that the parallel-transmission rule reflects the genealogical principle that may in part govern transmission of this status. Yet another possibility is that Siriono names are transmitted in parallel fashion, father to son, mother to daughter, and the rule of parallel transmission of kin-class status reflects this. But again, this is not the case. Siriono are named by their fathers and commonly after animals, though they may be known by a variety of nicknames (Holmberg 1950: 74–75). In short, the motivation for this rule is not determinable from the available data, or if it is so determinable, it is a kind of motivation not yet encompassed in our theory of the sociology of kinship systems, and so not apparent to us.

Be this as it may, parallel transmission *is* a feature of Siriono kin classification; recognition of the fact cannot be allowed to depend on our ability to state conclusively just exactly where, or even whether or not, the same structural principle occurs elsewhere in Siriono culture or social structure. The definitive test must be whether or not Siriono employ the rule; we suggested in Chapter 7 how this test might be carried out.

As noted earlier in this chapter, the sociological interest of rules of kin-class or terminological extension is not exhausted when we have considered how their presence in a particular case might be explained. It may be that knowledge of the principles of kin classification will sometimes help us to understand social phenomena that otherwise seem relatively inexplicable. In this case it seems to us that, given the existence of the rule of parallel transmission, it is possible to suggest why a man's MBD is his most appropriate potential spouse and why his FZD is forbidden to him along with other close *ari* and *akwani*.

First, it is virtually certain that most Siriono will have to marry kin, so the question for Siriono must be what kinds of kin they shall marry and what kinds they shall determine to be forbidden. Second, we take it to be a general phenomenon that men prefer to marry women of about their own age or younger, and that generally these will be women of their own generation. (This is not a necessary or universal preference, but it is a common one of obvious relevance in this case.) Therefore, if a society is to single out any kinswomen as particularly appropriate spouses, these are likely to be (but not necessarily) women of a man's own generation who are most likely to be of his own age or younger. (A society might of course "experiment" with other arrangements but the experiments would probably prove unsuccessful—largely because they would simply fail to meet the needs of very many men.) Third, it is also a general phenomenon that opposite-sex siblings are forbidden as sexual and marital partners; where marriage has to be with a kinsman, distant kin are preferred over close kin (except in situations where marriages are contracted between close kin in order to avoid the dispersal and attenuation of rights over certain valuable resources, including, e.g., "royal blood." This leaves second-degree (or greater) collateral kinswomen of a man's own generation (i.e., cousins). Where some such kinswomen are singled out as particularly appropriate spouses, it is almost universally one or another or both of the cross cousins, i.e., a man's MBD, or his FZD, or both.

Anthropologists have puzzled over this fact for some time (for a review of the literature see Lévi-Strauss 1969) and have tended to ask why the two kinds of cousins, parallel and cross, are treated differently, as though cross cousins were more distant kin than parallel cousins when "in fact" they are equally close or distant. But "close" and "distant" are matters for cultural definition; there are many different ways of computing degrees of kinship, and kintypes that are equidistant by one measure may be of different degrees by another. Thus, in some cases a classificatory (and perhaps social) distinction between the two kinds of cousins may be a product of the local system of reckoning degrees of kinship.

Even we, in our own cultural tradition, have more than one way of reckoning degrees. Thus we sometimes describe the first-cousin types as being kin of the fourth degree (for legal purposes, in the so-called civil degree), or as kin of the second degree (by canon reckoning), or as second-degree collaterals (by yet another measure, appropriate to the structure of our system of everyday kinship terminology). By any of *our* customary measures, however, these first-cousin types are of equal degree or distance. But we ought to ask whether, in a system like that of the Siriono, these four types (MZD, FBD, MBD, FZD) reasonably could be expected to be of the same kinship distance, or whether their respective "distances" from ego might more reasonably be viewed as different from one another.

We have shown (see Chapter 2) that there is ample evidence that the Siriono ascribe an essential role in procreation to both of a child's presumed parents and that this lays the necessary groundwork for genealogical reckoning whenever or in whatever context it may be appropriate. Moreover, we have shown (as did Needham also, 1961: 251–52) that there are contexts in which a genealogical manner of reckoning is indeed appropriate and necessary, for the class *yande* clearly has focal types, and these focal types can be singled out by no other means than by a chain of relative products: "female *edidi* of male *anongge* of *ezi* of male ego" (i.e., ♂ MBD), and the reciprocal of this, viz., "male *edidi* of female *anongge* of *eru* of female ego" (♀ FZS). If this can be done, as it must be, for these kintypes, it can surely be done for any other kintypes for which genealogy or presumed genealogy is known, as for example, the remaining ones of those which (in English) we call first cousins. All of this, then, might well seem to argue that the Siriono are in as good a position to reckon at least a putative "civil degree" as we are, and that therefore the four cousin types mentioned above might be seen, even in Siriono eyes, as being equidistant from ego. This would have to be true for any two or more kintypes if the number of links is the same in each case, *and if* the links are "equi-valent," i.e., given the same value, or given the same weight, in the evaluation of "closeness" of kinship. The first of these conditions is fulfilled in the case of the cousin types mentioned, but it appears most likely that the second condition is not.

The Siriono kinship system is distinguished by its same-sex sibling merging rule (a feature shared of course with many other systems) and by its parallel-transmission rule—to mention only those bearing on the point here under consideration. These rules, together with the others set forth in Chapter 5, govern the extensions of the terms of the system. It is possible that they may also govern notions of "closeness" and "distance" between kinsmen, and not only between those belonging to different terminological classes, but even among those within a single class. (The extensionist approach allows for the recognition of differences of distance or degree—however conceptualized—*within* the broader categories, as well as for differences of both distance and kind between members of different categories.) Here, then, it is appropriate to press one of the reasonable implications or expectable correlates of the same-sex sibling merging rule.

Siblings of same sex may be seen not only as more "like" each other (which they obviously are) than siblings of opposite sex, but also perhaps as more "closely related." (A basis for this, which is especially appropriate in the Siriono case, will become apparent shortly.) Thus, although both types of siblings are classed as one's *anongge*, subcategorical differences of both kind and degree may, and apparently are, recognized between them. In any event, this is the net effect of the operation of the same-sex sibling merging rule. In accord with this rule, among the four kintypes FBD, MZD, FZD, and MBD, the first two of these are treated as if in some significant sense "like" FD and MD respectively, and are categorized with these as *anongge*. The latter two, however, are not affected by this equivalence rule; they are left as kin of (apparently) different and more "distant" kinds than the first two, i.e., so far as the consequences of *this* rule are concerned (but see below). Now, the first two, FBD and MZD, like a man's own sister, and like other familial and familial-like kin, are subject to the incest taboo. Holmberg writes:

> . . . it is strictly forbidden to have intercourse with any member of one's nuclear family, except one's spouse. Among the Siriono these incest taboos are generalized to include nonfamily members who are designated by the same kinship terms as those used for members of the nuclear family. Consequently, one may not have relations with a parallel cousin, with the child of a sibling of the same sex, with the child of a parallel cousin of the same sex, with a sister or parallel cousin of the father, or with the child of anyone whom one calls 'potential spouse' (1950: 64).

Thus, in this important matter the parallel cousins are indeed "like" one's own siblings and other familial kin.

But the same-sex sibling merging rule, as can be seen, introduces a difference of "degree" (and of kind) only between the parallel cousins and cross cousins, allowing the former to be treated as "closer" than the latter. A man's MBD, however, is still no more "distant" by *this* reckoning than is his FZD, or the latter is no "closer" than the former. Why then, one may ask, is his FZD strictly forbidden? And why is his MBD his "rightful spouse"?

With regard to the first of these two questions, it is relevant now to press one of the apparent implications of the parallel-transmission rule a bit further. The implication is that, in a society having a kinship system with premises like those of the Siriono system, women must be regarded as not only more "like" their mothers (which of course they are) but also as in some special sense more "closely related" to them than they are to their fathers, so that in some contexts they are classified together or are otherwise (i.e., covertly) treated as equivalents; and similarly, that men must be regarded as more "like" and more "closely related" to their fathers than to their mothers, so that in some contexts these, too, are classified together or otherwise treated as equivalents. Now if male ego is "like" and covertly equivalent to his father, and if his FZD is "like" and covertly equivalent to her mother, then by implication the genealogical relationship of a man to his FZD is also in some significant way "like" and covertly equivalent to that of a man to his sister. And so indeed it is for the Siriono. Holmberg continues:

> In addition to these taboos [the ones quoted in the previous citation], which are clearly reflected in the kinship system, relations with the following relatives are also regarded as incestuous: Grandparent and grandchild, parent-in-law and child-in-law, uncle and niece, aunt and nephew, *a woman and her mother's brother's son*, and *a man and his father's sister's sister's daughter* (1950: 64, italics ours).

A man is not only prohibited from marrying his FZD, he is also prohibited from having sexual relations with such a woman, this being regarded as incestuous. In these important ways, then, a man's FZD *is* like a sister.[10] Moreover, we have already seen that the kinship terminology employs a rule that covertly equates a man's FZD with his sister. To be sure, a man's FZD is not herself called *anongge* (she is called *ari*), but this is because of context limitations on the parallel-transmission rule such that, for purposes of determining the use of kinship terms, the rule is not applied simultaneously to both ends of the genealogical chain. But the underlying principle of parallel transmission of kinship status, or of attributes of these statuses, finds fuller expression in the incest prohibition and in the covert structural equivalence between FZD and Z. The use of

---

[10] See also Kulp (1925: 168; cited in Leach 1961: 67): In one region of South China, MBD-FZS marriage is permitted but marriage with the FZD is "taboo because of the traditional attitude that the boy has only his father's blood and the girl has only her mother's blood . . . but the mother has the blood of her brother's son because the latter, being a son, has the blood of his father . . . In other words a girl and her mother are conventionalized, so far as mating is concerned, into siblings . . . ." As Leach comments, it would appear that "a woman is identified with her mother and a man with his father, so that sex relations between a man and his father's sister's daughter are the equivalent of brother–sister incest" (1961: 67).

kinship labels, in *any* kinship system, is only one of the means that people employ in "classifying" types of relatives. Covert structural equivalences, as well as other forms of behavior, may go even further than the labels do in classificatory merging, just as, in the opposite direction, covert non-equivalences, optional specifiers, and yet other kinds of behavior may introduce finer and finer discriminations whenever such are in order. In the present case, the covert structural equivalence and the incest taboo equate FZD with Z (*anongge*) even though the terminology stops short of that; and these same factors thus also make implicit discriminations of "closeness" and "distance" within the terminological category *ari*.

The situation is completely different in regard to a man's MBD. A man is not "like" his mother, and a woman is not "like" her father, so the genealogical relationship of a man to his MBD is not "like" that of a man to his FZD and to his sister. It is thoroughly unlike that relationship. No reduction assimilates it directly to any closer genealogical type, whether the rules operate under their specified context restrictions or be given wider latitude. Rather, the reductions lead to affinal types (WBD under the specified constraints, or WBW if the constraints are lifted on the parallel-transmission principle), which are classifiable by a male ego only under the rule that one follows one's spouse in applying kinship labels to spouse's relatives who are not otherwise relatable to oneself, and vice versa (rule 1.13, Table 6). These latter types are *akwani* in the special sense of "*akwani* by marriage," which is what the type ♂ MBD would be also were it not for the overriding defining rule that specifies this type as a focus of the class *yande* (see Chapter 5, pp. 92–98).

In brief, then, our hypothesis is that the demographic situation being what it is, a Siriono's sexual and marital partners in general have to be from among his kin. The natural choices are "distant" kin. Given the factors that may be expected to control the perception of "kinship distances" in this system, a man's MBD is the proper and only choice within the first-cousin range. His FZD, FBD, and MZD are all "like" sisters in one or more ways. His MBD is not, but instead is the logical candidate for being the prototype of the relation of "distant" or "minimal" kinship within one's narrower circle of kin. Demographic as well as genealogical factors might well contribute to the singling out of this type as against other more remote classificatory equivalents.

As Holmberg noted, there are *yande* types more distant than MBD (at least by our ordinary notions of kinships distance). But in one statement (1950: 81) he distinguishes a man's true MBD as "his rightful spouse" in contrast to other "classificatory cross cousins" (i.e., more distant classificatory *yande*) who are also potential spouses. If we may take this single statement at its face value, then there are *two* aspects to this problem.

A man's MBD is not only *an* appropriate spouse, a "potential" spouse; she is *the* appropriate type of relative, his "rightful" spouse.

The first aspect of the problem, then, has to do with potentiality or accessibility; the second has to do with a more narrowly defined rightful claim which applies only to the focal type of this class, and not to the class in its entirety. In regard to this latter, one can ask why this "right" in the first place, and, if there is to be one, why single out the closest genealogical type rather than a more distant type within the class. We can only suppose that by Siriono perception of kinship distance, the type ⚥ MBD satisfies the essential conditions for "kinship distance" and that further increments either do not really increase this in their view, or else are irrelevant, and further, that the Siriono may have found the recognition of a man's "right" to a woman, specifiable with minimum ambiguity, to be something of a necessity or at least an effective means for limiting conflicts over sex and marriage, which tend to be congenital to societies of this scale. An established prior right would reduce the free-for-all. Now, if one is to be assigned a "right" to a spouse from among one's kin, and if there is to be any way (through either formal or informal methods of social control) to assure or "enforce" that right, then it is probably easiest to put into effect when it is assigned to the genealogically simplest type of relationship within the eligible category. Not to do so would be to decrease the assurance of this right, for the longer the genealogical chain to the specified type of woman, the greater the number of competing claimants and the greater the difficulty in marshalling support from intervening concerned parties in pressing one's claim.

Siriono still quarrel over such matters, but it is interesting to note that such quarrels are reported as occurring not between men, but largely between husbands and wives (apparently over too frequent intercourse with other *yande*), between co-wives (presumably over the favors of their common husband), and otherwise between women (Holmberg 1950: 61). Quarrels between men over women and their access to them apparently are relatively infrequent, and it is difficult to avoid the conclusion that a clear system of rights and privileges in respect to kinswomen (or culturally discriminated categories of them) lies behind this relative tranquility.[11]

[11] The case of the Gidjingali, described by Hiatt (1965), does not conssitute negative evidence for this hypothesis. True, the Gidjingali have a system of rights over women in marriage yet engage actively in disputes over the acquisition of them. But this system of rights is by no means as simple as the Siriono system; the rights are more broadly defined, more kintypes are involved, and the nature of the system of rights itself is actually responsible for much conflict. We do not suppose, then, that all such systems of rights over women in marriage are designed, either by conscious intent or social-adaptive or evolutionary processes, to minimize conflict over women. This does not in the least rule out the possibility that some such systems have just that effect.

To conclude this matter, we may point out that it is not necessary to posit a system of asymmetric alliance between descent groups in order to give a reasonable and satsifactory account of the matrilateral cross-cousin marriage prescription of the Siriono. The present account is in better accord with the reported ethnography and is in agreement with the principles which underlie the structure of the system of kin classification. It is not necessary for a student of comparative social structure to anticipate that all instances of a so-called matrilateral cross-cousin marriage prescription may have a similar cause or similar function in relation to the same sort of larger social context.

9 Comparative and Theoretical Considerations

I: Parallel Transmission

Although Siriono kinship terminology is of a "type" not heretofore recognized in conventional typologies, it is not a unique specimen. Its most distinctive classificatory principle, the parallel-transmission rule, occurs also in the kinship systems of the Apinaye, Kayapo, Canella (or Ramkokamekra), and Nambikwara, all in Brazil, and in the kinship system of the Quechua of the Inca capital and surrounding area at the time of the Conquest. These systems are the subjects of studies now in preparation by us and others, so we note only briefly a few of their similarities to and differences from the Siriono system.

The published data for none of these systems are as extensive as those for the Siriono, and all offer some interpretational difficulties. Nevertheless, the basic structural principles are fairly apparent, and one of them is parallel transmission of kin-class status. This is evident in the fact that in all of these systems there is a pronounced tendency for cross-collateral kintypes to take the terminological statuses of their parents of the same sex. Beyond this, however, these systems appear to differ markedly from one another and from the Siriono system, but we think it can be shown that the "surface variation" is due in large part to differing context restrictions placed on the rule of parallel transmission in each case.

Apinaye

Nimuendaju's two accounts (1939: 110–12; 1956: 141–42) of the Apinaye kinship system differ substantially from one another, but this is probably due to editorial interference. For several reasons it seems to us that the Portuguese edition is probably the more reliable, and so we take it as the basic source. From this account it appears that the Apinaye system differs from the Siriono in classifying *all* cross cousins as "grandparents" and also as "grandchildren": an individual of a particular cross-cousin kin-

type may be classified in either way. The principles governing these seemingly alternative classifications are not reported by the ethnographer, but
on analogy with the relative-age opposition evident in the case of the sibling categories, we would hypothesize that a cross cousin is classified as
"grandparent" if he or she is older than ego and as a "grandchild" if younger. It would seem that this is the Apinaye way of maintaining the consistency of reciprocals in the face of the difficulties imposed by the
parallel-transmission rule. (Cf. the Siriono mode, which is to assign
father's sister's children the status "senior" regardless of relative age.)

In addition to this difference from the Siriono system, the Apinaye
lacks a spouse-equation rule. As a corollary, it has a number of distinct
affinal categories. The data on these seem rather meager, but they suggest
that the principle of parallel transmission is operative in the affinal as well
as the consanguineal domain. It is certainly operative in the classification
of the cross step-kin types (FZH, MBW, HZC, WBC) who are "grandparents" and "grandchildren." Unfortunately, there are no data on the
classifications of more remote collaterals such as the children of cross
cousins and their reciprocals the cross cousins of parents. In the Siriono
system, these classifications are affected by the spouse-equation rule, as
well as by considerations of simple generational status (junior or senior),
but since the Apinaye system lacks such a rule it may handle these kintypes
somewhat differently. In the absence of the relevant data, it is not possible
to formulate the precise context restrictions on the principle of parallel
transmission.

Canella

In the Canella or Ramkokamekra kinship system, also reported by Nimuendaju (1946: 104–5), we find some further differences. This system appears
even more Crow-like than the Siriono, for here FZS = F, FZD = FZ =
FM, and conversely, $\male$ MBC = $\male$ C, $\female$ MBC = $\female$ BC = $\female$ CC. In
other words, the cross-cousin classifications meet Murdock's criteria (1949:
224) for a Crow-type system. Again, however, there are no data on the
classifications of cross cousins' children. Even so, it seems clear that this
system does not employ a Crow-type skewing rule, and the extensive
Omaha-like equations which it shares with the Siriono system suggest
quite strongly that it, too, features the rule of parallel transmission.[1] Our
hypothesis is that in this system, as in the Siriono, father's sister's children

---

[1] The Canella system has been the subject of previous studies by Carol Steffens
Schilling and by Roger M. Keesing (both unpublished). We are indebted to them for
their exploration of the possibilities in interpreting Nimuendaju's data and for their
insights into the problems of Gê kinship terminology, though the hypothesis which we
present here differs from both of theirs.

are (arbitrarily) ascribed senior generational status. However, this system does not feature a spouse-equation rule and, apparently, it does not extend parallel transmission into the domain of step-kin by means of a rule like 1.13 (Table 6), an auxiliary of the MBD-FZS spouse-equation rule of the Siriono system, which it could do even though it lacks a spouse-equation rule. FZH is not classified as "grandfather" and WBC is not classified as "grandchild"; these step-kin types are classified under two *affinal* terms, *wawe* or "son-in-law," and *paye* or "man's parent-in-law," respectively. (The classifications of MBW and HZC are not reported.) In the Siriono system, both the FZH classification as "grandfather" and the MBW as "grandmother" are dependent on rule 1.13, and it is the absence of this rule which, apparently, determines that FZH has no consanguineal or kin-class status in the Canella system. FZS cannot take the kin-class status of his father if his father has no such status, but FZS could of course be classified as equivalent to FZH anyway. This would mean that he would have to be classified as a "son-in-law." But he is instead classified as "father," and, conversely, MBC are classified as "children" by male ego, and as "grandchildren" by female ego, exactly as they are in some Crow-type systems (i.e., systems that employ Crow-type skewing rules) but, it would seem, for somewhat different reasons.

FZS may be reckoned as "father" via the parallel-transmission rule if we dispense with the auxiliary 6.3 to that rule, which requires that ♀ S be reckoned as equivalent to ♀ HS (in certain specified contexts). If so; FZS, SR, so apply $6.2^+ \rightarrow$ FMDS, $6.1^+ \rightarrow$ FMS, $3 \rightarrow$ FB, $2 \rightarrow$ F. It must be remembered that rule 6.3 is an auxiliary to the parallel transmission rule, not an essential part of nor a necessary accompaniment to that rule itself; therefore, the presence or absence of the auxiliary constitutes one of the context restrictions on the parallel-transmission rule.

To all appearances, the Canella system extends the parallel-transmission rule into the domain of affinal relatives. Note, for example, the denotata of the "man's parent-in-law" term (*paye*). The foci of this term are WF and, apparently WM,[2] and its additional denotata are WB, WZ, WBS, WBD, the latter two of which are step-kin rather than affinal relatives. The classification of WB and WBS as equivalent to WF and, apparently, of WBD as equivalent to WM are, again, Omaha-like features; the classification of WZ as equivalent to WM is, again, a Crow-like feature.

---

[2] We say "apparently" because *our* inclusion of WM in this category is based on a reconstruction premised on the principle of consistency of reciprocals. Nimuendaju lists WM as *čwei*, along with ♀ BW and male ór female ego's SW. But he lists ♀ BH as *piyoye*, along with ♂ DH, the reciprocal of which is *paye*, WF. It seems that if ♀ DH is *piyoye*, the reciprocal WM should also be *paye*, and thus the listing of WM as *čwei* may be an error. It may also be that we have to deal here with a more complex form of the consistency of reciprocals which is not yet apparent to us.

In other words, the same principle as applies in the consanguineal domain appears to apply in the affinal domain. Exactly how this principle is extended into the affinal domain, and consequently affects the classification of some step-kin, is not determinable from the available data (which is incomplete and, in a few details, also internally inconsistent). Since this system has no spouse-equation rule, which would require that all affinal relations be reckoned as equivalent to certain kinds of consanguineal relations, and which would determine the SENIORITY status to be attributed to affines of one's own generation and to step-kin of other generations, it must posit some other rule for dealing with the latter problem. But, again, it does not seem possible, on the basis of the available data, to specify the nature of that rule. Presumably, FZH is attributed JUNIOR status (even though related to ego through a senior kinswoman), and, conversely, WBC are attributed SENIOR status (even though they are junior kinsmen of ego's wife). This would follow from the attribution of SENIOR status to a man's wife's siblings as linking and as designated relatives.

Another peculiarity of the Canella system must be noted. Nimuendaju reports that MZC are classified *not* as "siblings," as we might expect since FBC are so classified, but as "grandparents" if older than ego and as "grandchildren" if younger than ego. If these data are correct (we have no reason to suppose that they are not), there are at least two ways in which they might be accounted for. The first is that the same-sex sibling merging rule may be weaker in this system than in the Siriono; it may be that MZ is merged with M as a designated kinswoman (and ♀ ZC with ♀ C) but as a linking kinswoman MZ (and ♀ ZC) is subject to the effects of the parallel-transmission rule. This rule would then have to be written in a somewhat stronger form than it was for the Siriono system, in order to reckon MZC as "grandparent" or "grandchild," depending on relative age. The classifications of MZH as "father" and of WZC as "child" are not necessarily a difficulty for this hypothesis, since it is clear from Nimuendaju's data that step-kin merging does not follow the usual pattern either.

The second possibility is that the usual same-sex sibling merging rule may operate in this system, thus reducing MZC to MC. If so, the half-sibling rule may be more restricted than usual, leaving MC to be reckoned as a "second degree relative" and, in this respect, as like a grandparent or grandchild, depending on relative age. Nimuendaju does not report the classifications of half-siblings, though his discussion of the effect of the Canella concept of "co-paternity" on name transmission (1946: 78) suggests that paternal or agnatic half-siblings do call one another "sibling." It would not necessarily follow from this that maternal or uterine half-siblings call one another "sibling," and so we must leave open the pos-siblity that the sibling terms reported by Nimuendaju are in fact paternal or agnatic sibling terms.

Kayapo

So far as we can tell, the Siriono and Canella "decision" to ascribe SENIOR status to father's sister's children was quite arbitrary; they might just as well have chosen to assign that status to mother's brother's chil-dren. It appears that the Kayapo (Dréyfus 1963: 64–68; Turner 1969) have done just that! In this system MBS is classified as "grandfather" (along with MB), and MBD is classified as "mother"; conversely, female ego classifies FZC as "child" and male ego classifies him or her as "grand-child." This is the mirror-image of the Crow-like pattern we find in the Canella system (and, less pronounced, in the Siriono system). Presumably, it is explicable in the same general way. In this system, however, the cross step-kin types *are* assigned categorical statuses as kinds of kin; MBW and FZH are skewed into the grandparent categories, and HZC and WBC are skewed into the grandchild categories. Thus it would seem that MBD could be ascribed the same kin-class status as her mother, i.e., "grand-mother," but she is classified as "mother." However, the extension of the parallel-transmission rule into the domain of the cross step-kin does not necessarily entail the classification of MBD as "grandmother." Again, this is dependent on whether or not the system employs both or only one of the two possible auxiliaries of the parallel-transmission rule. We must suppose that this system, like the Canella, does *not* employ one of the auxiliaries we posited for the Siriono system (again, rule 6.3, Table 6), though it does employ a rule like 1.13, but of course not as an auxiliary of any marriage rule.

T. Turner (1969) reports that Kayapo classify the descendants of certain cross cousins as follows:

"grandfather"	:	MBSS
"sister"	:	MBDD
"brother"	:	MBDS
"child"	:	♂ MBDSC, ♀ MBDDC
"grandchild"	:	♀ MBDSC

Although these classifications are identical to those found in some systems featuring Omaha-type skewing rules, in this case they are most readily accounted for on the assumption that the SENIOR status of the maternal cross cousins as designated kin "carries over" to their statuses as linking kin, one of the reasons being that there is no spouse-equation rule in this system (see Chapter 6). The result is a rather pronounced Omaha-like pattern, but the resemblance is only superficial, just as the resemblance of the Canella system to certain Crow-type systems is only superficial.

Nambikwara

The published data on the Nambikwara kinship system are somewhat confusing (Lévi-Strauss 1948: 19–20), for the system is reported to contain a self-reciprocal term covering the grandchild kintypes *and* siblings of grandparents *but not* the grandparent kintypes themselves. Cecil Cooke, who has recently returned from an extended period among the Nambikwara, informs us that he found the conventional pattern of two reciprocal grandparent and grandchild terms and of extension of these terms to the siblings of grandparents and the grandchildren of siblings. Cross-collateral kin of the first ascending generation (MB, FZ) are classified as "grandparents," but the reciprocal kintypes in the first descending generation (♂ ZC, ♀ BC,) are placed in special "nephew" and "niece" subcategories of the "grandchild" category, as in the Siriono system. The cross cousins are *not* classified as "grandparents" or "nephew" or "niece." Instead there are four special categories for these kintypes: "male ego's male cousin," "male ego's female cousin," female ego's female cousin," and "female ego's male cousin." These are much like Siriono *yande*, in that they are "taken out of" the implicit GRANDKIN supercategory.

The Nambikwara practice *bilateral* cross-cousin marriage, and a classificatory rule expressing this practice is part of their terminological system. This is evident in the fact that spouses' parents are classified as "grandparents" (i.e., they are terminologically equivalent to MB, MBW, FZ, and FZH), and the children-in-law are classified as "nephews" and "nieces." Similarly, the spouses of siblings are classified as though they were cross cousins, as are spouses themselves. To all appearances, the spouse-equation rule in this case is not one that specifies covert structural equivalences between specific kin and affinal types but consists, simply, in the assumption that ego (or his or her sibling) marries a cross-collateral kinsman of his or her own generation (see Scheffler 1970*b*). According to Lévi-Strauss, marriage with cross collaterals of adjacent generations is also permitted, but it has no apparent effect on the *system* of kin classification (though if such marriages occur they may have an effect on how particular kinsmen are classified since they would create alternative possibilities of classification).

Inca

The data on Inca kinship terminology at the time of the Conquest are scattered but relatively full (especially Perez Bocanegra 1631; Gonzales

Holguin 1607; 1608; Santo Thomás 1560a; 1560b). There are of course gaps and certain ambiguities in the data, but they suffice nonetheless, and yield to analysis. They too reveal a principle of parallel transmission of kin-class status, as well as a MBD-FZS—spouse equation (in both respects similar to the Siriono).[3] The Inca system, however, had separate maternal uncle and paternal aunt terms, distinct from the grandparental terms (unlike Siriono in this respect), as well as reciprocal nephew-niece terms correlated with these. These terms were extended to the appropriate first-cross-cousin types by the rule of parallel transmission, and further, to the appropriate affinal types by the MBD-FZS—spouse equation rule. Thus SWF = WB = MBS = MB = WF, all of which are independently attested as being called *caca*. Similarly, and in mirror-image fashion, DHM = HZ (= FZD) = FZ, three of which items are independently attested as *ipa*. There was a separate term for a woman's husband's mother designating this affinal status distinctly, and taking precedence over the more general FZ term. But this term is also extended by the rule of parallel transmission. Thus ♂ DHM = HM = HMM, all independently attested as *quihuach*. It will be noted that these represent transmission in the male line for the male statuses of maternal uncle and (man's) father-in-law, and in the female line for the female statuses of paternal aunt and (woman's) mother-in-law. Similar patterns can be shown for some other terms. There was apparently more than one manner of resolving the "seniority" question, so as to establish complementarity between the domains of these principles, as alternatives are present in the data for certain of the kin-types affected. An additional feature of this system is an apparent three-generation-cycle in the sequence of lineal kinship statuses in both the male and the female lines, as well as among subcategories of sibling classes in their collateral extensions. A seemingly irregular feature of this system is an apparent alternative classification (suggested by data in only one of the sources) by which FB and FBS may be assigned the status (or *one* of the statuses) designated by the term *caca* (MB, MBS; WF, WB), rather than— or in addition to—the normal classifications of *yaya* "father" for FB, and *huauque*, (man's) "brother," for FBS. If the data on this apparent alternative are reliable (as one must assume, in the absence of convincing proof of the contrary supposition), the explanation may lie in the exceptional privileges, or perhaps obligations, involved in the marriages of nobility and royalty, which, in the latter case, could go so far as to permit or specify marriage with an agnatic half sister.

---

[3] A fuller treatment of the Inca kinship system will appear at a later date in a volume entitled *Historical Studies in the Language of Kinship*, by F. G. Lounsbury. This volume will include expanded versions of the Lewis Henry Morgan lectures presented at the University of Rochester in April 1970.

Similar Structures in Other Cultural Domains

Although in the available ethnography on Siriono there is little or nothing to suggest that some other domain of the culture or society is structured by the principle of parallel transmission, such isomorphism is found in many of the cases dealt with just above, most commonly in the form of name transmission. This isomorphism is not readily, if at all, apparent from the published ethnographic sources, and in this section we draw upon the recently completed field research of R. Da Matta, T. Turner, and C. Cooke.[4]

Apinaye social structure is in many ways similar to that of the Siriono. The Apinaye live (ideally) in circular villages which are divided into northern and southern halves. Each half is occupied by a nonexogamous yet allegedly matrilineal moiety (Nimuendaju 1939: 21). Postmarital residence is uxorilocal, and each house contains a number of nuclear families, the maximum number being six (1939: 73). Nimuendaju describes the families of a household as "matrilineally related" (1939: 72), but explicitly states that "there is no organized extended family of any kind." Households average ten "inmates." It would seem, then, that the female nucleus of a household is typically a pair or triplet of sisters (or "sisters"), their husbands, and their offspring (compare to the Siriono "extended family"). The moieties operate only in ceremonial, game, and sporting contexts; they have no religious or economic significance (1939: 22). Each moiety "owns" a series of "great" and "little" personal names, which are sex-linked. According to Nimuendaju (1939: 22), these are transmitted ceremonially from a man to his sister's son and from a woman to her sister's daughter; alternatively, a boy may receive his names from his MMB, and a girl from her MM, MMZ, or her mother's "adoptive" sister.

From this account it would appear that this system of personal name transmission and the system of kin classification are structurally dissimilar, but a more intensive investigation of the system of name transmission has established an interesting relationship. According to Da Matta (1969), Apinaye say a man may not give his names to his sons and a woman may not give hers to her daughters because "they already made the child." Instead, in the case of a boy, a brother or classificatory brother of the father, who is classified as "father" and described in this context as a "substitute father," acts as a "bringer" or "arranger of names." He chooses one of the boy's classificatory grandfathers to pass his names on to the boy. Since the names belong to one or the other of the moieties, the boy then belongs to the moiety to which the names belong. It may or may not be the moiety of his mother. Similarly in the case of a girl, one of her mother's

---

[4] We wish to thank Da Matta, Turner, and Cooke for their generous cooperation in making some of the results of their studies available to us prior to publication. We should note, however, that they do not necessarily endorse our analyses of the Apinaye, Kayapo, and Nambikwara systems of kin classification.

sisters or classificatory sisters chooses one of the girl's classificatory grandmothers to pass her names on to the girl, and the girl belongs to the moiety to which the names belong. The moieties are nonexogamous, but when a woman marries, if she does not belong to the moiety of her husband, she changes her moiety to that of her husband. The moieties, then, are neither matrilineal nor exogamous. It is interesting to note that despite the fact that boys do not take the names of their fathers or girls those of their mothers, the Apinaye, if asked who gave names to a child, always refer to the "arranger of the names," a boy's "fictive" or "substitute father" and a girl's "fictive" or "substitute mother."

After the transmission of the names, the "arranger of the names" is charged with the duty of paying indemnities in cases of defloration or divorce, and those whose names the child has acquired are charged with ceremonial duties in rites of passage (Da Matta 1969).

There is, in addition, a second set of moieties, membership of which is associated with the institution of "formal friendship." A boy's "fictive" or "substitute father" chooses a formal friend for him, and a girl's "fictive" or "substitute mother" chooses a formal friend for her, from whom he or she receives the "marks" of one of the two moieties. The rule is that a boy's formal friend should be the *son* of his "substitute father's" formal friend, and a girl's formal friend should be the *daughter* of her "substitute mother's" formal friend. That is, the formal friend relationship is transmitted from one generation to the next by the rule of parallel transmission; on one side the man and boy concerned are classificatory father and son; on the other they are actual father and son. The "marks" and names of these moieties are not, however, transmitted from actual father and mother to actual son and daughter, respectively.

The moieties composed of men and women who are formal friends of one another, and who share the same "marks," are named Ipognot-xoine and Krenotxoine, and the names signify "people of the center or plaza" and "people of the house or periphery," respectively. According to Nimuendaju (1939: 29–31), the groups with these names are only two of a set of four groups known generically as *kiye*. Nimuendaju reports that membership of the *kiye* is determined by what we have called the principle of parallel transmission, and also that the *kiye* are exogamous and that there are certain prescribed marital relations between them. However, Da Matta found that the other two names, Kraombedy ("beautiful hair") and Kre'kara ("eaves of the house") are *not* the names of additional groups but simply descriptions of certain ritual paraphernalia worn by members of the Ipognotxoine and Krenotxoine moieties. The conclusion must be that Nimuendaju somehow misunderstood his informants, and a system of four *kiye* has never been a part of Apinaye society (compare Maybury-Lewis 1960). However, in spite of his apparent error in regard to the precise nature of the phenomenon, Nimuendaju at least had ascertained that there was *some* kind of principle of parallel transmission operative in this system. So far as moiety membership is concerned (i.e., in the two genuine ones of Nimuendaju's "*kiye*"), the results of the actual principle of transmission and the purported principle as given by Nimuendaju must be the same.

Among the Kayapo the structural isomorphism is on a more tenuous footing. According to Turner (1969) the village consists of uxorilocal extended family households surrounding a central plaza. The plaza is divided into eastern and western halves and each contains a large men's house. The men who meet in these houses are divided into junior and senior age sets. A women's society, also divided into junior and senior age sets, is attached to each men's house. Boys are introduced into a men's house when they are about eight years old by a ceremonial sponsor called a "substitute father"; girls are similarly introduced by "substitute mothers." Here the "substitute fathers" and "mothers" must be nonrelatives. The moieties are nonexogamous and, again, on marriage a woman joins the women's society associated with her husband's men's house, if she is not already a member of it. Men, too, may change their moiety affiliation. In this case moiety affiliation is governed by the principle of parallel transmission, though the same-sex parent-child relationship between sponsor and inductee is fictionalized. One might describe it as being based on parallel transmission within a system of nonconsanguineous godparenthood, rather than within a system of consanguineous godparenthood and parenthood as among the Apinaye.

Name transmission among the Kayapo is determined in yet another manner, which, at least as far as "preferences" in the matter go, might be characterized as an opposite principle of "cross transmission." "Great names" are passed ceremonially from man to boy and woman to girl but not from father to son and mother to daughter; Kayapo say that this is not done because it would cause the early death of the child. The ceremony of transmission is elaborate and may last for several months; it is sponsored by the parents of the child who must provide food for the participants. Many Kayapo do not acquire "great names." According to Turner (1969) "there is a preference for a living mother's brother, especially if he is resident in the same village, to pass on his names to his sister's son," but the preferred name giver for a girl is her father's sister. However, the name giver may be any kinsman of the same sex and of the "grandfather" category (for a boy) or of the "grandmother" category (for a girl), including actual paternal and maternal grandparents.

From Nimuendaju's account (1946), the moiety and name transmission systems of the Canella would seem to be much the same as those of the Kayapo.

The Nambikwara apparently have a less complicated manifestation of the principle of parallel transmission. Although it is not reported in Lévi-Strauss's ethnography (1948), C. Cooke informs us that among the Nambikwara names are transmitted directly from father to son and from mother to daughter.

The evidence is also quite clear that inheritance of family names among the Inca followed this same principle, that is, they were transmitted from father to son and from mother to daughter. Apparently not all children bore an inherited family name, however; some took on "new names" (see Nuñez del Prado 1957; also Lounsbury n.d.).

Obviously, much remains to be said about the systems of kin classification and the social systems of these several societies. For example, it is interesting to note that Apinaye and Kayapo forbid the direct transmission of any names from father to son and mother to daughter, though in the case of the Apinaye *kiye* names the result is the same as it would be if the formal friendship relation were directly transmitted. But Nambikwara and Inca both practice direct father-to-son and mother-to-daughter name transmission (though note that in the Inca case family rather than personal names are involved). This suggests the hypothesis that underlying the parallel transmission of kin-class status there is some (perhaps variable) notion of an essential identity between same-sex parent and child, and that although this notion finds expression in the systems of kin classification of all these societies, opposite conclusions have been drawn from this postulate or premise, at least with respect to its implications for other forms of behavior. In some cases it is reasoned that it is therefore "natural" to transmit names directly in the same way, but in others it is reasoned that this identity implies that it is dangerous to transmit names directly. In these latter cases names are still transmitted from generation to generation and between kin, but being sex-linked they are passed from MB to ZS, FZ to BD, MZ to ZD, or between persons otherwise related as "grandparent" and "grandchild," or they are transmitted by means of fictionalized father–son and mother–daughter relationships. Thus, the transmission of names in "cross" (MB $\rightarrow$ ZS, FZ $\rightarrow$ BD) or fictionalized "parallel" fashion, rather than actual "parallel" (F $\rightarrow$ S, M $\rightarrow$ D) fashion, might equally be a consequence of a posited essential identity of same-sex parent and child. It seems probable that different supplementary premises would underlie this drawing of opposed conclusions from the same cultural premise.

These brief notes will suffice to make our point: the Siriono system of kin classification is not unique. Aside from the fact that it shares several of its more familiar principles (i.e., the same-sex sibling merging rule, the half-sibling rule, and the step-kin rule) with a vast number of otherwise quite different kinship terminologies, its most fundamental and characteristic principle of classification probably occurs also in several other systems. One of these (the Inca) also shares the MBD-FZS–spouse equation rule. All of these systems are found on the South American continent, but they belong to societies widely separated in time and space, and widely divergent in language, culture, and social structure. So far as the available data permit us to say, there is no necessary correlation between type of terminological system (as determined by the distinctive equivalence rules of a system) and one or another particular aspect of social structure. This is not to suggest that no correlations are to be found or that systems of kin classification exist *in vacuo*, not being affected by or themselves affecting other domains of social life—as we see it, the evidence is all to the contrary. It is rather that a correlation noted in one case is not *necessarily* to be expected in another, and that the correlations may be either direct or indirect (as where name transmission follows a rule that is different from but complementary to that which governs the intergenerational transmission of kin-class status).

II : The MBD-FZS–Spouse Equation Rule

The other distinctive rule of the Siriono system of kin classification is the MBD-FZS–spouse equation rule, and just as the parallel transmission rule is not confined to the Siriono system, neither is this one. At this point it hardly bears repeating that certain classificatory systems which feature this rule have been interpreted in other ways, principally as systems of "social categories" which are integral parts of systems of asymmetric affinal alliance between unilineal descent groups or major social categories. In claiming that these classificatory systems are in fact kinship systems and that they feature MBD-FZS–spouse equation rules, we have not intended to suggest that the social structural bases or ramifications of these rules are the same as those outlined for the Siriono case in Chapter 8. Indeed, at the conclusion of Chapter 8 we indicated that we would not expect the rule necessarily to have the same basis or functions in all cases, any more than we would expect the same of *any* rule of kin classification. But to allow for convergent development of the same rule in different systems and for different reasons, causes, motives, etc., is not necessarily to rule out the possibility of a strong tendency for a particular rule of kin classification to develop in a particular kind of social or cultural context, which context may be widely recurrent. We suggested, for example, that the Siriono MBD-FZS–spouse equation rule rests on the right of each man to claim his MBD as a wife and that this right may represent one form of adjustment to the problem of access to women, a problem that tends to recur in societies of this scale. But we see no evident need to suppose that this is the only possible way of dealing with these problems, or to suppose that these are the only problems to which rightful claims over particular kinds of kins-women might constitute a reasonably adaptive response.

The point, then, is that it could be that the Siriono case is highly exceptional in some respects; in particular, it could be that in most other cases of the occurrence of the MBD-FZS–spouse equation rule, the social structural basis of the rule is a system of intergroup marital exchange. One or two other cases similar to the Siriono could be cited (see Petrullo 1939 on the Yaruro of Venezuela) to show that the Siriono case is not unique, at least insofar as the social structural base of its spouse-equation rule is concerned. Yet, a fairly extensive search of the ethnographic litera-ture has convinced us that the MBD-FZS–spouse equation rule is, by and large, confined to societies featuring asymmetric political-affinal alliance between unilineal descent groups (see below). It should be evident that in acknowledging this we are not conceding to the arguments of those who maintain that the systems of kin classification of these societies are really systems of social classification; note that we do not speak of "asymmetric alliance systems" in Needham's (1960: 99–106) holistic sense (see also Lévi-Strauss 1969: 365), but simply of asymmetric political-affinal alli-ance between unilineal descent groups, which we show below is a quite different matter.

In order to avoid further confusion and needless bebate, we should document our claims for at least some of these other societies and their systems of kin classification. We do not regard the following discussions of a few relevant cases as providing anything like adequate demonstrations of our claims about them. Such demonstrations will have to await another occasion—for each would require almost as much space and discussion as Chapters 4, 5, 6, and 8, which are devoted specifically to the Siriono data. We limit our observations to specification of the exact phrasing of the most distinctive equivalence rules of each of these systems, and where necessary we note those aspects of the superclass and subclass structure that may tend to obscure the basically simple structures of these systems. Lexical forms that may be employed (largely in referential usage) to distinguish between primary and extended senses of the terms are reported—but sel-dom systematically—for all of the systems dealt with below. It hardly seems necessary to analyze these in detail here, though of course analysis of them is necessary to a complete account of the semantics of any system of kin classification.

Kinship terminologies employing the MBD-FZS–spouse equation rule are, it seems, most common in Asia, for example, in the systems of the Purum (Das 1945), Thado (Shaw 1929; Hutton 1922), and Lakher (Parry 1932; Lorrain 1951), who are Kuki-speaking peoples living in the Assam-Burma border region. Many linguistically and culturally related Chin-speaking peoples have similar systems of kin classification, e.g., Kachin (Leach 1945; 1954) and Haka Chin (Lehman 1963). The kinship terminology of the Gilyak of Sakhalin Island (Sternberg 1933 [1964]) also features this rule, and so do several systems found in Indonesia, e.g., those of the Toba and Karo Batak of Sumatra (on the latter see Singarimbun 1965), and that of the people of the Manggarai region of Flores Island (see Fischer 1957). Indeed, aside from the Siriono and Inca cases noted above, we cannot cite another genuine example of the occurrence of this rule outside of Asia.

In most of these cases, the MBD-FZS–spouse equation rule is superimposed on systems whose other most distinctive equivalence rule is some form of Omaha-type skewing rule. But this is not a necessary relationship. The Toba Batak have a system based on a variant of the Omaha principle,[5] and the Karo Batak and Manggarai systems feature no rules of intergenerational transmission of kin-class status (see below).

The Gilyak Kinship System

Sternberg's (1933 [1964]) data on the Gilyak system of kin classification are presented in Table 9, which has been constructed from observations scattered throughout his report.[6] The structure of the table presupposes the following comments.

The only problematic aspect of this system concerns its interesting subclass structure (see Table 10 and Figure 8). We may begin by considering the term *akhmalk* (Number 6). Sternberg glosses this term as "father-in-law," but it is used by both male and female ego to designate the mother's brother. Therefore, its focal denotatum must be MB; the term is extended, via an Omaha-skewing rule, to the male agnatic descendants of the MB, and via the MBD-FZS–spouse equation rule, to a man's WF and his male agnatic descendants. Sternberg does not report what a woman calls her HF. Any man classified as "mother's brother" may also be classified as *atk*, "grandfather," but kinsmen of the second ascending generation may not be classified as *akhmalk*. It is clear from this that "mother's brother" is a subclass of the "grandfather" class; and MB (like ♂ ZC and ♀ BC for Siriono) must be treated as a subfocus, as a

---

[5] Batak data available to us are from Mrs. H. L. Tobing, Instructor in Indonesian at Yale University and herself a Batak, who has been Lounsbury's collaborator in a seminar on the analysis of kinship systems. Analysis of the Batak data will be presented in another publication.

[6] The data as presented here are from the English translation of Sternberg's reports compiled by the Human Relations Area Files, 1964. The data presented in Lévi-Strauss (1969: 292–94) were taken from another translation and are sometimes confusing and self-contradictory. The translation from which Lévi-Strauss worked appears to have contained a number of errors. In particular, the Human Relations Area Files translation shows that HF is not classified as *akhmalk* (MB), although WF is. This obviates the necessity of Lévi-Strauss's argument on the subject of female ego's classification of her affines (1969: 296–98).

Table 9

GILYAK KINSHIP TERMINOLOGY

Term	Focus*	Derivative Denotata
1. *ytk*	F	FB, FFBS, FMZS, MFZS, MH, MZH, WFZH, HMB
2. *ymk*	M	MZ, MFBD, MMZD, FMBD, FW, FBW, WFZ, HMBW
3. *ogla*	S, D	♂ BC, ♀ ZC, ♂ MBDC, ♀ FZSC, WC, HC, WZC, HBC, ♂ FZSSW
	[CC]	[also: all kin, step-kin, and affines two or more descending generations removed from ego]
	[♂ ZC]	[also: male ego's FZC, FFZC, DH, ZH, FZH, FZSC, etc.]
4. *atk*	FF, MF	all male kin, step-kin, and affines two or more ascending generations removed from ego;
	[MB]	[also: MBS, MBSS, WF, WB, WBS, etc.]
5. *achik*	FM, MM	all female kin, step-kin, and affines two or more ascending generations removed from ego; also: MBW, MBSW, WM, WBW, WBSW, etc.
6. *akhmalk*	MB (cf. 4)	MBS, MBSS, FMBS, FMBSS, WF, WB, WBS, etc.
7. *ymgi*	♂ ZS (cf. 3)	male ego's FZS, FFZS, FFZSS, DH, ZH, FZH, FFZH, etc. female ego's DH, HZS, HFZS, etc.
8. *nern*	♂ ZD (cf. 3)	male ego's FZD, FZSD, FFZD, FFZSD, DHZ, ZHZ, FZHZ, etc. female ego's HZD, HFZD, HZH, etc.
9. *tuvn*	B, Z	FBC, MZC, FMBDC, MFZSC, FZSW, MBDH, WFZC, HMBC, WZH, HBW, ♀ BW
akhand	[B⁺]	
nanakhand	[Z⁺]	FZ, HM,
askhand	[B⁻, Z⁻]	♀ BC
10. *angej*	♂ MBD	male ego's WZ, BW, MZSW, MBSD, FBSW, FMBSD, MFBSD, MMZSD,
	[♂ SW]	[WBD, WBSD]
11. *pu*	♀ FZS	female ego's HB, ZH, MZDH, FBDH, FFZSD, FFBDD, FMZDD, etc.
12. *navkh*	♂ WB, ♂ ZH	male ego's WBS, MBSS, ZH, FZH, FFZS, FFZSS, FFZH, MBS, FZS, etc.
13. *jokh*	♂ SW (cf. 10)	WBD, WBSD
14. *mam*	W	
15. *yrkh*	H	

*Brackets indicate subcategories

193

Table 10

RECIPROCAL SETS IN GILYAK KINSHIP TERMINOLOGY

1.	$\dfrac{atk\ [akhmalk] + achik,}{ogla\ [ymgi + nern],}$	i.e.,	$\dfrac{(\text{FF} + \text{MF [MB]}) + (\text{FM} + \text{MM})}{(\text{SS} + \text{SD}) + (\text{DD [\male ZS]} + \text{DD [\male ZD]})}$
2.	$\dfrac{ytk + ymk}{ogla}$	i.e.,	$\dfrac{(\text{F}) + (\text{M})}{(\text{S} + \text{D})}$
3.	$\dfrac{tuvn\ [akhand + nankhand]}{tuvn\ [askhand]}$	i.e.,	$\dfrac{(\text{Sb}^+ [(\text{B}^+) + (\text{Z}^+)])}{(\text{Sb}^- [\text{B}^- + \text{Z}^-])}$
4.	$\dfrac{navkh}{navkh}$	i.e.,	$\dfrac{\male\ \text{WB}}{\male\ \text{ZH}}$
5.	$\dfrac{angej\ [jokh]}{pu}$	i.e.,	$\dfrac{(\male\ \text{MBD} [\male\ \text{SW}])}{(\female\ \text{FZS} [\female\ \text{HF}])}$
6.	$\dfrac{mam}{yrkh}$	i.e.,	$\dfrac{(\text{W})}{(\text{H})}$

labeled node in a pathway of reduction. The reduction in this case termi-
nates in the kintype MF. The reciprocal "man's sister's child" class is
likewise a subclass (divided into two sexually distinguished classes, *ymgi*
and *nern*) of the "grandchild" class. The "grandchild" class is here labeled
by the same term as the "child" class. This is not an unusual arrangement;
it is found in many Omaha-type systems (see Hutton 1921) and in some
Crow-type systems too (see Goodenough 1956; Scheffler 1970a). It is
evident that this system employs an Omaha-type skewing rule, but the
question is which one. Since MB must be reduced to MF, it would seem
that the Omaha-type-III rule

$$(\dots \female\ \text{B} \longrightarrow \dots \female\ \text{F}) \equiv (\male\ \text{Z} \dots \longrightarrow \male\ \text{D} \dots)$$

is appropriate. Note, however, that FZ is classified as "elder sister" and,
conversely, a woman classifies her brother's children as "younger siblings."
These classifications are characteristic of Omaha-type-II systems, i.e.,
those using the rule

$$(\text{FZ} \longrightarrow \text{Z}) \equiv (\female\ \text{BC} \longrightarrow \female\ \text{Sb}).$$

Combined with classifications generated by an Omaha-type-III skewing
rule, these classifications indicate that the skewing rule utilized in this
system is stronger (i.e., more pervasive) than either the Omaha-type-II or
Omaha-type-III rule. The appropriate rule in this case is one that treats
a woman's brother as structurally equivalent to her father in all genealogical contexts other than female ego's brother as a designated kinsman;
conversely, a man's sister is regarded as structurally equivalent to his

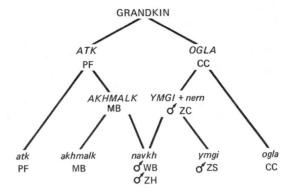

Figure 8.   Gilyak Kinship Terminology: Some subclass relations

daughter in all genealogical contexts other than male ego's sister as a designated kinswoman. This is an example of the Omaha-type-IV skewing rule, one that "evacuates" both the paternal aunt and maternal uncle classes (Lounsbury 1964a: 377). The fact that there is a "mother's brother" category in this system does not contradict this interpretation since the "mother's brother" class is a subclass of the "grandfather" class.

The appropriate phrasing of the Omaha-skewing rule in this case is:

$$(\ldots/\venus\ B/\ldots \rightarrow \ldots/\venus\ F/\ldots) \equiv (\ldots/\mars\ Z/\ldots \rightarrow \ldots/\mars\ D/\ldots).$$

The slashes in the formula indicate that a sequence of three dots must be prefixed *or* postfixed, or both, to the kintypes ♀ B and ♂ Z; or, in other words, a woman's brother and a man's sister are to be regarded as structurally equivalent to their father and daughter, respectively, in all genealogical contexts *other than* as designated kinsmen. Apparently, the rule is only optionally applicable to the kintypes MB and male ego's ZC as designated kinsmen; it is always applied to them as linking kinsmen. Thus, MB may be designated as *akhmalk* or *atk* and male ego may designate his sister's child as *ymgi* or *nern*, or as *ogla*. Sternberg's account gives no indication of the conditions under which Gilyak chose to apply or not to apply the rules in these genealogical contexts.

The nature of the *navkh* category is problematic, but the accuracy of the interpretation offered here is not particularly critical to our analysis of the system as a whole. There is no question that this term is used self-reciprocally between male cross cousins and male siblings-in-law. Sternberg apparently understood it to be primarily a "man's brother-in-law" term. However, he reports that it is used also between MBS–FZD; and a woman may address her "sweethearts," which would include her FZS, as *navkh*. Also, *navkh* is the term "which the members of the *ymgi* and *akhmalk* clans of the corresponding generations give to one another (1933 [1964: 193]) (though it may be that the intended reference here is to male ego only). It may be, then, that *navkh* is a general "cousin" term which is extended to at least some siblings-in-law, but it may also be that it is a "man's brother-in-law" term that may be used metaphorically by both sexes of ego in the sense of "comrade." We treat *navkh* as a "man's brother-in-law" term, though, again, this interpretation is not particularly critical to our analysis. From this perspective, *navkh*, like Siriono *yande*, is a subclass of the grandparent and grandchild classes. The designation as *navkh* is, again, optional; men designated as *navkh* may also be designated *atk*, *akhmalk* or *ymgi*, *ogla*. Thus, a man's MBS, for example, may be classified as if he were MF, MB, or WB, and, conversely, a man's FZS may be classified as if he were DS, ZS, or ZH.

It should be virtually self-evident that this system employs a MBD-FZS–spouse equation rule. What we have to determine is exactly how that rule should be phrased. Although a man may call his wife *angej* and a woman may call her husband *pu*, there are special terms for "wife" and "husband" (literally "old woman" and "old man," the "old" indicating respect). Thus it would seem that, like Siriono *yande*, *angej* and *pu* connote a potential affinal status and designate the categories of the kin ($\male$ MBD, $\female$ FZS) to which that status is ascribed. Like Siriono *yande*, these terms are extended to siblings-in-law of the appropriate sex.

It would seem, however, that a Gilyak man may at times refer to his wife by the term designating the kind of kinswoman she is, and a woman may refer to her husband by the term designating the kind of kinsman he is. Thus, we may write the MBD-FZS–spouse equation rule in kin classification in much the same way as we did for the Siriono system. Here, however, we know which second cousins are classified as potential spouses and we may say definitely that a man's MBD and a woman's FZS are regarded as structurally equivalent to W and H, respectively, in all contexts other than as designated kinsmen. Yet the data concerning distant collateral kintypes are less than full, and it is therefore not entirely clear which corollaries and possible auxiliaries of the marriage rule should be posited for this system. Sternberg reports that the *akhmalk* of one's own *akhmalk* are regarded as one's *akhmalk*, too, and conversely the *ymgi* of one's own *ymgi* are regarded as one's *ymgi*, though as "distant *akhmalk*" and "distant *ymgi*." That is, the men of one's mother's mother's clan (e.g., MMBS) are classified as *akhmalk* or as *atk*. By the Omaha rule they are *atk* and their sisters are *achik* ("grandmothers"), but it is difficult to be certain about how these men may be classified as *akhmalk*. One possible way is by means of the same auxiliary to the spouse-equation rule as we posited for the Siriono system in order to account for the fact that there a man's FZDC is classified as though he or she were a man's "sister's child" (see rule 1.14, Table 6). However, Sternberg does not report how a man classifies his FZDC in the Gilyak system; by the Omaha rule these kintypes would be classified as "grandchilden," but they would be ("ideally" at least) members of ego's *ymgi's ymgi* clan and of the first descending generation, so they may be classifiable as *ymgi* and *nern*. If so, the Siriono spouse-equation rule auxiliary 1.14 is appropriate here too.

The other auxiliary (1.13, Table 6) we posited for the Siriono spouse-equation rule also seems appropriate, but in an even stronger form. Note that a woman's HZC is classified as though he or she were a "man's sister's child." A pair of terms normally used by male ego only may be used by female ego in this special circumstance. (Likewise, a woman's DH is classified as *ymgi*, but this is by a corollary of the spouse-equation rule which equates ♀ DH with ♀ HZS.) But note also that a woman classifies her BW as "sibling"; though unreported, the reciprocal HZ must be "sibling" also. In this case, then, the auxiliary to the spouse-equation rule must be written:

$$(.♀ \text{ HZ} \longrightarrow .♂\text{Z}) \equiv (♀ \text{ BW.} \longrightarrow ♀ \text{ B.})$$

This is to say that a woman classifies her HZ as though she were a male ego's sister (i.e., the woman takes the perspecitve of her husband). Thus, it seems likely that female ego's FZD and MBD are classified as "siblings," though Sternberg does not report this.

The spouse-equation rule here takes priority over the Omaha-skewing rule, just as it takes priority over the transmission rule in the Siriono system.

Gilyak Society

Gilyak, like Siriono, regard a man's MBD as his most appropriate potential spouse and ascribe him a rightful claim over her in marriage; she belongs to him "by right of birth." As among Siriono, MBD and FZS have not only the right to marry but also privileges of sexual access both before and after their respective marriages. This latter privilege extends to *angej* and *pu* in general, but after marriage it is exercised largely by the brothers of a woman's husband. Among some Gilyak groups the privilege is not extended to elder brothers, who therefore classify the wives of their younger brothers as *jokh*, i.e., as though they were the wives of sons. When a man marries his MBD he does not have to pay brideprice for her, because she is his rightful spouse. Note, however, that in some other societies where men have rightful claims over their MBD as wives, they must pay brideprice for these women. Here, again, we encounter a situation in which the same cultural premise may lead to opposed conclusions in different societies.

Unlike the Siriono, Gilyak are ordered into an indeterminate number of small, corporate descent groups (patrilineal). They distinguish between kin of one's own clan ("clan people"), kin of the mother's (or MB's) clan (*akhmalk* kin), and, conversely, kin of the sister's son's clan (*ymgi*) kin. All such persons are regarded as *pandf*, "cognates" or kin (from the verb *pandynd*, "to be born"). Clans whose members are "mother's brothers" and "sister's sons" in respect of one another are linked by affinal as well as consanguineal ties, by virtue of the fact that men have rightful claims over their MBDs in marriage. The right is based on the nature of the cognatic link.

According to Sternberg (1933 [1964: 76]) Gilyak, say "you must take your wives from whence you came, from the clan of your mother," and he adds that Gilyak "prefer" to marry their MBDs, or agnatic kinswomen of their mothers. Although he notes that there is a "persistent tendency" to do just this, he reports that choice of a spouse is *not* restricted to women of the mother's clan. Not only may a man take a wife from his mother's mother's brother's clan (his "distant *akhmalk*" clan), he may take a wife from any clan in which he has *akhmalk* and therefore *angej* (e.g., his FMB's clan, which may or may not be the same as his mother's clan), from among even more distant *akhmalk* clans, or from among nonkin. Furthermore, he may marry a woman from a clan related to his own clan as the *ymgi* of its own "distant *ymgi*." Thus it is not so much that marriage is prescribed with an *angej* as it is that a man is prohibited from marrying a woman he classifies as *nern*, if she is related to him within second-cousin range; beyond that range, he may marry even a *nern*. Thus, choice of a spouse is not restricted to women of clans which have already given wives to men of ego's clan, but if a man marries a nonkinswoman, her kin are classified as though they were ego's *akhmalk*, etc., and her clan becomes a potential source of wives for other men of ego's clan.

Sternberg (see also Lévi-Strauss 1969: Chapter 18) argues that the Gilyak system of kin classification is predicated on a system of interclan marital alliance wherein each clan has a rightful claim over all the women of another clan, but his detailed ethnographic account makes it clear that this is not the case. A man has the right to marry any *angej*, but he has a rightful claim over only one or a few *angej*, i.e., his proper *angej* or his MBD. It would appear that when a man chooses to exercise his rightful claim and to marry a MBD, he perpetuates or further consolidates a marital (and consanguineal) alliance that already exists between two clans; the same thing may be accomplished by marriage between classificatory *angej* and *pu*. But when a man chooses to marry a nonkinswoman, this establishes an alliance between their clans. However, while it would seem that marriages between their individual members may have implications for relations between clans, the arranging of marriages is not the concern of clans as corporate wholes. Sternberg's account contains little to suggest that clans as such figure in the formation of marital contracts.

The Kachin (Jinghpaw) Kinship System

A somewhat similar system of kin classification is found among the Kachin of Burma. Our data on this system are presented in Table 11 and Figure 9.[7] Again, this is just an Omaha-type system with an overlaid MBD-FZS–spouse equation rule. As such, the essential problem in its analysis is to specify the exact forms of the Omaha-skewing rule and the spouse-equation rule.

The solution requires first the recognition of certain subclass relations, which are perhaps less readily apparent than are those in the Siriono and Gilyak cases. Once these are recognized, however, the nature of the system is clearly evident and its solution is straightforward. The skewing rule is of the Omaha-type-II variety (FZ $\longrightarrow$ Z$^+$) $\equiv$ ($\female$ BC $\longrightarrow$ $\female$ B$^-$/Z$^-$), and the spouse-equation rule can be expressed simply as an equation of a man's father-in-law with his maternal uncle (WF $\longrightarrow$ MB) and, conversely, of a man's daughter's husband with his sister's son ($\male$ DH $\longrightarrow$ $\male$ ZS).

The critical subclass relations are those between *moi* and *na*, between *gu* and *khau*, and between *nam*, *nau*, and *khau*. These are diagrammed in Figure 9 (a, b, c).

Moi and *na* are related as special subclass and residue subclass respectively, of a larger unlabeled structural class symbolized here as *NA* (see Figure 9a). This latter is nothing other than an Omaha-type-II "elder sister" class based on an equivalence of FZ with elder sister. That there is some underlying categorical equivalence between these subclasses in Kachin can be seen, among other ways, in the fact that for female ego the husbands of both *na* (Z$^+$, etc.) and *moi* (FZ, FFZ, etc.) are *gu*. That this is not also true in the case of male ego is due only to the priority of the self-reciprocal "man's own-generation brother-in-law" term *khau* (see below). As between *na* and *moi*, *moi* is the marked term of this opposition and *na* is the unmarked term. The distinctive feature of *moi*, over and above those of the superclass *NA*, is "not own-generation" ($\sim$g$^=$). The residue class *na*, then, is confined to ego's own generation.

Khau and *gu* are related to each other, and to a larger unlabeled structural class symbolized here as *GU*, in a somewhat similar way (see

[7] Kachin data at our disposal are from Dr. LaRaw Maran, himself a Kachin as well as a social anthropologist and linguist. The use of the Kachin kinship terminology will be dealt with more fully in another study.

Table 11

KACHIN KINSHIP TERMINOLOGY

Term	Focus	Some Derivative Denotata
1. *ji*	FF, MF	FFB, MFB, FMB, MMB, MMBS, MMBSS, WMB, WBWB, FMZH, MFZH, MMZH
2. *woi*	FM, MM	MFZ, FMZ, MMZ, FFBW, MFBW, MMBW
3. *šu*	SS, SD, DS, DD	reciprocals of (1) and (2)
4. *wa*	F	FB, FFBS, FMZS, MFZS, MH, MZH, FMBDH, MFBDH, MMZDH, HMB
5. *nu*	M	MZ, MFBD, MMZD, FMBD, FW, FBW, MFZSW, FFBSW, FMZSW, WFZ
6. *ša*	S, D	reciprocals of (4) and (5)
7. *phu*	B$^+$	FBS, MZS, FMBDS, MFZSS, FFBSS, FMZSS, MMZDS, MFBDS, if older
8. *na*	Z$^+$	FBD, MZD, FMBDD, MFZSD, FFBSD, FMZSD, MMZDD, MFBDD, if older
9. *nau*	B$^-$, Z$^-$	reciprocals of (7) and (8), WFZC, HMBC
10. *tsa*	MB	MMZS, MFBS, ♀ MBS, ♀ MBSS, ♀ MBSSS, WF, WFB, ♀ BWF, ♀ BWB, ♀ BWBS
11. *ni*	MBW	MMBD, MMBSD, MMBSSD, MBSW, MBSSW, WM, WMZ, WBW, ♂ SWM, ♀ BSWM, ♀ BWM
12. *khri*	♂ ZS, ♂ ZD	reciprocals of (10) and (11)
13. *moi*	FZ	FFZ, HM, HFM, ZHM, ZHFM
14. *gu*	Z$^+$H	FZH, FFZH, FZHF, HF, HFF, ZHF, ZHFF, ♀ FZS$^+$, ♀ MFZDS$^+$, ♀ FFZSS$^+$, ♀ FFBDS$^+$, ♀ FMZDS$^+$
15. *nam*	♀ BS, ♀ BD	reciprocals of (13) and (14)
16. *rat*	♂ MBD$^+$	male ego's MMBDD, FMBSD, MFBSD, MMZSD, B$^+$W, WZ$^+$
	♀ FZS$^-$	female ego's MFZDS, FFZSS, FFBDS, FMZDS, Z$^-$H, HB$^-$
17. *khau*	♂ ZH, WB	male ego's FZS, MBS, MMBDS, FMBSS, MFZDS, FFZSS, MFBSS, MMZSS, FFBDS, FMZDS
18. *ning*	♀ BW, HZ	female ego's MBD, FZD, MMBDD, FMBSD, MFZDD, FFZD, FFZSD, MBSD, MFBSD, MMZSD, FFBDD, FMZDD, HFZ, HFFZ, BSW, BWBD, BWBSD, FZHZ, FFZHZ

Figure 9b), but with two differences from the arrangement just described for *na*, *moi*, and *NA*. The denotata of *khau* are drawn only in part from *GU*; since it is a self-reciprocal term, it draws similarly from the reciprocal structural class *NAM* (see below), and since it neutralizes the elder-young-

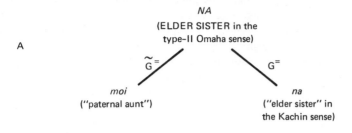

A

NA
(ELDER SISTER in the
type-II Omaha sense)

$\tilde{G}^{=}$ $G^{=}$

moi
("paternal aunt")

na
("elder sister" in
the Kachin sense)

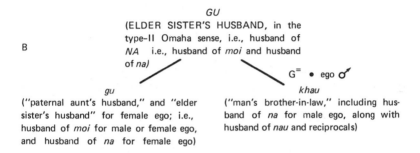

B

GU
(ELDER SISTER'S HUSBAND, in the
type-II Omaha sense, i.e., husband of
NA i.e., husband of *moi* and husband
of *na)*

$G^{=}$ • ego ♂

gu
("paternal aunt's husband," and "elder
sister's husband" for female ego; i.e.,
husband of *moi* for male or female ego,
and husband of *na* for female ego)

khau
("man's brother-in-law," including husband of *na* for male ego, along with
husband of *nau* and reciprocals)

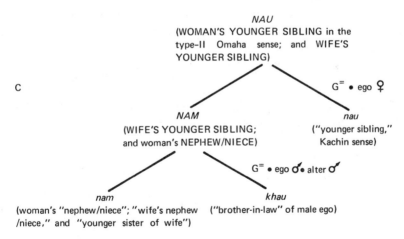

C

NAU
(WOMAN'S YOUNGER SIBLING in the
type-II Omaha sense; and WIFE'S
YOUNGER SIBLING)

$G^{=}$ • ego ♀

NAM
(WIFE'S YOUNGER SIBLING;
and woman's NEPHEW/NIECE)

nau
("younger sibling,"
Kachin sense)

$G^{=}$ • ego ♂• alter ♂

nam
(woman's "nephew/niece"; "wife's nephew
/niece," and "younger sister of wife")

khau
("brother-in-law" of male ego)

Figure 9. Kachin Kinship Terminology: Some subclass relations

er opposition, it includes certain members outside of both *GU* and *NAM*.
The other difference from the *na-moi-NA* arrangement is that whereas
the special subclass *moi* was defined by only a single additional distinctive
feature ($\sim g^{=}$), the special subclass drawn from *GU* by the overlapping and

higher-priority category *khau* is defined by a double criterion: the designated types must be of ego's generation ($g^=$), and ego must be male (ego ♂). *Khau* is the marked term in its opposition to *gu*, as it is also in its opposition to *nam*. Since the special class drawn from *GU* and designated by *khau* is defined by the conjunction of two distinctive features (rather than by one), the residue class designated by *gu* is only disjunctively definable. (The complement of a class product, if greater than zero, is a class sum.) Thus *gu* applies to the husbands of all *moi* for either male or female ego, and to the husbands of all *na* for female ego only.

Finally, since *nam* is reciprocal to both *moi* and *gu*, and since *nau* is related to *nam* in the way in which *na* is related to *moi*, and since *khau* is related to *nam* in the way in which *khau* is related to *gu*, the class and subclass taxonomy involving *nam*, *nau* and *khau* is superficially more complex in appearance (see Figure 9c), but it derives entirely from the two reciprocal sets just described. It results in a three-level taxonomy, the structure of which is adequately shown in the diagram. It needs only to be noted that the unmarked term *nau* which is unrestricted as to sex of ego, draws only half of its membership from the structural superclass *NAU*, this portion, of course, being just those cases where ego is female. Since this subclass of *NAU* is defined by the conjunction of two features ($g^= \cdot$ ego ♀), the residue class *NAM* is necessarily disjunctive. And since the special subclass of *NAM* covered by the overlapping higher-priority term *khau* is defined by the conjunction of three features ($g^= \cdot$ ego ♂ $\cdot$ alter ♂), the residue class designated by the term *nam* is still further disjunctive. But since *NAU* is reciprocal to both *NAU* and *GU* (as the term *nam* is the common reciprocal of both *moi* and *gu* throughout their entire ranges, on the basis of a husband's using his wife's term for her cross nephews and nieces), the structural class *NAU* is disjunctive to begin with: for female ego it is a consanguineal category, but for male ego it is an affinal category. This underlying disjunctivity remains in the polysemy of the term *nam*; it is only modified by the restrictions resulting from the overlap of the higher-priority terms *nau* and *khau*.

With these details about the relations between classes, subclasses, and reciprocal classes made clear (as they have to be in any case, no matter what hypothesis one may entertain about the underlying nature of the categories themselves and of the system), it becomes possible to recognize the fundamental equivalence rules of the system. As noted in advance, it is an Omaha-type-II system with an overlaid spouse-equation rule which is most simply specified as an equivalence of wife's father with mother's brother and of a man's daughter's husband with his sister's son. We specify the spouse-equation rule in this way for essentially structural reasons, but the sociological appropriateness of this specification is indicated below. Note, however, that if the rule (WF → MB) ≡ (♂ DH → ♂ ZS) is posited, the rule ($\triangle$ MBD ... $\longrightarrow$ $\triangle$ WZ ...), etc. has to be drawn as a corollary of it. Therefore, we may speak of a MBD-FZS–spouse equation rule in kin classification in this system, though it should be remembered that there the rule has the status of a corollary of a more fundamental rule.

Besides these, the usual same-sex sibling merging and half-sibling rules hold; and an additional rule must describe the fact that a man uses his wife's term for her brother's children (as noted above in the discussion of *nam*), and a woman uses her husband's term for his sister's children (*khri*, reciprocal to both *tsa* and *ni*). All of the rest follows from these rules, including a number of other class and subclass relations that follow from the marriage rule. For example, a man's *gu* and his patrilateral *khau* (both affinal categories) are taken out of, or overlaid on, the male half of his *KHRI* (a consanguineal category), thus restricting his male *khri*, his "nephews," to the first descending generation. No such affinal categories are overlaid on or withdrawn from the female half of his *KHRI*, allowing a man to have female *khri*, "nieces," not only in the generation of his male *khri* but in all generations above that as well, including the sisters of his *gu* and of his patrilateral *khau* as well as the sisters of his male *khri*, i.e., in the usual extension of this category in Omaha-type-II systems.

Kachin Society

According to our information, a Kachin man is entitled to claim one of his sisters' sons as a husband for one of his daughters; thus, a man may be obliged to marry a MBD, but he is so obliged if and only if his MB asserts his rightful claim. There is no general obligation of MBD-FZS marriage and if a man marries a MBD his brothers are not free to marry her sisters. Furthermore, it is thought fitting and proper for sisters to marry in order of their relative ages, and an elder unmarried sister has the right to marry before her younger sisters. Thus, if a man has several unmarried MBDs and his MB asserts his rightful claim, the man is obliged to marry the eldest. She may be his *rat* or *nam* (since designation by these terms is determined by the relative ages of ego and alter) (cf. Leach 1945 [1961: 36]). If he does not want to marry her, but instead one of her younger sisters or some other woman, he is obliged to obtain a release from his MB and to compensate her and his MB. Furthermore, if he marries some other woman, not of a group established by precedent as being his "wife-giver" (*mayu*), he may have to pay compensation not only to his MB but also to certain men of the "wife-taking" (*dama*) groups of his new "wife-givers" (see Leach 1945 [1961: 46]). This suggests that while a man's MB has a rightful claim over him as a potential DH, a man (or one man in each sibling set) also has rightful claim to a MBD.

Marriages are often arranged for essentially political purposes, in order to establish or to consolidate political alliances between lineages or incipient lineages. As described by Leach (1945; 1954), the typical arrangement is for a village to be composed of several lineage (*amyu*) segments known as *htinggaw amying*, "household name." The members of each of these units worship the same set of household ancestor spirits, usually no further removed than great grandfathers (Leach 1954: 110). These shallow lineages are strictly exogamous, but at higher levels of segmentation lineages may or may not be regarded as exogamous. The lowest-order lineage segments of which a village is composed may or may not be segments of the same higher-order lineage and, in any event, they may intermarry. Thus, the component lineage segments of a village may be related both consanguineally and affinally. Each village is "owned" by a chiefly lineage segment, and the other lineage segments living in the village are typically the clients and political inferiors of the chiefly lineage. Villages may also form "village clusters" which are similarly organized. In the case of the village cluster:

> Constituent villages are 'owned' by lineages which, locally, are of inferior status to the chief's lineage. Those which are not of the same clan as the chief's lineage are normally in 'son-in-law' relationship to that lineage (Leach 1961: 92).

According to Leach, "from the *individual's* point of view" (1954: 73–74, emphasis ours), every lowest-order lineage segment within the community falls into one or the other of four categories:

1. *kahpu-kanau ni*, or lineages of the same clan as ego's and so closely related as to form, with ego's group, an exogamous unit.
2. *mayu ni*, or lineages from which men of ego's lineage have recently taken brides.
3. *dama ni*, or lineages into which women of ego's lineage have recently married.
4. *lawu-lahta ni*, or lineages recognized as "relatives" but not so closely related as to preclude marriage and, consequently, assimilation of the lineage in question to category 2 or 3.

The lineages thus categorized are the lowest-order lineage segments or "household names." The *mayu-dama* relationship "is effective as between lineages of the *htinggaw* group scale; it does not operate consistently at the clan level although Kachins sometimes talk as if it should" (1954: 81). Thus two lineage segments classifiable as "brothers" (*kahpu-kanau ni*) because they belong to the same clan, may be related also as *mayu-dama ni*.

In theory the *mayu-dama* relationship is permanent. However, one marriage per generation is sufficient to maintain a political alliance between two lineage segments. There is no requirement that all men must marry women of lineages already established as wife-givers in respect to their own lineages, and marriages are often arranged with women of unrelated lineages in order to establish new interlineage alliances. Furthermore, not all marriages between previously unallied lineages are regarded as having implications for relations between the lineages as wholes. That is to say, some *mayu-dama* relationships are cultivated and elaborated; other are not (Leach 1954: 77).

Kachin marriages ideally involve the transfer of wealth or, in other words, payment of brideprice. But often marriages are contracted without brideprice or with a substantially reduced brideprice. In such cases, the groom (who is often a younger son of a chief) takes up residence with the bride's father and becomes his "follower and tenant," as well as the potential head of a new, independent lineage segment. Leach remarks:

> If the *mayu-dama* relationship thus initiated continues for several generations with orthodox patrilocal residence, the ultimate position will be that the descendants of the father-in-law and the descendants of the son-in-law will be living side by side in the same community in landlord-tenant relationship. This probably is the most usual history of present day Kachin villages (1961: 87).

Elsewhere Leach notes that "in orthodox marriages where residence is patrilocal and brideprice is paid in full, there is not the same emphasis on the political inferiority of the *dama*" (1954: 84). In these cases, which often involve marriage to a woman from outside the village or village cluster, there is no significant difference in the relative statuses of *mayu* and *dama*.

In keeping with the political asymmetry of the *mayu-dama* relationship, there is a ban on FZD-MBS marriage, for this would constitute a marriage with a woman of a normally wife-taking group and complicate and confound the system of reciprocities already established between the groups. But such marriages are banned also on the ground that they would result in defective offspring (Leach 1954: 136–40; 1961: 45–46; compare Lévi-Strauss 1969: 481–85). Beyond approximately third-cousin range, however, people are free to marry without regard to kin class or *mayu-dama* relationships between lineages, provided that the lineages concerned are not politically closely allied. Thus, a man may marry a woman he classifies as *khri* ("♂ ZC") and, conversely, a woman may marry a man she classifies as *tsa* ("MB"), provided that they are not genealogically closely related or that their lineages are not close political allies (Leach 1954: 84, 138). Similarly, there is no objection to marriage between persons who classify one another as some kind of "sibling," or "grandparent," or "grandchild," again provided that they are not genealogically closely related and that their lineages are not close political allies (Leach 1954: 84, 138). Of course, where such marriages do occur, the parties to them are both kin to and affines of one another, and they have the possibility of classifying one another according to either relationship.

There are, it seems, no fixed rules governing these situations, and certainly new affines are not automatically classified as though they were MBs, etc. Where two lineages of the same clan intermarry, they may continue to speak of one another as "brother" lineages (Leach 1961: 46, note 2), though particular individuals may make the appropriate terminological adjustments (Leach 1961: 45–46). Thus, an individual's classification of his kin and affines is not necessarily "consistent" with or determined by the political-affinal alliances of his or her lineage, and it is therefore unwarranted to argue, as Leach (1945) does, that the system of kin classification is in fact a system of social category labels designating positions in a system of asymmetric alliance (see also Lévi-Strauss 1969). Nor is it accurate to assert that the Kachin have a *prescriptive marriage rule* in the sense that marriage is prescribed exclusively with a woman of one and only one category (see Needham 1962a: 55).

Some Similar Cases

Similar systems of kin classification and marriage are found among many if not most other Chin- and Kuki-speaking peoples. The kinship terminology of the Haka Chin, for example, employs the Omaha rule

$$(\dots \female\ B \longrightarrow \dots \female\ F) \equiv (\male\ Z \dots \longrightarrow \male\ D \dots)$$

(i.e., the type-III rather than the type-II rule) and, apparently, the MBD-FZS–spouse equation rule. However, the data on this system (see Lehman 1963: 137–38; Newland 1897), and the apparently similar systems of the Lakher (Parry 1932; Lorrain 1951), Purum (Das 1945), and the Thado (Shaw 1929; Hutton 1922), for example, are too limited to permit definite analyses. Yet, one interesting terminological feature of the Lakher, Purum, and Thado systems deserves mention here. By and large, the ethnographers have given systematic accounts of vocative rather than referential usage, and these contain some apparent inconsistencies. However, since the same apparent inconsistencies are reported for all of these systems, it seems that they are not really inconsistencies. For example, $\male$ MBS is reported equated with MB (and in some cases MF), but $\male$ FZS is typically reported as "sibling" rather than as "sister's son" or "grandchild." This and other apparent internal contradictions may be resolvable as follows.

Throughout the Kuki-speaking groups, kin terms are used in direct address somewhat differently than in reference. In general, younger kin and affines of ego's generation and below are not addressed by kinship terms but by name or teknonym (e.g., "father of X"). Elder kin and affines of ego's generation and above are addressed by the appropriate term of reference *if it is a senior category term* (e.g., *pu* for MBS). However, if it is a junior category term (e.g., *tu* for ♂ FZS), the term is not used and one of the "sibling" terms is employed in its place. By this rule, however, we would expect an elder MBD to be addressed as "mother," but it is only in the Thado case that she is reported as such; otherwise MBD is given as "sibling." The presumption must be that the "sibling" terms are extended to siblings-in-law, and MBD is classified as though she were BW or WZ. Again, however, the data are too incomplete to permit a definitive interpretation.

The Haka Chin case as described by Lehman (1963: 103 ff.) is strikingly similar to that of the Kachin, though of course there are some interesting differences (see Leach 1969; Lehman 1970). Of particular interest is the fact that "a woman's family has a lien on her offspring by virtue of her irrevocable membership in her natal lineage or of the enduring relationship between the lineages established by marriage" (1963: 123–24). This "lien" is more specifically described as a right held by MB in respect to ZC. It consists in part of a man's claim to a portion of the brideprice of his ZD, and in his claim to receive prestations from his ZS, partly, it seems, as a consequence of the marriage of his sister, but also as a potential or actual WF. We would suppose that another part of this "lien" consists in a right to claim one's ZS as a DH.

According to Lehman, Haka Chin regard marriage as establishing a political alliance between the descent groups (i.e., small-scale lineages) of the parties to it. The alliance "is by definition enduring, but the Chin do not conceive of it as perpetual" (1963: 129). Whether or not a particular alliance endures depends on the desires of the parties to it, who may revalidate it from time to time either by the giving of prestations to the wife-givers (who may refuse to accept them) or "by a subsequent marriage within a few generations (three or four, but there is no formal rule)" (1963: 130).

Lehman emphasizes the political nature of Haka Chin marital alliance, and he stresses the fact that there is no "positive" (see Dumont 1968) rule of marriage. He argues that "enduring structural relations among local descent groups" are maintained quite simply by "the injunction not to give wives to groups who are wife-givers . . . . " Haka Chin "*prefer* to marry a real or classificatory mother's brother's daughter. No other prescription or preference is given" (Lehman 1963: 123). This emphasis on the political nature of Chin marriage alliance leads Lehman to observe that it probably is mistaken "to think of systems of prescriptive marriage" as "primarily systems of 'indirect exchange' and reciprocity, or dualistic ideology, as Lévi-Strauss (1949) and Needham have treated them" (1963: 98).

Lehman's central argument is directed against one of the principal tenets of "alliance theory," viz., "that the *structural logic* of systems of prescriptive marriage can be understood only in terms of their function as ideally well-ordered, cyclical exchange" (1963: 98). This is false, he argues, inasmuch as it suggests that the peoples in question conceive of their societies as wholes and as composed of three types of intermarrying groups. While it is true that they sometimes do speak of three or five such types of group and of "cycles" of exchange between them, this does not imply that they have an "ideology" (i.e., a system of concepts and rules) in which the whole society is conceived as divided into three or five types of groups formally implicated in a system of cyclical marital alliances (see also Lehman 1970).

The societies in question may best be understood, Lehman argues, by starting with the assumption that what we have to deal with is a "general political strategy of making marriage serve as a particular kind of differentiated alliance where the obligations between the parties are asymmetrical" (1963: 98). From this perspective, one of the most distinctive characteristics of societies allegedly ordered as asymmetric prescriptive alliance systems is the political function of marriage: marriage allies (or may ally) small-scale lineages or lineage segments (not whole lineages or clans) and does so asymmetrically. This notion entails no rules of marriage other than: (1) the alliance should be maintained; and (2) the asymmetry of the relationship should be maintained by the avoidance of taking a wife from a wife-taking group. Conformity to the first rule is readily accomplished by an occasional further marriage between the groups concerned. Since the groups allied by marriage are not lineages or clans as wholes but only "particular household-sized units" (1963: 99), conformity to the second rule may entail little more than avoidance of marriage between FZD and MBS. The practice of assymmetric political-affinal alliance between such groups may give rise to short-lived "cycles" of "indirect exchange" of women or of goods (e.g., parts of brideprice) among them, but it is not one of the concerns of the people involved either to initiate such "cycles" or to maintain any such "cycles" as may arise (Lehman 1963: 99; 1970).

Despite these observations, Lehman (1963: 99, note 4) adds that he agrees with Needham's contention that "the complementary opposition between the conceptual categories, wife-giver and wife-taker, is . . . the formal logical foundation of prescriptive asymmetric marriage." He suggests that his observations on the actual operation of asymmetric marital alliance between groups do not disconfirm this view but "go beyond the analysis of the formal, conceptual distinctions to which [Needham's] wide-ranging comparative interests restrict him for the time being." What Lehman overlooks, however, is that, prior to about 1964, both Lévi-Strauss and Needham regarded systems of generalized exchange or asymmetric alliance systems as having two "indissoluble" aspects, a system of concrete affinal alliance between groups, and a system of "social" (or, for Lévi-Strauss, "kin") classification, both of which are ordered by the principles of "descent" and "alliance." Thus, if this view of the "logical foundation of prescriptive asymmetric marriage" is to be maintained, it has to be shown that the systems of kin classification of the societies in question do make use of the "complementary opposition" between the categories "wife-giver" and "wife-taker." This is especially critical since Needham's more recent difficulties with the Siriono case have led him to disclaim any suggestion that a terminology of asymmetric prescriptive alliance is *necessarily* associated with a system of concrete intergroup marital alliance (see Chapter 2, pp. 28–30).

In 1963, Lehman took the position that "A prescriptive marriage system undoubtedly exercises a notable influence on kinship terminology" (1963: 137). Although he refrained from arguing "the merits of the theory that kinship terminologies are primarily reflections of certain kinds of marriage rules," his brief discussions of the Haka Chin (1963: 137–39) and Southern Chin (1963: 96, 101–2) systems are primarily concerned with the degree to which their equations "are in . . . harmony with a prescriptive, asymmetric marriage system," i.e., the degree to which they can be understood as based on a distinction between three types of asymmetrically intermarrying groups. Therefore, it is especially interesting that, in his most recent comments on the Haka and other Chin groups, he states "we are not motivated by the ethnographic evidence to postulate any rule or rules referring to a marriage cycle in any proposed formal description of asymmetrical marriage alliance" (1970: 120). Although he refers in the same paragraph to a forthcoming analysis of the Haka Chin system of kin classification—thus suggesting that this analysis does not posit "a rule or rules referring to a marriage cycle"—he does not state whether or not he still finds it necessary to speak of "the three ideal lines of agnates, wife-takers, and wife-givers" (1963: 138) which, in 1963, he found were *not* consistently distinguished in the terminology of kin classification.

From the Haka and other Chin cases, it seems quite clear that the fundamental difficulty with "alliance theory" is not the concept of an "ideology" which posits "marriage cycles." It is rather the concept of a "total system" consisting of a "symbolic order" and a "social order," both of which are structured by the principles of "descent" and "alliance." The concepts of wife-giver and wife-taker certainly are present and, certainly, these are complementary, opposed categories, but they are not the "logical foundation" of any "total" social and cultural systems.

The Manggarai Kinship System

Though the Gilyak and Kachin systems of kin classification feature Omaha-skewing rules and are essentially nothing more than simple Omaha-type systems on which MBD-FZS–spouse equation rules are superimposed, there are no structural reasons preventing such a rule from being superimposed on systems of kin classification that do not feature rules of intergenerational transmission of kin-class status. The kinship systems of many Indonesian peoples offer pertinent examples. The data on most of these systems are rather limited, but those for the Manggarai (Flores Island) system are perhaps sufficient to illustrate the apparent essential structural features of these systems.

The data on Manggarai kinship terminology are presented in Table 12. The principal sources are Coolhaas (1942) and Verheijen (in Fischer 1957) and they are in essential agreement. Though Verheijen reports *empo* as "grandchild," he notes elsewhere that it may also mean "ancestor" (1951: 65), so it probably is a self-reciprocal "grandparent"–"grandchild" term, and *ema lopo* and *ende lopo* probably are descriptive labels for the two kinds of grandparents (see also Needham 1966c: 149). The other difference concerns the cross cousins. According to Coolhaas (1942: 347), MBD and FZS call each other *wina* and *rona* "husband" and "wife"; FZS and MBS call each other *kesa*, "brother-in-law"; FZD and MBD call each other *ipar*, "sister-in-law"; and a man calls his FZD *weta*, "sister." However, according to Verheijen, cross cousins as such classify one another as one or another kind of sibling, and it is only under certain circumstances that they classify one another as reported by Coolhaas. Since Verheijen's account (in Fischer 1957) is the more detailed and specific, we have chosen to work with it rather than that of Coolhaas.

According to Verheijen, where MBD and FZS have been betrothed to one another by their parents, their parents refer to them as the wife (*wina*) and husband (*rona*) of one another, but they themselves continue to use either personal names or sibling terms (*weta* and *nara*) in address. Perhaps they may refer to (but not address) one another as *wina* and *rona* in the sense of potential wife and husband. However, a man refers to (addresses?) his future wife's sisters as *kae* or *ase*, and a woman refers to (addresses?) the brothers of her future husband as *kae* or *ase*, too. Note that *kae* and *ase* are "elder same-sex sibling" and "younger same-sex sibling" terms, respectively, but they are used also for the same-sex siblings of one's spouse. That is, in classifying siblings-in-law of the same sex as the spouse (or same-sex siblings of one's future spouse or spouse

Table 12

MANGGARAI KINSHIP TERMINOLOGY

Term		Foci	Derivative Denotata
1.	*ema*	F	FB, FFBS, MZH
2.	*ende*	M	MZ, FBW
3.	*anak*	S, D	♂ BC, ♀ ZC, HBC, WZC
4.	*empo*	FF, MF (also *ema lopo*) FM, MM (also *ende lopo*) SC, DC	
5.	*amang*	MB	FZH, WF, HF
6.	*inang*	FZ	MBW, WM, HM
7.	*to'a*	♂ ZC, ♀ BC	WBC, HZC
8.	*kae*	♂ B⁺ ♀Z⁺	♂ ego's elder FBS, MZS, FZS, MBS; ♀ ego's elder FBD, MZD, FZD, MBD; WZ, HB, WZH, HBW, ♀ ZH, ♂ BW
9.	*ase*	♂ B⁻, ♀ Z⁻	same as *kae* but younger than ego
10.	*nara*	♀ B	♀ ego's FBS, MZS, FZS, MBS
11.	*weta*	♂ Z	♂ ego's FBD, MZD, FZD, MBD
12.	*rona*	H	♀ FZS*
13.	*wina*	W	♂ MBD*
14.	*kesa*	♂ ZH, WB	♂ FZS*, ♂ MBS*
15.	*ipar*	♀ BW, HZ	♀ FZD*, ♀ MBD*, WBW, HZH
16.	*koa*	DH	♂ ZS*
17.	*wote*	SW	♀ BD*

*Indicates classification when also affinally related or when designated as a future affine of the appropriate type.

designate), ego "follows" his or her spouse's usage. The relevant equivalence rule here is:

$$(. \, ♂ \, WZ \, . \longrightarrow . \, ♀ \, Z \, .) \equiv (. \, ♀ \, ZH \, . \longrightarrow . \, ♀ \, Z \, .)$$
$$(. \, ♀ \, HB \, . \longrightarrow . \, ♂ \, B \, .) \equiv (. \, ♂ \, BW \, . \longrightarrow . \, ♂ \, B \, .)$$

It would seem from Verheijen's account that cross cousins classify one another as though they were related affinally only when a marriage has actually been arranged between persons of the two sibling sets involved.

The important question for our purposes is: Is there, beyond this, a general presumption of MBD-FZS marriage, at least for purposes of kin classification, such that parents' cross cousins and the children of one's own cross cousins are classified as if one's father had married his MBD, one's mother her FZS, etc.? Unfortunately, the most directly relevant data are not reported, and we have to infer the answer to this question from less direct evidence.

To begin with, note that FZH is classified as "mother's brother" and MBW as "father's sister"; WBC and HZC are likewise classified as "cross nephew" and "cross niece," as in the Siriono system. Since, in Manggarai, MBD-FZS marriage is "preferred" and FZD-MBS marriage is flatly proscribed, it is evident that these equations are not attributable to any rule of bilateral cross-cousin marriage or to a "two-section system" (cf. Fischer 1957: 18–19, 20; Needham 1966c: 150). They could result from equivalence rules similar to those that generate the same classifications in the Siriono system (see p. 120). That they must do so seems evident from the fact that WBW and HZH are classified as *ipar*, "woman's same-sex sibling-in-law." All of these classifications may be generated by the rules:

$$(. \, \male \, WB \ldots \rightarrow . \, \female \, B \ldots) \equiv (\ldots \, \male \, ZH . \rightarrow \ldots \, \male \, Z .)$$
$$(. \, \female \, HZC . \rightarrow . \, \male \, ZC .) \equiv (. \, \female \, MBW . \rightarrow . \, \female \, MB .)$$

The second rule is almost the mirror image, but in fact a slightly more restricted form of the mirror image, of the first. It has to be so restricted, for to write it as generally as the first would be to offer two possibilities for reduction of WBW and HZH, one of which would require them to be classified as *kesa* rather than *ipar*.

Rules like these occur in the Siriono, Gilyak, and Kachin systems, and we have seen that they have the status of auxiliaries of the MBD-FZS–spouse equation rule. They probably have the same status in this system. An additional reason for supposing that they do and that this system does employ the MBD-FZS–spouse equation rule is the following: In Manggarai society, as in Gilyak and Kachin, marriages may ally lineages as well as individuals, and ideally these alliances are enduring. Again, however, two brothers are not permitted to marry two sisters; if a man marries a MBD, his brothers must take their wives from other families. Indeed, according to Fischer (1957: 17), they "have to choose their marriage partners in other patrilineages." Be this as it may, each lineage has at least several others from which its men may take wives. If a man may not marry his MBD, then he may marry his FMBSD (who would not be his MBD if his F or his FB had married some woman other than a MBD). Now Fischer does not report the classification of FMBS or FMBSD, but by the MBD-FZS–spouse equation rule, FMBS would be equivalent to FWB or MB, *amang*, and FMBSD would be a "potential wife." If this rule were not employed, it is difficult to see how FMBS might be classified other than as FB or "father." It seems likely that appropriate potential spouses are specified as the daughters of male ego's *amang* and that FMBS is classified as *amang*.

In short, although the evidence is inconclusive, it is probable that one's own cross cousins are classified as siblings unless they have been singled out as one's future siblings-in-law, but one's parents' cross cousins are classified as if the appropriate MBD-FZS marriage had occurred; conversely, the children of one's own cross cousins also are classified as if the appropriate MBD-FZS marriage had occurred.

Assuming that the MBD-FZS–spouse equation rule is employed in this system, its appropriate phrasing seems to be:

$$(\male \text{ MBD} \rightarrow \male \text{ WZ}) \equiv (\female \text{ FZS} \rightarrow \female \text{ ZH}), \text{ etc.}$$

It must be understood, however, that according to Verheijen's account the rule does not apply to the MBD who is male ego's spouse-designate when she is considered as a designated kinswoman.

Two final observations. The categories *koa* (DH) and *wote* (SW) must be assumed to be specially marked subcategories of *to'a* ($\male$ ZC, $\female$ BC). They designate actual children-in-law but may be used also in reference to $\male$ ZS and $\female$ BD who have been singled out as future children-in-law. The reciprocal senior categories *amang* and *inang* are not so divided. Note that FZH is treated as equivalent to FZ, and MBW as equivalent to MB, as in the Siriono system, but here FZ and MB are not then skewed into the grandparent category. Here *amang* is opposed to *inang* as a "cross first-degree collateral kins*man* of the first ascending generation" versus a "cross first-degree collateral kins*woman* of the first ascending generation." The extension rule equating FZH with MB and MBW with FZ may be regarded as requiring that FZH, for example, be regarded as a "cross first-degree collateral relative (not kinsman) of the first ascending generation," and, being a male, as an *amang*. This rule simply neutralizes the distinction between cross collateral kin and cross step-kin.

Manggarai Society

Some aspects of Manggarai society have been noted already. It is unclear from the available ethnographic accounts whether or not men have rightful claims over their MBDs in marriage, or whether or not men have the right to claim their ZSs as DHs (as is perhaps more likely to be the case since we are told that MBD-FZS marriages are arranged by parents). In contrast, it is quite clear that there is no general obligation to marry a MBD or even a woman who is the daughter of an *amang*. Although certain lineages or clans are traditionally allied as wife-givers and wife-takers (Coolhaas 1942: 348–49; Mennes 1931: 375–80), these groups are not obliged to contract all of their marriages with one another, and, indeed, the rules of marriage positively prohibit them from doing so. Patrilineages or the "branches" of clans are exogamous in principle, but the clans are not, However, the patrilineages themselves seem to be quite shallow: marriages are tolerated between second and third agnatic parallel cousins (e.g., FFBSD-FFBSS), and it seems likely that such marriages either lead to or are symptomatic of lineage segmentation (see also Leach 1961: 44; Lehman 1963: 98–99). Marriage between uterine parallel cousins (MZD-MZS) is also permitted in certain circumstances: if two sisters marry men of different lineages, which are lineages that may intermarry, then MZD-MZS may marry (Fischer 1957: 17–18).

Manggarai marriage rules, then, may be characterized thus: The minimal patrilineage is exogamous and a man should not marry a woman from a lineage traditionally related to his own as a wife-taker (at the very least, he should not marry a FZD; in the light of the nonexogamous status of the clans, it is unlikely that there is a rule forbidding marriage to a woman of the clan of one's FZD, other than the FZD herself). Beyond this, lineages traditionally allied as wife-givers and wife-takers should maintain their alliances, which they may do quite simply by means of an occasional additional marriage.

Some Similar Cases

A somewhat similar system of kin classification probably occurs among the Yaruro of Venezuela (Petrullo 1939), though the Yaruro, like the Siriono, are not organized into corporate unilineal descent groups which could ideally or actually exchange women in marriage. While the Yaruro data are meager and perhaps unreliable, the data for the Karo Batak are quite good (see Singarimbun 1965) and provide conclusive evidence for the existence of a classificatory system with a MBD-FZS–spouse equation rule but no skewing or transmission rule. Unfortunately, Singarimbun's data are yet to be published, and so we cannot here present an analysis of Karo Batak kinship terminology.

The case of the matrilineal Garo of Assam (Burling 1963) is similar, also, but in this case it is clear that the jural basis of the rule is the right of a man to claim a ZS as a DH. Here each couple chooses one of their daughters to be their "heiress," and she alone stays in the parental home with her husband and their children. All other children move away on marriage or shortly thereafter. A boy from another family also is chosen to marry the heiress and to be the heir of her family. The girl's father chooses the heir, and Garo say "a man always wants to get his own 'nephew' (i.e., *gritang* [ZS]) . . . to come in to be his heir, the husband of his heiress daughter" (Burling 1963: 80). He may have to settle, however, for a classificatory ZS, since he may not have a ZS or since none of his ZSs may wish to be chosen. Burling states that, although it is "not an obligatory duty, it is at least a proper and worthy act to oblige a 'brother' by giving him one's son, and to oblige an 'uncle' by becoming his son-in-law" (1963: 81). But he notes also that "a boy who agrees to become an heir explains his action by saying that he feels a sense of duty and believes he should help his father-in-law" (1965: 77). Moreover, "the 'uncle's' authority over his younger lineage mates, both his 'sister' (the mother of his prospective 'heir') and the 'nephew' himself, makes it somewhat difficult to give him an outright refusal," and "the weight of opinion [within the lineage] will aid a man who wants a 'nephew'. Everyone encourages the 'nephew' to undertake the duty and tries to overcome his doubts" (1963: 81–82). We conclude that a man does have a right to claim as ZS as a DH. The ZS, however, has the right to refuse, but he is under considerable moral pressure not to refuse.

The Garo system of kin classification (Burling 1963: 351 ff.) is a simple Dravidian-type system, i.e., one in which parallel collaterals within one degree of generational removal are merged with ego's parents, siblings, and children, and the residual cross collaterals are placed in specially marked categories. More distant collateral kintypes are attributed parallel or cross status depending on relative sex of the linking kin at *all* generational levels (see Lounsbury 1964*b*: 1079; Scheffler 1970*b*). Step-kin and affines are classified in a manner that is consistent with bilateral cross-cousin marriage, but while Garo do permit marriage between a man and his MBD or his FZD, they also permit marriage between individuals related in ways other than as cross cousins or classificatory cross cousins. There is no evidence that, when men marry women related to them in ways other than as cross cousins or classificatory cross cousins, they then classify their in-laws as though their wives were in fact their cross cousins, actual or classificatory. Thus, the pattern of extension of kin terms to in-laws cannot be accounted for by asserting that there is a presumption of marriage to a cross cousin, actual or classificatory (see Scheffler 1970*b*). But these extensions may be accounted for by means of the MBD-FZS–spouse equation rule—again best expressed as (WF → MB) ≡ (♂ DH → ♂ ZS). Since this rule is imposed on a Dravidian-type system—one in which MBD and FZD, and MBS and FZS, are not terminologically distinguished to begin with—the spouse-equation rule must result in WB and ♂ ZH, for example, being designated by the same term (the male cross-cousin term). This and many other terminological equations and distinctions of the Garo system may appear superficially to be inconsistent with MBD-FZS marriage. They are not inconsistent, however, because the particular terminological equations and distinctions affected by the MBD-FZS–spouse equation rule must depend in large part on the other rules of the system, including the primary defining rules.

Here, too, "marriage establishes or perpetuates not only a household but also an enduring relationship between the lineages of the husband and wife" (Burling 1963: 140). The relationship is usually asymmetrical, women coming from one lineage, men from another, but occasionally men from two households marry each other's sisters and "trade residences." But this "brother exchange," as Burling (1963: 159) calls it, happens when "one man marries first, and the kinship ties which he establishes help to facilitate the arrangement of a subsequent marriage between his wife's younger brother and his own sister." In a case like this, one of the men may be married to his own FZD. Such an arrangement may be perpetuated over several generations, each heir helping to arrange a subsequent match between his wife's younger brother and his own sister.

Discussion

So far as we have been able to determine, instances of MBD-FZS–spouse equation rules superimposed on Crow- or Omaha-type systems do not occur in North or South America, though the two continents provide a number of cases of societies with Crow- or Omaha-type systems of kin classification and in which MBD-FZS marriage is reportedly "preferred." Some anthropologists have argued that the kinship system of the Miwok Indians of central California is (or was) an asymmetric alliance system of social classification (Lévi-Strauss 1969: 359–70; Buchler and Selby 1968: 267). Thus it might be suspected to be an Omaha-type system on which a MBD-FZS–spouse equation rule is superimposed, but it is in fact nothing more than a simple Omaha-type system. Gifford's (1916) data are extensive and wholly reliable (cf. Lévi-Strauss 1969: 365–67) and they show quite clearly that classification in this system is *not* affected by a MBD-FZS–spouse equation rule. Furthermore, MBD-FZS marriages are (or were) permitted in only some of the Miwok groups, though all groups share the same system of kin classification. Where such marriages occur, and ego is therefore related to some of his kinsmen in more than one way, it is the shorter genealogical connection—the one reflecting the MBD-FZS marriage—that is taken as the basis of the classification. To take an extreme example, a man's MFZS is classified as his "brother," but in some cases ego's MFZS is married to ego's mother and ego classifies the man as "father"—because he *is* ego's father (Gifford 1916: 176). Neither does this system reflect WBD marriage, as Gifford supposed. The system features a distinct set of affinal terms, and WBD and WBS are classified as "sibling-in-law" along with WZ and WB, that is, the Omaha rule is applied in the step-kin as well as in the consanguineal domain, with the result that some step-kin are classified as if they were affines or in-laws. The same thing occurs in many other Omaha-type systems (see Tax 1955a on the Fox), none of which have anything to do with "prescriptive alliance" or "prescriptive marriage." Among the Miwok, marriage is permitted, perhaps in some sense even preferred, with a classificatory "mother's younger sister," a category that includes MBD, but MBD is often deemed "too close" and thus unmarriageable.

As noted earlier, one of the aims of Needham's analysis of the Siriono kinship system was to show that matrilineal asymmetric alliance systems are not only theoretically possible but do in fact occur. In addition to the Siriono case, Needham mentioned the Mnong Gar of Vietnam and the Belu of Central Timor, Indonesia, as "certainly" cases of the same sort. However, as far as the system of kin classification is concerned, the case of the Mnong Gar is similar to that of the Miwok: this system features a Crow-type skewing rule that is restricted to the elder sister of a male linking kinsman (Lounsbury 1964a: 368–69); the classification of collateral kin is not affected by a MBD-FZS–spouse equation rule. Like the Miwok system, the Mnong Gar features a distinct set of affinal categories (Condominas 1960). Thus, although the Mnong Gar are matrilineally organized and may establish and maintain interlineage alliances by means of MBD-FZS or "MBD"-"FZS" marriage, the latter structural feature is not reflected in the system of kin classification.

The terminological data for the Belu are rather meager (Vroklage 1953: 410 ff.) but are sufficient to demonstrate that the system does not feature a Crow-type skewing rule. Thus, even if Crow-type skewing rules were sufficient evidence for the existence of a "matrilineal" rule of kin classification, there is nothing in the available evidence to suggest (much less to confirm) the existence of a "matrilineal" rule of kin classification in the Belu case. The Belu system appears to be similar to that found in nearby Manggarai; it seems to employ a MBD-FZS–spouse equation rule, but it takes no cognizance of "matrilineal" (or simply uterine) kinship in the classification of kin. Again, the Belu are matrilineally organized and may ally matrilineages by means of MBD-FZS or "MBD"-"FZS" marriage, but because of the nature of the kinship terminology this case fails to meet Needham's criteria for a matrilineal asymmetric alliance system.

The Garo, again, are matrilineal and do "practice asymmetric alliance," but their kinship terminology has no "matrilineal" features. Although Needham describes this as "lineal descent terminology" (1966c: 142), the description refers to nothing more than the presence of terminological equations such as FB = F, MZ = M and such terminological distinctions as FZ ≠ M and MB ≠ F. These however, have to be accounted for in this case, as in many others, as products of the same-sex sibling merging rule, which leaves the cross first-degree collateral kin to be specified by special terms.

So far as we have been able to determine, MBD-FZS–spouse equation rules occur superimposed on systems that employ Omaha-type skewing rules or parallel-transmission rules and on systems that do not feature rules of intergenerational transmission of kin-class status. It seems that they do *not* occur superimposed on systems that employ Crow-type skewing rules.[8] The systems on which MBD-FZS–spouse equation rules are superimposed are similar, whether or not they employ skewing or transmission rules, inasmuch as they all distinguish between the same-sex and opposite-sex siblings of parents and classify the former with parents; conversely, they distinguish between the children of same-sex and opposite-sex siblings and classify the former with one's own children. In systems with skewing or transmission rules, one or the other (or both) of the opposite-sex siblings of one's parents is displaced into a kin category of another generation, or assigned to a category of its own into which kin of other generations are displaced. The spouse-equation rule (and its corollaries and auxiliaries) usually operates first to equate specific affinal types with specific collateral kintypes of the same generations, and these are then subject to the skewing or transmission rule. The spouse-equation rule also operates (as in the Siriono case) to reduce more distant collateral kintypes to step-kin or affinal types which are then classified according to the requirements of it and other equivalence rules. In systems lacking skewing or transmission rules, the opposite-sex siblings of parents are given separate designations (as are their reciprocals), i.e., they are made the foci of certain categories. Again, the spouse-equation rule then operates to assimilate affinal types to cross or parallel collateral kintypes, or it operates to reduce certain distant collateral kintypes to first-degree collateral kintypes, sometimes through several successively closer step-kin and kintypes.

To all appearances, the MBD-FZS–spouse equation rule is structurally compatible with several different "types" of systems of kin classification. The range of empirical variation seems to be limited, however, to systems which also distinguish between parents' same-sex and opposite-sex siblings and, conversely, between the children of same-sex and opposite-sex siblings, i.e., to systems in which the distinction of relative sex is employed in the definitions of kin categories and terms at their primary ranges. This is logically consistent with the obvious cultural and social significance of the relative-sex distinction as expressed in the spouse-equation rule itself. The distribution of this distinction (i.e., that between the same-sex and opposite-sex siblings of parents, etc.) is of course far broader than the distribution of the MBD-FZS–spouse equation rule; neither can be explained in terms of the other (cf. Lévi-Strauss 1969: 129–33, 143–45). But it may be that the distinction between parallel and cross kin (of the first degree of collaterality) is a necessary precondition for the MBD-FZS–spouse equation rule.

---

[8] The case of the Kaska Indians (see Honigmann 1954: 76 ff.) seems nonexceptional, but the data are limited and insufficient to support any strong claims, pro or con, about the structure of this system of kin classification. It is not clear that this system employs a Crow-type skewing rule, much less a MBD-FZS–spouse equation rule.

It is an interesting fact that, so far as we have been able to determine, MBD-FZS–spouse equation rules do not occur in conjunction with Crow-type skewing rules, though it would be easy to demonstrate (by constructing a purely hypothetical model or range of models) that such a combination is no less feasible than the empirically common combination of the MBD-FZS–spouse equation rule and Omaha-type skewing rules. The former arrangement would be nothing more than a mirror image of the latter. Similarly, we have been unable to locate a single positive example of a FZD-MBS–spouse equation rule of kin classification, and we can detect no purely formal reasons for its nonoccurrence; such a rule could be superimposed on Crow-, Omaha-, and many other types of kinship systems and be made to "work" perfectly well.[9]

The (apparent) nonexistence of these terminological arrangements seems to require a sociological explanation. No such explanation is attempted here for two reasons. First, adequate exposition of a theory (sociological or otherwise) that might account for the occurrence of certain kinds of rules and systems of kin classification, and the (apparent) nonoccurrence of others, would require further extensive analyses and theoretical discussion, both of which must be postponed to another occasion. Second, our central concern here has been to demonstrate a method of structural semantic analysis and to discuss some of the more important assumptions and concepts relevant to it. The method will have to be applied to a wide range of systems of kin classification, and the societies in which they occur will have to be carefully examined, before we will have a satisfactory empirical basis for a general sociological theory of systems of kin classification.

Thus we readily acknowledge that at this point we cannot offer a replacement for the demonstrably inadequate omnibus semantic and sociological theory that has become known as "the theory of prescriptive

---

[9] The Tismulun of Espiritu Santo Island, New Hebrides, provide a possible exception, but the terminological data (Deacon 1929) are insufficient to permit determination of the structure of the system; the sociological data are meager too, but there is no evidence that the Tismulun recognize rights over FZD in marriage. The Yaka of the Congo (Sousberghe 1965) have an interesting Crow-type terminology in which the FZD is designated by a "potential spouse" term which is extended, in accordance with the Crow-skewing rule, to the female uterine descendants of the FZD if she is not chosen as one's spouse. This system certainly does not employ a FZD-MBS–spouse equation rule in kin classification, but it does mark a man's FZD as his "potential spouse." The case of the Chipewyan Indians (Legoff 1889; Curtis 1928) is somewhat different. This system appears to employ a Crow-type skewing rule, and it features a number of terminological equations and distinctions that are highly suggestive of a FZD-MBS–spouse equation rule; but there is also some evidence that distant collateral kin are classified as in Iroquois-type systems, not in accordance with such a marriage rule (see Legoff 1889: 328). There has been considerable discussion among anthropologists about whether or not a "system of prescribed patrilateral cross-cousin marriage" is either theoretically possible or operationally feasible. Unfortunately, the discussion has been confounded by a failure to distinguish between the feasibility of a certain kind of system of kin classification and the feasibility of a system of patrilateral political-affinal alliance between unilineal descent groups.

asymmetric alliance systems." But that theory was developed largely to account for the fact that in certain societies affines, step-kin, and more remote collateral kin are classified as if each and every man has married or will marry a MBD and, conversely, each woman a FZS. To many anthropologists the theory of prescriptive alliance systems has seemed to offer an adequate explanation of this and many other features of the same societies, but it has only seemed to do so, and at the expense of ignoring or denying many linguistic and ethnographic facts. The most critical of these facts is that the classificatory systems in question are systems of kin classification whose terms have multiple significata, though of course in many cases the terms have semantic functions other than or in addition to their kin-category designating functions.

Given the appropriate generally relevant semantic concepts, it is a relatively simple matter to demonstrate that the terminological phenomenon in question is nothing more or less than the product of the MBD-FZS–spouse equation rule in kin classification, a rule of terminological or kin-class *extension*. Since this rule may be superimposed on a wide variety of otherwise quite different systems of kin classification, it is evident that the most distinctive feature of those systems which do employ the MBD-FZS–spouse equation rule is that rule itself. So, of course, one of the things that has to be explained about these systems is the occurrence of that rule.

We have seen, however, that this rule of kin classification is sometimes associated with the right of a man to claim his MBD in marriage (though in some cases the claim is restricted to one man from each sibling set), and sometimes with the right of a man to claim a ZS as a DH. At this point we cannot say that the existence of such rights provides the necessary and sufficient conditions for the institutionalization of the MBD-FZS– spouse equation rule. It may be that the rule occurs in the absence of such rights, or that the rights occur in some societies without receiving expression in the associated systems of kin classification. The available ethnographies, though often suggestive, do not provide unequivocal evidence on these points, so we cannot fairly argue that the rule of kin classification is uniformly associated with such rightful claims of men over their MBDs or their ZSs; we can only say that we know of no clear-cut negative instances.

If it is the case that MBD-FZS–spouse equation rules are commonly (though perhaps not necessarily) expressions of such rightful claims of men over MBDs or ZSs, the sociological problem is to explain the existence of such rights. We suggested in Chapter 8 that in the Siriono case a man's MBD is regarded (perhaps because of the distinctive Siriono mode of reckoning kin-class extension) as the prototypical "distant" kinswoman of his own generation and therefore as marriageable; the ascription of a rightful claim over her probably is a device designed to minimize conflicts over sexual and marital access to women. We cannot say why or how Siriono chose to express this jural relationship in the form of the MBD–FZS–spouse equation rule; we can only say that it "makes sense" to do so in a society in which one's affines are almost certain to be one's kin and in which the jural status-relationships ascribed between reciprocal types or classes of kin are neither highly specific nor highly differentiated.

Clearly, this interpretation does not apply in any simple, straight-forward fashion to the other cases we have noted (except perhaps the Yaruro), for in some of them we have to deal (perhaps in addition) with a different kind of right, viz., the right of a man to claim a ZS as a DH, and this right is associated with, and no doubt has considerable significance for, formalized and ideally enduring political-affinal alliances between unilineal descent groups. In these societies any marriage may serve either to establish or to maintain an alliance between the lineages of the principal parties; marriage in Siriono society can have no such function, if for no other reason than there are no lineages or other kinds of corporate kin groups which could be so allied.

To the extent that the theory of "alliance systems" has taken any notice of the marital rights of men over particular kinds of kinswomen, or over particular kinds of kinsmen, the tendency has been to regard such rights, under the guise of "preferential" or "prescriptive marriage rules," as structurally derivative, and to argue that "rules" of interkin marriage restate a generalized jural relationship between descent groups as a highly specific jural relationship between types of kin. We have already noted (Chapter 2) that, in Lévi-Strauss' view, this is the "simplest" and "most effective" means for ensuring the perpetuation of particular exchange relationships and, thus, the overall integration of the total social system. The more specific requirement is alleged to be the simplest illustration and the most direct expression of the more general requirement (to maintain established alliances). Quite aside from the fact that how this is so is far from self-evident—the generalized requirement is itself already quite simple and direct and certainly easier to realize in social action—this theory purports to explain ethnographic phenomena whose very existence, in many cases, is open to question, i.e., preferential or prescriptive (i.e., obligatory) MBD-FZS marriage.[10]

Yet, rightful claims over MBD or ZS in marriage are probably often integral components of systems of political-affinal alliance between line-ages, and this in itself does not seem difficult to explain. But it requires the assumption that, far from being the simplest illustration and the most

---

[10] We do not claim that such preferences and prescriptions do not exist anywhere, but anyone at all familiar with the relevant ethnographic literature will realize that these terms have been used rather loosely by various anthropologists to describe widely diverse ethnographic phenomena, and often without adequate description of the phenomena themselves.

direct expression of a more generalized requirement (to maintain established alliances), such rights are in fact the very keystones of any systems of intergroup political-affinal alliance. Since an alliance, once established, is not automatically perpetuated but always has to be revalidated, either by further prestations on the part of the wife-taker or by additional marriages, the right of a man over his ZS as a potential DH gives the wife-giver (usually the status-superior in the intergroup relationship) the power either to revalidate the relationship or to allow it to atrophy simply by refraining from claiming what is rightfully his. It is not his right to claim just any "ZS," however, and so the wife-takers are free to make marriages and to contract alliances elsewhere. Where, as may be true of the Kachin case, there is also a rightful claim on the part of a man to one of his MBDs, this may be a complementary right giving the wife-takers the power to demand the continuation or reinforcement of the alliance. Since wife-givers are usually regarded as the status-superiors in the intergroup relationship, the interests of the status-inferiors are perhaps thus protected against arbitrary termination of the relationship on the part of the status-superiors. After all, their status-superiority is not merely a matter of their wife-giving status; it is at least as much a matter of politics and land tenure.

Furthermore, note that in the Gilyak case, which is not at all atypical, the relationship between wife-givers and wife-takers is described as one between "mothers' brothers" and "sisters' sons," i.e., it is described by means of kinship terms, and the description is based on the presumed relations of kinship between members of the lineages involved. The appropriateness of the description must rest on the fact that particular lineages are defined as wife-givers and wife-takers, and they are allied in marriage *precisely because* their respective members are related as true and classificatory mothers and mothers' brothers to children and sisters' children (or in some other cases as mothers and grandfathers to children and grandchildren), and because men have rightful marital claims over their sisters' sons or their mothers' brothers' daughters. Of course, alliances may be contracted between previously unrelated groups, and so a consanguineal relationship is not prerequisite to the initiation of an alliance. Neither, then, can it be the sole normative basis for the perpetuation of an alliance. Yet the consanguineal relationship does determine in principle which groups shall be allied in marriage. As Lévi-Strauss has observed:

> ... if we exclude all considerations of marriage preferences [e.g., rights] expressed in terms of kinship degrees, the definition of the social structure will become empty and tautological, since all we shall know about the marriage system of these tribes is that each group is supposed to receive its wives from 'wife-giving' groups and to give its daughters to groups concerning which nothing can be said either, except that they are 'wife-takers' in relation to the former (1965: 17). (See also Schneider 1965b: 65–67.)

Insofar as the rightful claims of men over their ZSs or MBDs are the keystones of systems of enduring political-affinal alliance between lineages, it is not inappropriate that the kinship terminologies of these societies employ MBD-FZS–spouse equation rules in kin classification, even though there is no obligation, or even a general preference, for men to marry MBDs. If it is presumed that any marriage may serve to initiate an alliance between two lineages and if the right to claim continuance of that alliance rests on the rights of men to claim their ZSs as DHs or their MBDs as wives, it follows that a marriage to a non-MBD (or non-"MBD") must establish jural relations (or the potential for them) between lineages which are precisely analogous to those which are maintained or reinforced by marriage to MBD or "MBD". The relationship established by a marriage between previously unrelated lineages is not merely that of wife-giver to wife-taker. While there may be a generalized obligation incumbent on lineages to continue to give wives to or to take wives from certain other lineages (i.e., to maintain established alliances), rights of bestowal of women (where such rights are recognized) are vested not in lineages as wholes but usually in the fathers of those women; and the right of a man over his MBD in marriage is a right over a woman of a specific kintype, not a right over women of "mother's" lineages in general. That is to say, lineages related as wife-givers and wife-takers are jurally related through the consanguineal relationships of their members and the rights and duties those consanguineal relationships imply. These latter jural relationships are not mere artifacts of the former but are, indeed, their very basis. Again, lineages are related as wife-givers and wife-takers precisely because their members are related as mothers and mothers' brothers to children and sisters' children (or in some cases as mothers and grandfathers to children and grandchildren). Thus, newly established interlineage relationships receive their concrete expression (not necessarily their only concrete expression) in specific jural relationships between the constituents of those groups, and these are jural relationships proper to specific classes of kin.

So when previously unrelated lineages become related as wife-givers and wife-takers, their individual members become jurally related as though they were certain kinds of kin, and in subsequent generations they are in fact kin of the appropriate types. By virtue of the jural relationships between lineages, the members of those lineages are appropriately classified as if they were kin of one another, but only because the jural relationships established by marriage between them are, in the first place, proper to particular classes of kin. In the first instance, the extension of kin terms to affines who are not kin has a jural basis, or a jural or social "cause." The formal equivalences are nonetheless those expressed in the corollaries of the MBD-FZS–spouse equation rule. There is no evident need to interpret this terminological extension as a practice designed to define "exceptional" or "irregular" marriages out of existence and so to create the appearance of unbroken and unbreakable marriage rules (cf. Needham 1962*b*: 87).

From our perspective, a number of features of societies allegedly organized as asymmetric alliance systems are not particularly puzzling, though from the perspective of alliance systems theory they must be seen as problematic and only indirectly related to the "idealized form of the social order" (see Leach 1961: 50), or they must be ignored (see Needham 1962*b*). For example, it seems only reasonable that the rights of men with respect to their ZS or their MBD should be limited by the rule that two brothers may not marry two sisters, that not all marriages are regarded as serving to establish or to maintain interlineage alliances, that men are typically free to marry women who are not of the same kin category as MBD (provided those women are not closely related kin), and that MBD-FZS marriages are relatively infrequent.

Where any marriage may serve to establish or to maintain an interlineage alliance, and where a single marriage between lineages is sufficient to establish their alliance for several generations, there may be considerable political disadvantage in concentrating one's marital contracts. The rule that two brothers may not marry two sisters absolves both lineages of the conflicts of interest that would necessarily follow from a general and unrestricted right over ZS or MBD. For similar political reasons there would seem to be little advantage in a rule that marriages should take place only between certain specified groups "traditionally" related as wife-givers and wife-takers, and so it is not surprising that such rules are quite uncommon. It seems probable, as Lehman (1963: 99) has observed, that where they do occur, as among the Purum, they reflect the special demographic circumstances of a small remnant population with a reduced range of lineages which are not undergoing extensive segmentation, and not necessarily a conceptualization of the society as a "closed asymmetric prescriptive alliance system."[11]

In these societies MBD-FZS marriage is not prescribed, although it may have political functions for allied lineages. Also, there is no apparent "preference" for MBD-FZS marriage, i.e., no notable tendency to marry MBD, or "MBD," or even women of the mother's or a "mother's" descent group. Insofar as such data are available and reliable (they seldom are), the reported frequencies of actual MBD and classificatory MBD

---

[11] There is some further evidence that this is a reasonable interpretation of the Purum case. Although Das offers a model of interclan marriage among the Purum, it is *his* construct from certain data on the use of kinship terms, and he notes that it differs from the *one* offered by *one* Purum informant, but he fails to specify exactly how if differs (see Das 1945: 131–32). It is far from certain that Purum themselves are in total agreement about how their five clans should intermarry, though there are, as far as the data go, no reasons to doubt that they agree there are rules of this sort. Such rules need not imply or be part of a "closed system of asymmetric alliance."

marriage vary considerably from society to society. The highest figures are those reported by Das (1945: 241) for the Purum: of 85 marriages recorded in three villages, 74 percent were to MBD and an additional 13 percent were to women of the mother's "sib" or clan. The data do not show how many of the latter could be described as marriages to the daughters of men called "brother" by ego's mother, but Das himself reports census data which disconfirm his claim that 74 percent of the marriages were to actual MBDs. In one village. for which Das asserted that all 42 couples were related as MBD-FZS, analysis of his census data reveals that only 22 of the 25 marriages noted therein were to women even of "mother's" or wife-giving clans, much less actual MBDs. Sternberg (1933 [1964]) reports a "strong tendency" among the Gilyak to marry women of a "mother's" clan, but he gives no figures on these or actual MBD marriages. In other cases, however, the frequencies are uniformly much lower. Bruner (1959: 120) reports 2.3 percent MBD marriages and 18.8 percent classificatory MBD marriages among rural Toba Batak and notes that the percentages are even lower among their urban relatives. Singarimbun (1965: 266–67) reports only slightly higher figures of 5.5 and 29 percent for rural Karo Batak; and Tugby (cited in Singarimbun 1965) reports 3.4 and 4 percent for the Batak of upper Mandailang. For another case of reputed "prescriptive" MBD-FZS marriage (though the kinship terminology has yet to be reported), Kunstadter (1966: 78) gives figures of 3.6 and 14.3 percent for the Lawa of Thailand. Kunstadter also observes that the frequency of actual MBD marriage among the Lawa is "not much higher than would be expected by chance" (1966: 80). It would seem, however, that Kunstadter's computations did not take account of the highly significant fact that Lawa do *not* express a "preference" for MBD-FZS marriage in general; as among Kachin, Batak, etc., "if one brother marries his matrilateral cross cousin, other brothers may not wed their brother's wife's sisters. To do so would transgress the rule that brothers cannot marry sisters" (Kunstadter 1966: 76).[12]

[12] The computations were based on estimates of expected frequencies of MBD-FZS marriage in simulated populations of varying sizes with and without expressed "preferences" for MBD-FZS marriage (see Kunstadter, *et al.* 1963: 517, Figure 2). Kunstadter estimates that in a relatively large (over 200) and stable population and *without* a preference for MBD-FZS marriage, a 1–2 percent incidence of MBD-FZS marriage is expectable by chance alone (provided there is no prohibition on such marriages). He also estimates that even where there is a general preference for MBD-FZS marriage only about 25–30 percent of the marriages could conform to the "ideal," simply because of the nature of the demographic constraints. Thus, he argues, "among the Lawa, prescriptions are followed relatively infrequently" (1966: 80). But, again, his own ethnographic data demonstrate that the Lawa neither prescribe nor express a general preference for MBD-FZS marriage. It would be more reasonable to ask in this case, and no doubt many others, how often men exercise their rightful claims (or even obligations, if there are any) with respect to their MBDs by marrying them, given the limitation that only one of each set of brothers is entitled (or obliged) to marry a MBD.

Therefore, it is not yet known whether the rates of MBD-FZS marriage in societies in which men have qualified rights in marriage over their MBDs, or over their ZSs as potential DHs, are significantly greater or less than the frequencies that might be expected by chance. There are, however, some reasons to suppose that in at least some of these societies men prefer *not* to marry their MBDs if they can avoid it. Bruner (1959: 123) reports that urban Toba Batak boys "claim that they find no challenge in courting their *pariban* (MBD), as they have rights to the girl," and Singarimbun reports a similar situation among the rural Karo Batak (1965: 269 ff.). Among the Karo Batak there is a strong feeling that any particular marriage should, in the final analysis, result from the free choice of the boy and girl; in the rare case a girl used to be forced to marry her FZS against her will, but this was avoided because the girl might then commit suicide. Also, they say, it is improper to court your *impal* (MBD) for she is like your sister, with the difference that you may marry your *impal* but not your sister. And, again, some men may not want to marry their MBD because if they marry a MBD they are obliged to marry the eldest available one, and she may not be the most desirable for other than political reasons.

It is clear, then, that in many societies MBD-FZS marriage has certain political functions for allied lineages, and these functions have a profound effect on the extent of rights over a MBD and the frequency of this type of marriage. In its total social significance, MBD-FZS marriage in these societies is therefore radically different from the institution of MBD-FZS marriage as it occurs among the Siriono.

We should be careful, however, and not conclude from these observations that the institution of MBD-FZS marriage in Siriono society is a totally different thing from the institution involving the same kintypes in, say, Kachin, Batak, and Gilyak societies. There are some similarities. The prohibition on FZD-MBS marriage, typically associated with the concept that individual marriage *may* create or maintain an asymmetric political alliance between lineages, is not solely, or perhaps even primarily, justified in terms of the incompatible obligations that would result if a man were simultaneously a wife-taker and a wife-giver of the same household:

> As a matter of fact one of the reasons most commonly given by Kachins in explanation of the ban on marriage between *tsa* and *hkri* is that such unions result only in stillborn or malformed children (Leach 1954: 139).

The reference here is clearly to the foci and other close kin of the categories *tsa* (MB) and *hkri* (♂ ZD), for marriage between distant *tsa* and *hkri* is not forbidden, and "in flirtatious poetry . . . it is normal for lovers to address one another as *hkri* and *tsa*" (Leach 1954: 138). The difference between MBD and FZD in these societies is not simply a difference between women of wife-giving and wife-taking groups, and, far from being thought of as radically different "types" of women, they are sometimes placed in the same kin category or described as being "like sisters" (note the Manggarai, Karo Batak, and Purum cases), even though jurally differentiated from sisters and from one another. The ethnography offers no justification for reducing rules of interkin marriage in these cases to rules of intergroup marriage, or for treating the former as epiphenomena of the latter.

Further still, there would seem to be good reasons to suppose that the institution of MBD-FZS marriage as found in Kachin, Haka Chin, Batak, Purum, etc. societies is not a totally different thing from the institution involving the same kintypes in a great many other societies. The vast majority of societies in which a man's MBD is regarded as his rightful spouse, or in which a man has the right to claim his ZS as DH, are found in east and southeast Asia, where in a great many more societies a man's MBD is regarded as his most appropriate and fitting spouse, if not a woman over whom he has a rightful claim. It is well known that in many east and southesat Asian societies marriage often serves as a means of establishing and maintaining intergroup alliances; and it is equally well known that in many Asiatic societies a distinction is drawn between "relatives of the bone" and "relatives of the flesh," which distinction, as we have already noted (Chapter 8, p. 175), sometimes serves (for the people who make it) to explain a prohibition on FZD-MBS marriage and a preference for MBD-FZS marriage. These societies are therefore comparable to one another in many respects, and it seems likely that those recognizing rights over MDB or ZS and interlineage relations of enduring political-affinal alliance have developed these institutions from a more common cultural and social-structural stock, one important feature of which is a set of notions about relations of kinship per se, in accordance with which it is deemed appropriate to marry a MBD but not a FZD. That is to say, it seems reasonable to suppose that rightful claims over particular types of kin in marriage and interlineage relations of enduring political-affinal alliance are but "specialized" forms of social and cultural institutions having a much broader distribution throughout Asia (cf. Needham 1966a: 30–32).

Though we could carry this speculation further, there is no need or warrant to do so at this point. Our concern here is with the *structure* of certain systems of kin classification and to some extent with the structures of the societies in which they occur. The main point we wish to make is simply this: There is no inherent contradiction in recognizing the genealogical or kinship foundations of certain classificatory and jural systems and their political and ritual functions for allied descent groups—where such exist. Where such groups are absent, as in the Siriono and Yaruro cases, the classificatory system can be said to reflect only "rules" of individual marriage and other principles of kin classification. Where such groups are present and may be regarded as politically allied by virtue of marriages contracted between their members, such an arrangement does not in the least preclude the simultaneous existence of "rules" of individual marriage, the expression of such "rules" in systems of kin classification, and the use of kinship terms to describe certain aspects of the system of intergroup relations. Such usage of kinship terms is of course possible only to the extent that there is some structural isomorphism between, some common principles of structure which are shared by, the interindividual and intergroup domains or subsystems of the social system. To recognize such usages for what they are (simple though highly attenuated extensions) is not to reduce one subsystem of a society to another—it is not to reduce the political system of intergroup alliances to a kind of "kinship system" or to a simple "system of MBD-FZS marriage" It is only to acknowledge the simple fact that where there are political relations between groups of kin these relations are readily and commonly expressed, by extension, in the idiom of kinship. This arrangement is of course not confined to societies in which lineages are politically allied via the rightful claims of men over their ZS or their MBD in marriage (see Fortes 1945; 1949).

Bibliography

The following abbreviations have been used:

AA = American Anthropologist
Bijd. = Bijdragen tot de Taal-, Land- en Volkenkunde
IJAL = International Journal of American Linguistics
JRAI = Journal of the Royal Anthropological Institute of Great Britain and Ireland
SWJA = Southwestern Journal of Anthropology

Alston, W. P.
1964. *Philosophy of language.* Englewood Cliffs, N. J.: Prentice-Hall, Inc.

Barnes, J. A.
1961. Physical and social kinship. *Philosophy of Science* **28**: 269–99.
1962. African models in the New Guinea Highlands. *Man.* **62**: 5–9.

Beattie, J. H. M.
1958. Nyoro kinship, marriage and affinity. *Internatl. African Inst. Mem.*, No. 28.
1964. Kinship and social anthropology. *Man* **64**: 101–3.

Bendix, E. H.
1966. Componential analysis of general vocabulary: the semantic structure of a set of verbs in English, Hindi and Japanese. *IJAL* **32.2** (pt. 2): Publ. No. 41. Indiana University Research Center in Anthropology, Folklore, and Linguistics.

Berlin, B., D. E. Breedlove, and P. Raven
1968. Covert categories and folk taxonomies. *AA* **70**: 290–99.

Berlin, B. and P. Kay
1969. *Basic color terms: their universality and evolution.* Berkeley: Univ. of California Press.

Bloomfield, L.
1933. *Language.* New York: Holt, Rinehart and Winston, Inc.

Boas, F.
1940. The relationship system of the Vandau. In *Race, language and culture*, pp. 384–96. New York: The Macmillan Company.

Bocanegra, J.
1631. *Ritual formulario*. Lima. [Manuscript, copy deposit in John Carter Brown Library, Providence, R. I.]

Bock, P.
1968. Some generative rules for American kinship terminology. *Anthropological linguistics* **10**: 1–6.

Bourne, L. E., Jr.
1966. *Human conceptual behavior*. Boston: Allyn & Bacon, Inc.

Bréal, M.
1900. *Semantics: studies in the science of meaning*. Trans. Nina Cust from 1897 French ed. New York: Henry Holt.

Bright, J. O., and W. Bright
1965. Semantic structures in northwestern California and the Sapir-Whorf hypothesis. In E. A. Hammel, ed., Formal semantic analysis. *AA* (Spec. Publ.) **67.5** (pt. 2): 249–58.

Bright, W. and J. Minnick
1966. Reduction rules in Fox kinship. *SWJA* **22**: 381–88.

Bruner, E. M.
1959. Kinship organization among the urban Batak of Sumatra. *Trans. New York Acad. Sci.* (Series 2) **22**: 118–25.

Bruner, J. S., J. J. Goodnow, and G. A. Austin
1956. *A study of thinking*. New York: John Wiley & Sons, Inc.

Buchler, I. R.
1964. Measuring the development of kinship terminologies: scalogram and transformational accounts of Crow-type systems. *AA* **66**: 765–88.

————, and H. Selby
1968. *Kinship and social organization: an introduction to theory and method*. New York: The Macmillan Company.

Burling, R.
1963. *Rengsanggri: Family and kinship in a Garo village*. Philadelphia: Univ. of Pennsylvania Press.
1964. Cognition and componential analysis: God's truth or hocus-pocus? *AA* **66**: 20–28.
1965. Burmese kinship terminology. In E. A. Hammel, ed., Formal semantic analysis. *AA* (Spec. Publ.) **67.5** (pt. 2): 106–17.
1970. American kinship terms once more. *SWJA* **26**: 15–24.

Condominas, G.
1960. The Mnong Gar of central Vietnam. In G. P. Murdock, ed., Social structure in Southeast Asia. *Viking Fund Publ. in Anthro.*, No. 29: 15–23.

Conklin, H. C.
    1962. The lexicographic treatment of folk taxonomies. In F. W. House-
        holder and S. Saporta, eds., *Problems of lexicography*, pp. 119–41.
        Bloomington: Univ. of Indiana Press.
    1964. Ethnogenealogical method. In W. Goodenough, ed., *Explorations in
        cultural anthropology*, pp. 25–55. New York: McGraw-Hill Book
        Company.

Coolhaas, W.
    1942. Bijdrage tot de kennis van het Manggaraische volk (West Flores).
        Tijdschrift van het Nederlandsch Aardrijkskundig Genootschap **59**:
        148–77; 328–57.

Copi, I. M.
    1953. *Introduction to logic*. New York: The Macmillan Company.

Coult, A.
    1966. A simplified method for the transformational analysis of kinship
        terms. *AA* **68**: 1476–83.
    1967. Lineage solidarity, transformational analysis and the meaning of
        kinship terminologies. *Man* (n.s.) **2**: 26–47.

Crawley, E.
    1927. *The mystic rose* (2nd ed.), 2 vols. London: Methuen and Co.

Curtis, E. S.
    1928. *The North American Indian*, vol. 18. Cambridge, Mass: The University
        Press.

Da Matta, R.
    1969. A reconsideration of Apinaye social morphology. [Unpublished paper
        presented at the 1969 annual meeting of the American Anthropological
        Association, New Orleans.]

Das, T.
    1945. *The Purums: an old Kuki tribe of Manipur*. Calcutta: Univ. of Calcutta.

Deacon, A. B.
    1929. Notes on some islands of the New Hebrides. *JRAI* **59**: 461–515.
    1934. *Malekula: a vanishing people in the New Hebrides*. London: George
        Routledge and Sons Ltd.

Dréyfus, S.
    1963. *Les Kayapo du nord*. Paris: Mouton and Co.

Dumont, L.
    1953a. The Dravidian kinship terminology as an expression of marriage.
        Man **53**: 34–39.
    1953b. Dravidian kinship terminology. *Man* **53**: 143.
    1957. Hierarchy and marriage alliance in South Indian kinship. *Occ. Papers,
        Roy. Anthro. Inst.* (London), No. 12.
    1968. Marriage alliance. In *International Encyclopedia of Social Sciences*,
        vol. 10: 19–23. New York: The Macmillan Company.

Eggan, F.
  1950. *Social organization of the Western Pueblos.* Chicago: Univ. of Chicago Press.
  1955. Social anthropology: methods and results. In *Social anthropology of the North American tribes* (rev. ed.), p. 485–554. Chicago: Univ. of Chicago Press.
  1960. The Sagada Igorots of northern Luzon. In G. P. Murdock, ed., Social structure in Southeast Asia. *Viking Fund Publ. Anthro.,* No. 29: 24–50.

Elkins, R. E.
  1968. Three models of Western Bukidnon Manobo kinship. *Ethnology* 7: 171–89.

Empson, W.
  1967. *The structure of complex words.* Ann Arbor: Univ. of Michigan Press.

Epling, P. J.
  1967. Lay perception of kinship: a Samoan case study. *Oceania* 37: 260–80.

Evans-Pritchard, E. E.
  1932. Heredity and gestation as the Azande see them. (Reprinted in *Social anthropology and other essays.* 1964. New York: The Free Press.)
  1951. *Kinship and marriage among the Nuer.* London: Oxford Univ. Press.

Eyde, D., and P. Postal
  1961. Avunculocality and incest: the development of unilateral cross-cousin marriage and Crow-Omaha kinship systems. *AA* 63: 747–71.
  1963. Matrilineality and matrilocality among the Siriono: a reply to Needham. *Bijd.* 119: 284–85.

Fabian, J.
  1965. Kung bushman kinship: componential analysis and alternative interpretations. *Anthropos* 60: 663–718.

Firth, R.
  1936. *We, the Tikopia.* London: Allen and Unwin.
  1968. Rivers on Oceanic kinship. In W. H. R. Rivers, Kinship and social organization. *London School of Economics Monographs on Social Anthropology,* No. 34: 17–36. New York: Humanities Press.

Fischer, H. T.
  1957. Some notes on kinship systems and relationship terms on Sumba, Manggarai and South Timor. *Internatl. Arch. for Ethnog.* 48: 1–31.

Fison, L.
  1880. Kamilaroi marriage, descent, and relationship. In L. Fison and A. W. Howitt, eds., *Kamilaroi and Kurnai.* Melbourne: G. Robertson.

Fock, N.
  1963. *Waiwai: religion and society of an Amazonian tribe.* National museets skrifter, Ethnografisk Raekke 8. Copenhagen: The National Museum.

Fortes, M.
  1945. *The dynamics of clanship among the Tallensi.* London: Oxford Univ. Press.

1949. *The web of kinship among the Tallensi.* London: Oxford Univ. Press.
1950. Kinship and marriage among the Ashanti. In A. R. Radcliffe-Brown, ed., *African systems of kinship and marriage,* pp. 252–85. London: Oxford Univ. Press.
1959. Descent, filiation and affinity: a rejoinder to Dr. Leach. *Man* **59:** 193–97, 206–12.
1963. The 'submerged' descent line in Ashanti. In I. Schapera, ed. Studies in kinship and marriage. *Occ. Papers, Roy. Anthro. Inst.* (London), No. 16: 58–67.

Fox, R.
1967. The Keresan bridge: a problem in Pueblo ethnology. *London School of Economics Monographs on Social Anthropology,* No. 35. New York: Humanities Press.
1969. Review of Buchler and Selby, Kinship and social organization. *Man* (n.s.) **4:** 469–70.

Frake, C.
1962. The ethnographic study of cognitive systems. In T. Gladwin and W. C. Sturtevant, eds., *Anthropology and human behavior,* pp. 72–85. Washington, D. C.: The Anthro. Society of Washington.

Friedrich, P.
1969. Metaphor-like relations between referential subsets. *Lingua* **24:** 1–10.

Gifford, E. W.
1916. Miwok moieties. *Univ. of California Publ. in American Archaeology and Ethnology* **12.4:** 139–94.

Gilbert, W. H.
1955. Eastern Cherokee social organization. In F. Eggan, ed., *Social Anthropology of the North American tribes* (rev. ed.), pp. 285–340. Chicago: Univ. of Chicago Press.

Glick, L.
1967. The role of choice in Gimi kinship. *SWJA* **23:** 371–82.

Gonzales Holguin, D.
1607. *Arte de la lengua Qqechua* Lima. [Reprinted 1901 as *Arte y diccionario, Qqechua-Español.* Lima.]
1608. *Vocabulario de la lengua general de todo el Peru, llamada lengua Qquechua o del Inca.* Lima. [New ed., Raul Porras Barrenechea, ed., Lima: Universidad Nacional Mayor de San Marcos.]

Goodenough, W.
1951. Property, kin, and community on Truk. *Yale Univ. Publs. in Anthro.,* No. 46.
1956. Componential analysis and the study of meaning. *Language* **32:** 195–216.
1965a. Rethinking 'status' and 'role': toward a general model of the cultural organization of social relationships. In The relevance of models for social anthropology, *Assoc. of Social Anthro. Monogr.,* No. 1: 1–24. London: Tavistock.

1965b. Yankee kinship terminology: a problem in componential analysis. In E. A. Hammel, ed., Formal semantic analysis. *AA* (Spec. Publ.) **67.5** (pt. 2): 259–87.

1967. Componential analysis. *Science* **156**: 1203–9.

1968. Componential analysis. In *International Encyclopedia of the Social Sciences*, vol. 2, pp. 186–92. New York: The Macmillan Company.

Goswami, B. B.
1960. The kinship system of the Lushai. *Bull. of the Anthrop. Survey of India* **9**: 81–88.

Greenberg, J. H.
1966. Language universals. In T. E. Sebeok, ed., *Current trends in linguistics*, Vol. 3, *Theoretical foundations*, pp. 61–112. The Hague: Mouton and Co.

Grottanelli, V. L.
1961. Pre-existence and survival in Nzema beliefs. *Man* **61**: 1–5.

Guemple, D. L.
1965. Saunik: name sharing as a factor governing Eskimo kinship terms. *Ethnology* **4**: 323–35.

Hammel, A.
1964. A factor theory for Arunta kinship terminology. *Univ. of Calif., Anthro. Rec.*, No. 24.
1965a. Formal semantic analysis. *AA* (Spec. Publ.) **67.5** (pt. 2).
1965b. Introduction. In *Ibid.*, 1–8.
1965c. A transformational analysis of Comanche kinship terminology. In *Ibid.*, 65–105.
1965d. An algorithm for Crow-Omaha solutions. In *Ibid.*, 118–26.
1966. Rejoinder to Coult. *AA* **68**: 1483–88.

Hammer, M.
1966. Some comments on the formal analysis of grammatical and semantic systems. *AA* **68**: 362–73.

Hanson, O.
1896. *A grammar of the Kachin language*. Rangoon: American Baptist Mission Press.
1906. *A dictionary of the Kachin language*. Rangoon: American Baptist Mission Press.

Henderson, R. N.
1967. Onitsha Ibo kinship terminology: a formal analysis and its functional applications. *SWJA* **23**: 15–51.

Hiatt, L. R.
1965. *Kinship and conflict*. Canberra: Australian National Univ. Press.
1967. Authority and reciprocity in Australian aboriginal marriage arrangements. *Mankind* (Sydney) **6**: 468–75.

Hocart, A. M.
1937. Kinship systems. *Anthropos* **32**: 545–51.

Holmberg, A.
1948. The Siriono. In Handbook of the South American Indians, Vol. 3, The tropical forest tribes. *Bulletin, Bureau of Am. Ethnol.* **143**: 455–63.
1950. Nomads of the long bow: the Siriono of eastern Bolivia. *Inst. of Social Anthro. Publ.*, No. 10. Washington, D. C.: Smithsonian Institute. [Reprinted in 1969. Garden City, N. Y.: The Natural History Press.]

Homans, G. C. and D. M. Schneider
1955. *Marriage, authority, and final causes: a study of unilateral cross-cousin marriage.* New York: The Free Press.

Honigmann, J. J.
1954. The Kaska Indians: and ethnographic reconstruction. *Yale University Publ. in Anthropology*, No. 51.

Hopkins, N. A.
1969. A formal account of Chalchihuitán Tzotzil kinship terminology. *Ethnology* **8**: 85–102.

Hunt, E.
1969. The meaning of kinship in San Juan: genealogical and social models. *Ethnology* **8**: 37–53.

Hutton, J. H.
1921. *The Sema Nagas.* London: Macmillan and Co., Ltd.
1922. Thado Kuki terms of relationship. *Man in India* **2**: 108–11.

Jakobson, R.
1957. *Shifters, verbal categories, and the Russian verb.* Harvard University: Russian language project.

Kaberry, P.
1941. The Abelam tribe, Sepik District, New Guinea: a preliminary report. *Oceania* **11**: 233–58; 345–67.

Kay, P.
1966. Comment on B. N. Colby, Ethnographic semantics: a preliminary survey. *Current Anthro.* **7**: 20–23.

Keesing, R.
1968. Step-kin, in-laws, and ethnoscience. *Ethnology* **7**: 59–70.

Kintsch, W.
1970. *Learning, memory, and conceptual processes.* New York: John Wiley and Sons.

Kroeber, A. L.
1909. Classificatory systems of relationship. *JRAI* **39**: 77–84.
1917. Zuni kin and clan, *American Museum of Natural History, Anthropological Publications*, 18 (pt. 2).

Kulp, D. H.
1925. *Country life in South China: the sociology of familism*, Vol. 1. N. Y. City: Bureau of Publications.

Kunstadter, P.
1966.   Residential and social organization of the Lawa of northern Thailand. *SWJA* **22**: 61–84.

———, R. Buhler, F. F. Stephan, and C. F. Westoff.
1963.   Demographic variability and preferential marriage patterns. *Am. J. of Physical Anthro.* **21**: 511–19.

Lamb, S. M.
1964.   The sememic approach to structural semantics. In A. K. Romney and R. G. D'Andrade, eds., Transcultural studies in cognition. *AA* (Spec. Publ.) **66.3** (pt. 2): 57–78.
1965.   Kinship terminology and linguistic structure. In E. A. Hammel, ed., Formal semantic analysis. *AA* (Spec. Publ.) **67.5** (pt. 2): 37–64.

Landar, H.
1962.   Fluctuation of forms in Navaho kinship terminology. *AA* **64**: 985–1000.

Lang, A.
1903.   *Social origins*. London: Longmans, Green and Co.

Layard, J.
1942.   *Stone men of Malekula: Vao*. London: Chatto and Windus.

Leach, E. R.
1945.   Jinghpaw kinship terminology. *JRAI* **75**: 59–72. (Reprinted in Leach, 1961.)
1954.   *Political systems of highland Burma*. Cambridge, Mass.: Harvard Univ. Press.
1958.   Concerning Trobriand clans and the kinship category tabu. In J. Goody ed., The developmental cycle in domestic groups. *Cambridge Papers in Social Anthropology*, No. 1: 120–45.
1961.   Rethinking anthropology. *L. S. E. Monogr. on Social Anthro.*, No. 22. London: Athlone Press.
1967.   The language of Kachin kinship: reflections on a Tikopia model. In M. Freedman, ed., *Social organization: essays presented to Raymond Firth*, pp. 125–52. London: Cass and Co.
1969.   'Kachin' and 'Haka Chin': a rejoinder to Lévi-Strauss. *Man* (n.s.) **4**: 277–85.
1970.   *Lévi-Strauss*. Fontana Modern Masters series. London: Wm. Collins and Co., Ltd.

Leech, G. N.
1969.   *Towards a semantic description of English*. London: Longmans, Green and Co.

Legoff, L.
1889.   *Grammaire de la langue Montaganise (ou Chippeweyane)*. Montreal.

Lehman, F. K.
1963. The structure of Chin society. *Illinois Studies in Anthro.*, No. 3. Urbana: Univ. of Illinois Press.
1970. On Chin and Kachin marriage regulations. *Man* (n.s.) **5**: 118–25.

Lévi-Strauss, C.
1948. *La Vie familiale et sociale des Indiens Nambikwara.* Paris: Société des Americanists.
1949. *Les Structures élémentaires de la parenté.* Paris: Presse Universitaires.
1963. *Structural anthropology.* New York: Basic Books, Inc., Publishers.
1965. The future of kinship studies. *Proc. R. A. I. for 1965:* 13–22.
1969. *The elementary structures of kinship.* Trans. from the French 2nd ed. 1967 (1st ed. 1949) by J. H. Bell, J. R. von Sturmer, and R. Needham, ed. London: Eyre and Spottiswoode.

Lorrain, R. A.
1951. *Grammar and dictionary of the Lakher or Mara language.* Shillong: Govt. of Assam, Dept. of Historical and Antiquarian Studies.

Lounsbury, F. G.
1955. The varieties of meaning. *Georgetown Univ. Monogr. Series on Languages and Linguistics*, No. 8: 158–64.
1956. A semantic analysis of Pawnee kinship usage. *Language* **32**: 158–94.
1962. Review of R. Needham, Structure and sentiment. *AA* **64**: 1302–10.
1963. Linguistics and psychology. In S. Koch, ed., *Psychology: a study of a science*, vol. 6., pp. 552–82. New York: McGraw-Hill Book Company.
1964*a*. A formal account of the Crow- and Omaha-type kinship terminologies. In W. Goodenough, ed., *Explorations in cultural anthropology*, pp. 351–93. New York: McGraw-Hill Book Company.
1964*b*. The structural analysis of kinship semantics. In H. G. Hunt, ed., *Proc. Ninth Internatl. Congr. Linguists*, pp. 1073–93. The Hague: Mouton and Co.
1965. Another view of the Trobriand kinship categories. In E. A. Hammel, ed., Formal semantic analysis. *AA* (Spec. Publ.) **67.5** (pt. 2): 142–85.
n.d. Some aspects of the Inca kinship system. [A paper read at the Internatl. Congr. of Americanists, Barcelona, 1964.]

Lowie, R. H.
1929. Relationship terms. *Encyclopedia Britannica* (14th ed.). London.
1935. *The Crow Indians.* New York: Rinehart and Co.

Lubbock, J. (Lord Avebury)
1875. *The origin of civilization and the primitive condition of man* (3rd ed.). London: Longmans, Green.

Lyons, J.
1967. Structural semantics: an analysis of part of the vocabulary of Plato. *Publ. Philological Society*, No. 20. Oxford: Blackwell.
1968. *Introduction to theoretical linguistics.* Cambridge: Cambridge Univ. Press.

Malinowski, B.
  1913. *The family among the Australian aborigines.* London: Univ. of London.
      [Reprinted in 1963. New York: Schocken Books.]
  1929*a*. *The sexual life of savages.* London: Routledge.
  1929*b*. Kinship. *Encyclopedia Britannica* (14th ed.), pp. 403–9. London.
      (Reprinted in *Sex, Culture, and Myth*, pp. 132–64. New York: Har-
      court, Brace & World.)
  1930. Kinship. *Man* **30**: 19–29.
  1935. *Coral gardens and their magic* (2 vols.). London: Allen and Unwin.

Marshall, L.
  1957. The kin terminology system of the !Kung Bushmen. *Africa* **27**: 1–55.

Martin, M. K.
  1969. South American foragers: a case study in cultural devolution. *AA* **71**:
      243–60.

Maybury-Lewis, D.
  1960. Parallel descent and the Apinaye anomaly. *SWJA* **16**: 191–218.
  1965. Prescriptive marriage systems. *SWJA* **21**: 207–30.
  1967. *Akwe-Shavante society.* Oxford: Clarendon Press.

Meek, C. K.
  1931. *Tribal studies in Northern Nigeria.* London: Kegan Paul

Meggitt, M.
  1962. *Desert people.* Sydney: Angus and Robertson.

Mannes, H.
  1931. Eenige aanteekeningen over de onderafdeeling Manggarai op het
      eiland Flores. *Koloniaal Tijdschrift* **20**: 242–66; 371–90.

Mills, J. P.
  1922. *The Lhota Nagas.* London: Macmillan.

Morgan, L. H.
  1871. Systems of consanguinity and affinity of the human family. *Smith-
      sonian contributions to knowledge*, No. 17. Washington, D. C.: The
      Smithsonian Institution.

Morris, C.
  1938. Foundations of the theory of signs. *Internatl. Encyclopedia of Unified
      Science*, vol. 1, No. 2. Chicago: Univ. of Chicago Press.
  1946. *Signs, language and behavior.* Englewood Cliffs, N. J.: Prentice-Hall,
      Inc.
  1964. *Signification and significance.* Cambridge, Mass.: MIT Press.

Murdock, George P.
  1949. *Social structure.* New York: The Macmillan Company.

Nayacakalou, R. R.
  1955. The Fijian system of kinship and marriage. *J. Polynesian Society* **64**:
      44–45.

Needham, R.
  1958a. A structural analysis of Purum society. *AA* **60**: 75–101.
  1958b. The formal analysis of prescriptive patrilateral cross-cousin marriage. *SWJA* **14**: 199–219.
  1960. A structural analysis of Aimol society. *Bijd.* **116**: 81–108.
  1961. An analytical note on the structure of Siriono society. *SWJA* **17**: 239–55.
  1962a. Genealogy and category in Wikmunkan society. *Ethnology* **1**: 223–64.
  1962b. *Structure and sentiment*. Chicago: Univ. of Chicago Press.
  1963. Some disputed points in the study of prescriptive alliance. *SWJA* **19**: 186–207.
  1964a. Descent, category and alliance in Siriono society. *SWJA* **20**: 229–40.
  1964b. The Mota problem and its lessons. *J. Polynesian Soc.* **73**: 302–14.
  1964c. Explanatory notes on prescriptive alliance and the Purum. *AA* **66**: 1377–86.
  1966a. Age, category and descent. *Bijd.* **122**: 1–35.
  1966b. Comments on the analysis of Purum society. *AA* **68**: 171–77.
  1966c. Terminology and alliance: I—Garo, Manggarai. *Sociologus* **16**: 141–57.
  1967. Terminology and alliance: II—Mapuche: conclusions. *Sociologus* **17**: 39–53.

Netting, R. McC.
  1968. *Hill farmers of Nigeria*. Seattle: Univ. of Washington Press.

Newland, A. G. E.
  1897. *A practical handbook of the language of the Lais as spoken by the Hakas and other allied tribes of the Chin Hills*. Rangoon: Govt. Printing Office.

Nimuendaju, C.
  1937. The social structure of the Ramkokamekra (Canella). *AA* **39**: 565–82.
  1939. The Apinaye. *Catholic Univ. of America, Anthro. Series*, No. 8. Washington, D. C.
  1946. The eastern Timbira. *Univ. of Calif. Publ. in Am. Archae. and Ethnol.*, vol. 41.
  1956. Os Apinaye. *Boletin do Museu Parcense Emilio Goeldi*, Tomo XII, Belém do Pará.

Nuñez del Prado, O. C.
  1957. *El hombe y la familia, so matrimonio y organizacion politico-social en Q'ero*. Cuzco.

Oberg, C.
  1955. Types of social structure among the lowland tribes of Central and South America. *AA* **57**: 472–88.

Opler, M. E.
  1937. Apache data concerning the relation of kinship terminology to social classification. *AA* **39**: 201–12.

Osgood, C. E., G. J. Suci, and P. H. Tannenbaum.
    1957. *The measurement of meaning.* Urbana: Univ. of Illinois Press.

Parry, N. E.
    1932. *The Lakhers.* London: Macmillan.

Pehrson, R. N.
    1957. The bilateral network of social relations in Konkama Lapp district.
        Indiana Univ. Publ., Slavic and East European Series, vol. 5. Bloom-
        ington.

Pelto, P.
    1966. Cognitive aspects of American kin terms. *AA* **68:** 198–201.

Petrullo, V.
    1939. The Yaruros of the Capanaparo River, Venezuela. *Bulletin, Bureau of
        Am. Ethnol.* **123.11:** 161–290. Washington, D. C.: Smithsonian
        Institution.

Pospisil, L.
    1964. Law and societal structure among the Nunamiut Eskimo. In W. H.
        Goodenough, ed., *Explorations in cultural anthropology,* pp. 395–431.
        New York: McGraw-Hill Book Company.
    1965. A formal analysis of substantive law: Kapauku Papuan laws of land
        tenure. In E. A. Hammel, ed., Formal semantic analysis. *AA* (Spec.
        Publ.) **67.5** (pt. 2): 186–214.

Powell, H. A.
    1956. Trobriand social structure. [Unpublished Ph. D. dissertation. Univ.
        of London.]
    1968. Virgin birth. *Man* (n.s.) **3:** 651–52.
    1969*a*. Genealogy, residence and kinship in Kiriwina. *Man* (n.s.) **4:** 177–202.
    1969*b*. Terriotry, hierarchy and kinship in Kiriwina. *Man* (n.s.) **4:** 580–604.

Priest, A.
    1964. Method of naming among the Siriono Indians. *AA* **66;** 1149–51.

Priest, P. N.
    1966. Provision for the aged among the Siriono Indians of Bolivia. *AA* **68:**
        1245–47.

Radcliffe-Brown, A. R.
    1913. Three tribes of Western Australia. *JRAI* **43:** 143–70.
    1929. A further note on Ambrym. *Man* **29:** 50–53.
    1950. Introduction. In A. R. Radcliffe-Brown and C. D. Forde, eds., *African
        systems of kinship and marriage,* pp. 1–85. London: Oxford Univ.
        Press.
    1952. *Structure and function in primitive society.* New York: The Free Press.
    1953. Dravidian kinship terminology. *Man* **53:** 112.

Read, C.
    1918. No paternity. *JRAI* **48:** 146–54.

Ridington, R.
1969. Kin categories versus kin groups: a two-section system without sections. *Ethnology* **8**: 460–67.

Rivers, W. H. R.
1907. On the origin of the classificatory system of relationships. In N. W. Thomas *et al.*, eds., *Anthropological essays presented to E. B. Tylor*, pp. 309–23. Oxford: Clarendon Press.
1914*a*. *The history of Melanesian society* (2 vols.). Cambridge: Cambridge Univ. Press.
1914*b*. *Kinship and social organization.* London: Constable and Co. [Reprinted in 1968 as *L. S. E. Monogr. on Social Anthro.*, No. 34. London: Athlone Press.]

Romney, A. K.
1965. Kalmuk Mongol and the classification of lineal kinship terminologies. In E. A. Hammel, ed., Formal semantic analysis. *AA* (Spec. Publ.) **67.5** (pt. 2): 127–41.

———, and R. G. D'Andrade.
1964. Cognitive aspects of English kin terms. In Transcultural studies in cognition. *AA* (Spec. Publ.) **66.3** (pt. 2): 146–70.

Rowe, J. H.
1946. Inca culture at the time of the Spanish conquest. In Handbook of South American Indians, vol. 2, The Andean civilizations. *Bulletin, Bureau of Am. Ethnol.* **143**: 183–330.

Ruel, M. J.
1962. Genealogical concepts or 'category words'? a study of Banyang kinship terminology. *JRAI* **92**: 157–76.

Santo Tomas, Domingo de
1560*a*. *Grammatica o arte de la lengua general do los indios de los reynos del Peru.* [Facsimile edition, 1951. Raul Porras Barrenechea, ed. Lima: Universidad Nacional Mayor de San Marcos.]
1560*b*. *Lexicon o vacabulario de la lengua general del Peru.* Lima. [Facsimile edition, 1951. Raul Porras Barrenechea, ed. Lima: Universidad Nacional Mayor de San Marcos.]

Saussure, F. de
1959. *Course in general linguistics.* Trans. by W. Baskin from 1915 French edition. New York: Philosophical Library.

Scheffler, Harold W.
1966. Ancestor worship in anthropology: or observations on descent and descent groups. *Current Anthro.* **7**: 541–51.
1967*a*. On scaling kinship terminologies. *SWJA* **23**: 159–75.
1967*b*. On concepts of descent and descent groups. *Current Anthro.* **8**: 506–9.

1969. Kinship and adoption in the northern New Hebrides. In Vern Carroll, ed., *Adoption in Eastern Oceania*, pp. 69–89. Honolulu: Univ. of Hawaii Press.

1970a. Baniata kinship terminology: the case for extensions. In F. Eggan, ed., *Studies in social organization*. Chicago: Univ. of Chicago Press. (In press.)

1970b. Dravidian-Iroquois: the Melanesian evidence. In C. Jayawardena and L. Hiatt, eds., *Anthropology in Oceania: essays for H. I. Hogbin*. Sydney: Angus Robertson Ltd. (In press.)

1970c. Review of C. Lévi-Strauss, The elementary structures of kinship. *AA* **72**: 251–68.

1970d. Ambrym revisited: a preliminary report. *SWJA* **26**: 52–65.

Schermair, A.
1948. *Gramática de la lengua Siriono*. La Paz: Talleres Graficos de A Gamarra.

1958. *Vocabulario Siriono-Castellano*. Innsbrucker Beiträge zur Kulturwissenschaft, Sonderheft 5.

1962. *Vocabulario Castellano-Siriono*. Innsbrucker Beiträge zur Kulturwissenschaft, Sonderheft 11.

Schneider, D. M.
1965a. American kin terms and terms for kinsmen: a critique of Goodenough's componential analysis of Yankee kinship terminology. In E. A. Hammel, ed., Formal semantic analysis. *AA* (Spec. Publ.) **67.5** (pt. 2): 288–308.

1965b. Some muddles in the models: or, how the system really works. In The relevance of models for social anthropology. *Association of Social Anthropologists Monographs*, No. 1: 25–86. London: Tavistock Publications.

1967. Descent and filiation as cultural constructs. *SWJA* **23**: 65–73.

1968a. *American kinship: a cultural account*. Englewood Cliffs, N.J.: Prentice-Hall, Inc.

1968b. Rivers and Kroeber in the study of kinship. In W. H. R. Rivers, Kinship and social organization. *L. S. E. Monogr. on Social Anthro.*, No. 34. London: Athlone Press.

———, and G. C. Homans.
1955. Kinship terminology and the American kinship systems. *AA* **57**: 1194–1208.

Schneider, D. M., and J. M. Roberts.
1956. Zuni kin terms. *Laboratory of Anthro.*, Notebook No. 3, Monogr. 1. Lincoln: Univ. of Nebraska.

Shapiro, W.
1968. Kinship and marriage in Siriono society: a reexamination. *Bijd.* **124**: 40–55.

Shaw, W.
1929. *The Thadou Kukis*. Shillong: The Government of Assam.

Singarimbun, M.
  1965. Kinship and affinal relations among the Karo of North Sumatra.
         [Unpublished Ph. D. dissertation. Canberra: Australian National
         Univ.]

Singer, C.
  1959. *A history of biology* (rev. ed.). New York: Abelard-Schuman.

Sousberghe, L. de
  1965. Cousins croisés et descendantes: les systèmes du Rwanda et du Burundi
         compares a ceux du Bas-Congo. *Africa* **35**: 396–420.

Spier, L.
  1925. The distribution of kinship systems in North America. *Univ. of Wash-
         ington Publs. in Anthro.*, No. 1. Seattle.

Stern, G.
  1931. *Meaning and change of meaning.* Goteborg, Sweden. [Reprinted 1965.
         Bloomington: Indiana Univ. Press.]

Sternberg, L.
  1933. *The Gilyak, Goldi, Negidal, Ainu: articles and materials.* [Trans. from
         Russian by Leo Bromwich and Norbert Ward, and prepared for
         Human Relations Area Files, New Haven, 1964.]

Steward, J. and L. Faron.
  1959. *Native peoples of South America.* New York: McGraw-Hill Book
         Company.

Sturtevant, W.
  1964. Studies in ethnoscience. In A. K. Romney and R. G. D'Andrade, eds.,
         Transcultural studies in cognition. *AA* (Spec. Publ.) **66.3** (pt. 2): 99–
         131.

Swartz, M. J.
  1960. Situational determinants of kinship terminology. *SWJA* **16**: 393–97.

Tax, S.
  1955a. The social organization of the Fox Indians. In F. Eggan, ed., *Social
         anthropology of the North American tribes* (rev. ed.), pp. 243–84.
         Chicago: Univ. of Chicago Press.
  1955b. Some problems of social organization. In *Ibid.*, pp. 3–34.

Tugby, D. J.
  1958. The Batak of Upper Mandailing. [Unpublished Ph. D. dissertation.
         Canberra: Australian National Univ.]

Turner, T.
  1969. Kinship terminology and social structure among the northern Kayapo.
         [Unpublished paper presented at the 1969 annual meeting of the
         American Anthropological Association, New Orleans.]

Tyler, S. A.
  1966. Whose kinship reckoning? Comments on Buchler. *AA* **68**: 513–16.
  1969. The myth of P: epistemology and formal analysis. *AA* **71**: 71–78.

Ullmann, S.
1962. *Semantics: an introduction to the science of meaning*. Oxford: Blackwell.
1967. Semantic universals. In J. H. Greenberg, ed., *Universals of language* (2nd ed.), pp. 217–62. Cambridge, Mass.: MIT Press.
Urban, W. M.
1939. *Language and reality*. London: G. Allen and Unwin.

Vergouwen, J. C.
1964. The social organization and customary law of the Toba-Batak of Northern Sumatra. *Koninklijk Instituut voor Taal-, Land- en Volkenkunde Trans.*, Series 7. The Hague: Martinus Nijhoff.
Verheijen, J.
1951. Het hoogste wezen bij de Manggaraiers. *Studia Instituti Anthropos*, vol. 4. Wien-Mödling.
Vroklage, B.
1953. *Ethnographie der Beluin Zentral-Timor*. 2 vols. Leiden: E. J. Brill.

Waldron, R. A.
1967. *Sense and sense development*. London: Andre Deutsch.
Wallace, A. F. C.
1961. *Culture and personality*. New York: Random House.
1965. The problem of the psychological validity of componential analysis. In E. A. Hammel, ed., Formal semantic analysis. *AA* (Spec. Publ.) **67.5** (pt. 2): 229–48.
———, and J. Atkins
1960. The meaning of kinship terms. *AA* **62**: 58–80.
Warner, W. L.
1937. *A Black Civilization*. New York: Harper and Brothers.
Weinreich, U.
1966a. On the semantic structure of language. In J. H. Greenberg, ed., *Universals of language* (2nd ed.), pp. 142–216. Cambridge, Mass.: MIT Press.
1966b. Explorations in semantic theory. In T. Sebeok, ed., *Current trends in linguistics*, vol. 3, *Theoretical foundations*, pp. 395–477. The Hague: Mouton and Co.
Westermark, E.
1891. *A history of human marriage*. London: Macmillan and Co.
Wouden, F. van
1968. Types of social structure in eastern Indonesia. (Trans. by R. Needham from the 1935 Dutch ed.) *Koninklijk Instituut voor Taal-, Land- en Volkenkunde. Trans. Series*, No. 11. The Hague: Martinus Nijhoff.

Yalman, N.
  1967. *Under the Bo tree*. Berkeley and Los Angeles: Univ. of California
         Press.

Zuidema, R. T.
  1964. *The Ceque system of Cuzco. The social organization of the capital of the
         Inca*. Leiden: E. J. Brill.

Index

Accidental homonyms, 7
Affinal relatives, consanguineal and, 94, 116
Affinal rights, 95
Affinal types, terms for, *figure,* 85
Affines (in-laws)
  defined, 116
  rights of, 95
Aggression, sources of, among Siriono, 168–69
Ak-, 90, 93
Ake
  broadest range of, *table,* 102
  defined, 86, 101
  denotata of, *table,* 86
  foci of, *table,* 104
  narrowest range of, *table,* 101
  primary range of, *table,* 89
  reciprocals of, 89–90
Akwani
  defined, 86, 101, 102–4
  denotata of, *table,* 86
  foci of, *table,* 104
    are subfoci of *ake,* 91
  as hypothetical superclass, 95–96
  primary range of, *table,* 89
  reciprocals of, 89–90
Akwanindu
  defined, 86, 101, 102–4
  denotata of, *table,* 86
  foci of, *table,* 104
    are subfoci of *ake,* 91
  primary range of, *table,* 89
  reciprocals of, 89–90

Alliance systems, 18–48
  asymmetric prescriptive
    intergroup marital alliances and, 209
    matrilineal, 25–33
    Needham's theory of, 1, 14, 19, 21–25, 34, 67, 191, 209; shortcomings of, 219–20; terminological equations and, 31; test case for, 1
  described, 18–25
  generalized exchange, 14, 19–25, 28, 33, 67, 216, 221, 222
  MBD-FZS–Spouse Equation Rule and, 23–24, 35–36; see also *MBD-FZS–Spouse Equation Rule*
  relevance of semantic theory to, 33–35
  Siriono
    genealogical connection in, 37–40
    Needham on, 25–33
    Siriono kinship terms and, 42–48
  See also Marriage
Alston, W. P., 6
Alter-ego, extensions via, 58–59
Alternative classification of kintypes, 76–78
Ami
  broadest range of, *table,* 102
  defined, 86, 101
  denotata of, *table,* 86
  foci of, *table,* 104
  as hypothetical superclass, 95–97

Nuñez del Prado, O. C., 189

Oberg, C., 161
Omaha-type skewing rules, 118
in Gilyak kin classification, 195–97
in Haka Chin kin classification, 206
in Kachin kin classification, 199, 202
Omaha-type systems, 15–18
Kayapo kinship terminology and, 183–84
of Miwok, 216
occurrence of *MBD-FZS–Spouse Equation Rule* and, 217–19
patrilineal descent groups and, 155
terminological equations of, 109
Opler, M. E., 153
Opposite-Sex Sibling Rule, 121–23
Osgood, C. E., 12

Parallel descent, 111
Parallel-Transmission Rule
comparative and theoretical considerations on, 179–90
kin-class status and, 1, 111, 112
in Siriono kin classification, 110–12
structural correlates of, 171–73
Parry, N. E., 191, 206
Parsimony, 73
Paternity, social fatherhood and, 40–42
Patrilateral cross-cousin marriage, 21, 26
rules for, 24–25
Pawnee, kin classification system of, 138
Petrullo, V., 191, 214
Polygynous family, Siriono, 161
Polygyny, first cross-cousin marriages and, 26
Polysemic terms
primary senses of, 11
relationship among senses of, 7–8
Polysemy
in alliance systems theory, 17–18, 33–34, 54
defined, 6–7
and metaphor, 9

Polysemy *(continued)*
of Siriono kinship terms, 42–48, 54, 105
of Trobriand kinship terms, 71
of Trukese kinship terms, 138
Pospisil, L., 70
Postal, P., 25, 107, 160
Postmarital residence, Siriono, 159
Preferred marriage, defined, 163
Prescribed cross-cousin marriage, 21, 22, 23, 27, 36
Prescriptive alliance systems, *see* Asymmetric prescriptive alliance systems
Priest, P. N., 82, 124, 135, 158
Primary defining rules, 142
Primary meaning, 7, 8, 11, 17, 34–35, 65–66
Primary ranges of Siriono kinship terms, *table,* 89
Primary referent, defined, 18
Primary sense (structurally primary signification) of a polysemic term, 11
Priority
cognitive, 8–9, 66
historical, 8, 59–61, 66
in learning process, 61–63, 65
logical, 9
Property among Siriono, 161
Psychological reality of structural semantic analysis, 136–50
Purum
kin classification system of, 191, 206
marriage rules of, 225–26, 227

Radcliffe-Brown, A. R., 9, 16–17, 40, 63–65
Ramkokamekra, *see* Canella
Reciprocals
consistency of, 77
in Gilyak kinship terminology, *table,* 194
in Siriono kinship terms, 89–91
Reproduction, Siriono theory of, 39–40
Residence
descent and, 21
Siriono postmarital, 159, 161
See also Matrilocality